Startup Business Chinese

Cheng & Tsui Publications of Related Interest

Startup Business Chinese

An Introductory Course for Professionals

新世纪商用汉语初级会话

Level 1

Jane C. M. Kuo

CHENG & TSUI COMPANY

Boston

19 18 17 16   4 5 6 7 8
4th Printing, 2016

Published by
Cheng & Tsui Company, Inc.
25 West Street
Boston, MA 02111-1213 USA
Fax (617) 426-3669
www.cheng-tsui.com
"Bringing Asia to the World"™

Library of Congress Cataloging-in-Publication Data
Kuo, Jane.
    Startup business Chinese / by Jane Kuo.
        p. cm.
    Includes index.
    ISBN 0-88727-474-9 (pbk. : v. 1)
    1. Chinese language—Textbooks for foreign speakers—English. 2. Chinese language—Business Chinese. I. Title

PL1129.E5K86 2005
495.1'82421'02465—dc22

                        2005049711

ISBN-13: 978-0-88727-474-9
ISBN-10: 0-88727-474-9

Printed in the United States of America

Publisher's Note

The Cheng & Tsui Asian Language Series is designed to publish and widely distribute quality language learning materials created by leading instructors from around the world. We welcome readers' comments and suggestions concerning the publications in this series. Please send feedback to our Editorial Department (e-mail: editor@cheng-tsui.com), or contact the following members of our Editorial Board.

Contents

Appendices

Tables and Figures

Tables

Figures

Preface

Purpose of *Startup Business Chinese*

China has evolved by leaps and bounds since Deng Xiaoping set into motion the transformation of China's economy with the Open Door policy in 1978. Since then, China's agrarian-based economy has transitioned into one that is more diverse and more heavily industrialized. This growing industrial economy has subsequently progressed to such a high level of importance on the world stage that business professionals worldwide are now flocking to mainland China in a drive to advance their business prospects. This migration of commerce to China has created a demand for executives who not only have expertise in their particular industries, but also have an understanding of Chinese language and culture.

In the past few years, executives going to China have usually had true business acumen but have lacked the linguistic and cultural skills necessary to communicate well in China. This book is designed to rectify that imbalance by enabling business professionals entering the Chinese market to supplement their strong business skills with commensurate knowledge of Chinese language and culture.

This textbook is intended for students of Chinese in general, and more importantly for businesspeople. Therefore, the topics in this book are specially designed to enhance learners' business communication skills and cultural awareness. It is the author's hope that through business-oriented situational dialogues, which use industry and workplace-specific vocabulary and expressions, learners may become better equipped to interact with their local colleagues, employees, and clients in China. Relevant cultural points to assist beginning Chinese language learners to better understand basic social norms and modes of interaction in China are also included. Overall, interactive communication skills are prioritized to enable students to reach a basic level of Chinese language proficiency in a reasonable amount of time. Although the book is designed for a one-semester class that meets five hours per week, it can be adapted as necessary to meet student and curricular needs.

Features of This Book

Learning Objectives

At the beginning of each lesson, a brief introduction describes the setting and outlines the learning objectives. By using this task-oriented, functional approach, this text prepares students to act appropriately when confronted with similar situations in real life.

Situational Dialogues

This book consists of 12 units, each with two situational dialogues. The dialogues represent dynamic storylines, typical of what one would experience in the business environment in China. Each is characterized by a realistic setting in terms of both context and structure.

Each dialogue is presented in both simplified characters and pinyin romanization. An English translation of each dialogue can be found in the appendix at the end of the book, rather than in the lesson itself, so that students may use it as a reference without becoming overly dependent on the translation, and thus be more apt to understand the nuances of Chinese.

Vocabulary

There are two sets of vocabulary lists per lesson. The first set consists of those words that appear in the lesson's dialogues and can be found immediately following each dialogue. The second set, the Additional Vocabulary list, includes words that occur throughout the rest of the lesson, such as in the Sentence Patterns and the Cultural Points. This list is placed after the Cultural Points section. The choice of vocabulary in the Additional Vocabulary section, although focused on language used in the business environment, also includes more generic and frequently used terms, which are germane to beginners.

Sentence Patterns

In Chinese, there are both formal and informal methods of communication that occur frequently in business communication. Both methods are introduced throughout this book's sentence pattern sections. Each lesson introduces basic grammatical patterns and their usage, including usage examples and additional vocabulary. Students can use this additional vocabulary to generate their own sentences within the framework of the sentence pattern.

Cultural Points

As culture is an integral and inseparable part of learning any language, each lesson includes several cultural points that are reflected through either the situational dialogues or the vocabulary. These cultural points explore various aspects of business practices in China, focusing specifically on business communication, interpersonal relations, and overall socio-cultural competence.

Audio Downloads

The textbook includes supplementary audio downloads that contain all of the dialogues, vocabulary words, and example sentences in the sentence pattern sections, as well as the pinyin romanization for the first six units and listening comprehension exercises in the exercise book. The audio downloads should be used to facilitate the development of accurate pronunciation and listening comprehension in an interactive environment. In order to ensure the authenticity and quality of the pronunciation, the speakers on the audio downloads are all native Chinese speakers. The audio downloads are available at www.cheng-tsui.com/downloads. Please reference product key SBC1-AX63.

Exercises

Practice exercises based on the dialogues, vocabulary, and sentence patterns taught in this book can be found in the separate exercise book. The practice materials consist of a variety of exercises including speaking, writing, and listening comprehension, the latter being accompanied by the audio downloads. The exercises progress from simple questions and tasks to more complicated, open-ended questions. The script of the listening comprehension exercises is included in the appendix at the back of the exercise book.

Acknowledgments

I would like to acknowledge the following people for their assistance, support, and encouragement. Their efforts made it possible to complete this book.

First, I would like to thank Thunderbird, the Garvin School of International Management, for providing me with graduate assistants and technical support, as well as offering an environment conducive to my research. My special thanks go out to Dr. Robert Grosse, Director of CIBER (Center for International Business Education and Research), and Dr. F. John Mathis, Dean of Faculty, for their continued confidence in and support of my work.

Next, I would like to thank the team at my publishing company, Cheng & Tsui, especially Jill Cheng, President; Sandra Korinchak, Managing Editor; Kristen Wanner, Editor; as well as the rest of the staff, for their continued confidence and support. My sincerest appreciation goes to Vivian Ling, Chief Editor, for her tireless efforts to bring this project to fruition.

Last, but certainly not least, is my team of assistants, who sat with me for many hours, helping to perfect my vision. My humble thanks and gratitude go out to Yinghua Zhang, Erpeng Zhang, Renee Zhang, Aaron Wixom, Geoffrey Sanders, Sid Sohonie, and Brett Lee for assisting me, while at the same time pursuing their own goals through the MBA program. Thanks also to Patrick Winslade, Media Services Technician at Thunderbird, for his work on the audio downloads that accompany this book. The outstanding contributions of all of these individuals not only greatly expedited the publication of this book, but also made this book more meaningful and valuable to its intended audience.

Introduction to the Chinese Language

To many English speakers, Chinese seems to be *the* incomprehensible foreign language: strange-sounding with its tones, indecipherable in its written form, and totally unlike any Western language. While these stereotypes may be misleading—and as you'll learn in this book, untrue—it is true that Chinese is considered by linguists and laypeople alike to be a difficult language to learn, especially for those accustomed to non-tonal pronunciation and alphabetic writing systems. In fact, the Defense Language Institute, the U.S. military's foreign language school, considers Chinese to be among the four most difficult foreign languages to learn (the others being Arabic, Russian and Korean)[1].

Chinese has several characteristics that may seem especially challenging to a new student of the language. First, Chinese is a tonal language. Second, spoken Chinese contains certain sounds that are not found in the English language and that may be difficult for English speakers to produce. Finally, Chinese uses a writing system that is based not on a phonetic alphabet but rather on a large number of semantically-based characters, each one of which has its own meaning.

Though it can be difficult, the study of Chinese need not be intimidating. In fact, there are many facets of Chinese that students would find surprisingly simple:

- Chinese grammar shares the same basic subject-verb-object syntactical structure as that of English.
- Chinese words are not inflected for distinctions such as number, person, voice, or tense.
- There is no gender differentiation in spoken Chinese.
- Though a few words still have honorific counterparts, Chinese has, in contrast, for example, to Japanese, evolved to become less hierarchical in terms of verbal communication.
- There are not nearly as many distinct sounds in Mandarin Chinese as there are in English or other Western languages. In standard Mandarin, there are only about 1,300 distinct syllables, while there are as many as 10,000 in the English language.

Though achieving mastery of the Chinese language is decidedly challenging, determination and patience during the initial learning period will take the student far. This chapter is an introduction to the basics of spoken and written Chinese. Note: the information presented here is designed to give beginners the tools to get started speaking and writing Chinese. The special "In Depth" boxes contain additional information for learners who want more detailed explanations of the rules governing Chinese. Learners should feel free to skim these "In-Depth" boxes and to review them again at various stages in their learning process.

---

[1] The Osgood File, "US Intelligence Officials Scramble to find Arabic and Farsi Speakers." *November 14, 2001, ACFNewsource, http://www.acfnewsource.org/general/language_institute.html*

Spoken Mandarin Chinese

When the word *Chinese* is used in conversation, it commonly refers to Mandarin Chinese, which has become the standard across the Chinese-speaking world. Mandarin Chinese originated in the northern part of the country, in the area surrounding Beijing. It was subsequently adopted by the government as the official language of the country and its provinces. Other regional dialects are still used, but they are each spoken mainly in their respective areas of the country, whereas Mandarin is used throughout China. Indeed, the Chinese word for Mandarin, *Putonghua*, literally translates as "common speech." The most important regional dialects are:

Wu	spoken in Shanghai and Zhejiang province
Hakka	spoken near the borders of Guangdong, Fujian, and Jiangxi provinces, along with other parts of China and Southeast Asia
Min	spoken in Taiwan and part of Fujian province
Yue	also known as Cantonese, spoken in the provinces of Guangdong, Guangxi, and Hong Kong
Xiang/Gan	spoken in the provinces of Hunan and Jiangxi

Pinyin

Pinyin is the official romanization system of the People's Republic of China and has been adopted as the international standard for romanization of modern Mandarin Chinese. This system uses the Western alphabet to represent the sounds of the Chinese language; thus it also represents the pronunciation of Chinese characters. It is important to note that the pinyin letters, though taken from the English alphabet, do not necessarily have identical pronunciation to their English counterparts.

The Role of Syllables in Chinese

Chinese is often mischaracterized as a monosyllabic language. This characterization probably arises from the fact that in the Chinese writing system each character represents a single syllable. While it is also true that the syllable has an especially prominent place in the structure of the spoken language, this does *not* mean that "syllable = word" or that each character represents an independent word. Many characters do not occur as independent words but are "bound morphemes" which always occur together with one or more other characters to form words. One study has found that approximately 66 percent of the 6,000 highest frequency words in modern Chinese are words of two syllables, about 24 percent are monosyllables, and the remaining 10 percent are words of three or more syllables.

Basic Elements of Pronunciation

A Chinese syllable is composed of three elements: an initial, a final, and a tone. Initials are by and large consonants, while finals are simple vowels, diphthongs, or compound vowels followed by an ending consonant. There are only three consonant sounds that can occur at the end of a syllable: n, ng and r. In total, there are 21 initial sounds, 37 final sounds and five tones. You will often hear that Mandarin has four tones, but the neutral tone is also distinct from the other four and we therefore include it in the total count of tones.

A diphthong is a complex speech sound or glide that begins with one vowel and gradually changes to another vowel within the same syllable.

Each Chinese syllable carries a distinct tone. These tones are commonly referred to simply as first, second, third, and fourth tones and the neutral tone. In terms of pitch, first tone is high and level; second tone is rising; third tone spoken in isolation begins low, falls slightly, then rises; and fourth tone begins at a relatively high pitch and falls sharply. Neutral tone syllables are always unstressed, and the actual pitch of the tone varies depending on the tone of the preceding syllable.

The next few sections will elaborate on each of these three elements of the phonology of a Chinese syllable.

Initials

An initial, usually a consonant sound, is the beginning part of a syllable. A syllable that begins with a vowel is considered to have a "zero" initial.

The table below explains the initial sounds and gives approximate equivalent sounds in English. Unless otherwise noted, the English equivalents are intended to be spoken with a typical American accent. See Table 1.1 at the side for an explanation of linguistic terms used in the pronunciation guide.

Table 1. *Initials and their approximate English equivalents*

Category	Sound	Default Final	How to Pronounce	Similar Sounds in English
Labials *(lips touch each other, or, for f, lower lip touches upper teeth)*	b-	o	similar to English "b" or soft "p"; unvoiced, unaspirated	*b* as in "*b*oard"
	p-	o	same as English "p"; unvoiced, aspirated	*p* as in "*p*ort"
	m-	o	same as English "m"; voiced	*m* as in "*m*ore"
	f-	o	same as English "f"; unvoiced	*f* as in "*f*orm"
Alveolars *(tongue touches back of upper front teeth)*	d-	e	similar to English "d" or soft "t"; unvoiced, unaspirated	*d* as in "*d*irt"
	t-	e	same as English "t" unvoiced, aspirated	*t* as in "*t*urtle"
	n-	e	same as English "n"; voiced	*n* as in "*n*urse"
	l-	e	same as English syllable-initial "l"; voiced	*l* as in "a*l*ert"

Velars *(back of tongue is raised against soft palate)*	g-	e	roughly same as English hard "g"; but unvoiced; unaspirated	*g* as in "*g*irl"
	k-	e	roughly same as English "k"; unvoiced, aspirated	*k* as in "*K*irk"
	h-	e	similar to English "h" but in careful articulation displays friction between back of tongue and soft palate; unvoiced	*h* as in "*h*eard"
Palatals *(tip of tongue touches back of lower front teeth; front part of blade of tongue touches hard palate)*	j-	i	similar to English "j" but unvoiced and palatal; unaspirated	*j* as in "*j*eep"
	q-	i	same as Chinese j- but strongly aspirated, unvoiced	*ch* as in "*ch*eer"
	x-	i	similar to English "sh"; unvoiced	*sh* as in "*sh*eet"
Dental Sibilants *(tip of tongue touches back of upper front teeth, with friction when released)*	z-	i	similar to English "ds" but occurring in syllable-initial position; unvoiced, unaspirated	*ds* as in "li*ds*"
	c-	i	similar to English "ts" but occurring in syllable-initial position; unvoiced, strongly aspirated	*ts* as in "bi*ts*"
	s-	i	like English "s"; unvoiced	*ss* as in "ki*ss*"
Retroflexes *(tip of tongue rises to front part of hard palate)*	zh-	i	similar to English "j" but unvoiced and with tip of tongue raised against hard palate; unaspirated	Similar to *j* in "*j*ump"
	ch-	i	similar to English "ch" but with tip of tongue raised against hard palate; unvoiced, strongly aspirated	Similar to *ch* in "*ch*urch"
	sh-	i	similar to English "sh" but with tip of tongue raised against hard palate; unvoiced	Similar to *sh* in "*sh*irt"
	r-	i	similar to English "r" but with tip of tongue raised against hard palate; voiced	Similar to *r* in "*r*ule"

Term	Definition
voiced	vocal chords vibrate
unvoiced	vocal chords don't vibrate
aspirated	utterance of initial sound associated with puff of air
unaspirated	no puff of air during utterance of sound

Note: The hard palate is the front part of the roof of the mouth, and the soft palate is the back part.

Finals

Finals follow initials or, in some cases, can be stand-alone syllables pronounced without an initial. Finals include simple finals (which are single vowels) and compound finals (which involve vowel-vowel or vowel-nasal combinations). There are six simple finals.

Note: The term "nasal" refers to the "n" and "ng" sounds.

Table 2. *Finals and their approximate English equivalents*

Category	Sound	Sounds Like. . .
Simple Finals (but pronounced like uo below if the final is not in a compound with other finals)	a	*a* in "f*a*ther"
	o	*o* in "Ohi*o*"
	e	*u* in "*u*gly"
	i	*ee* in "s*ee*m"
	u	*oo* in "b*oo*t"
	ü	round lips as if to say *oo* in "r*oo*t" but push tongue toward palate as if to say *ee* in "b*ee*t"; similar to the German umlaut (French – *u* in "l*u*ne")
Special Simple Final	*-i*	*-i* with z-, c-, s-, zh-, ch-, sh- and r-, is a special case of the i final. It does not sound like the i in ji, qi, and xi but is rather a vowel continuation of the preceding consonant. It is written with italics throughout this introduction.

	ai	the word "*eye*"
	ei	*ay* in "w*ay*"
	ao	*ow* in "c*ow*"
	ou	*o* in "n*o*," *ow* in "l*ow*," or *ough* in "d*ough*"
	an	a + "n" sound (emphasize "n" sound, not "a" sound), similar to *awn* in "yawn" but without lip rounding
	en	*un* in "p*un*"
	ang	like *ang* in German "*Ang*st"
	eng	*ung* in "l*ung*"
	ong	similar to *ong* in "l*ong*" but lips more rounded, as with *o* in "*o*pen" plus –*ng*
	ia	German "ja" meaning "yes"
	iao	*yao* in name of NBA star "*Yao* Ming"
	ie	*ye* in "*ye*t"
	iu	*yo* in "*yo*del"
	ian	*y* in "*y*es" + *ain* in "ag*ain*"
Compound Finals	in	*ean* in "m*ean*"
	iang	*y* in "*y*es" + <u>ang</u>
	ing	*ing* in "do*ing*"
	iong	*y* in "*y*es" + <u>ong</u>
	ua	*wa* in "*wa*tch"
	uo	a very short combination of u + o
	uai	*wi* in "*wi*de"
	ui	the word "weigh"
	uan	*wan* in "*wan*ton"
	un	*wen* in "Bo*wen*"
	uang	u + ang
	ueng	u + eng
	üe	ü + something close to a short e sound (like e in "bet")
	üan	ü + *ain* in "ag*ain*"
	ün	ü + "n" sound
	er	similar to the word "are"

In Depth: Pinyin Spelling Rules

1. uo

    a. After *b-*, *p-*, *m-*, and *f-*, *u* is omitted but o is still pronounced as uo with a very light u.

    b. For all other initials sounds, the u remains. (e.g., *duo*)

2. ü and u

    a. When used in combination with *j-*, *q-* and *x-*, the umlaut (two dots) of ü are dropped leaving simply *ju*, *qu*, and *xu*. This applies to the compound finals üe, üan and ün as well. (e.g., qüe → *que*; jüan → *juan*)

    b. When the final ü and the compound finals occur without an initial, the umlaut is dropped and a "y" is added to the front of the syllable (e.g., ü → *yu*; üan → *yuan*)

    c. With *l-* and *n-* keep the umlaut for both ü and üe. (e.g., *lü* and *nüe*)

    d. In finals with no initial consonant, *u* is replaced by w. (e.g., uo → *wo*; uang → *wang*)
    The exceptions to this rule are:

        u → *wu*
        ui → *wei*
        un → *wen*

Note: w and y should not be considered initials. They are simply used as place-fillers and aids to pronunciation.

3. i and y

    In finals with no initial consonant, *i* is replaced by *y*. (e.g., ie → *ye*; ian → *yan*)
    The exceptions to this rule are:

        i → *yi*
        in → *yin*
        ing → *ying*
        iu → *you*

4. The Apostrophe

    In cases where the end of one syllable and the beginning of the next are both vowels, an apostrophe is used to separate the two syllables in order to avoid confusion. (e.g., nü and er → *nǚ'ér* meaning "daughter")

(See table 5 for a complete pinyin spelling chart.)

Tones

Chinese, and all of its dialects, are tonal languages. In a tonal language each syllable is spoken in a tone that is distinguished from other tones by relative pitch, or pitch change. Many people relate pitch used in music to pitch used in tones, but the two are quite different. A syllable never has a *fixed* pitch; variation in pitch is always *relative*, changing according to the voice range of individual speakers, sentence intonation, the speaker's mood, etc. In the case of Mandarin Chinese, each syllable is assigned one of the four principal tones or a fifth neutral tone.

Since Chinese characters provide no more than occasional hints at the phonetic properties of the spoken language, we cannot look at a character and be able to pronounce it unless we have already learned the spoken word or part of a word that it represents. This is true for tones, of course, as well as for consonants and vowels.

This means that tones, like consonants and vowels, are absolutely indispensable in spoken Chinese. If tones are ignored there are only about 450 different syllables in spoken Mandarin, but the presence of tones brings the total number of distinct syllables to approximately 1,300, alleviating what would otherwise be an untenable problem of homonyms in the language. Essentially, *spoken Chinese is unintelligible if the tones are not spoken properly!* There may be a temptation on the part of some to believe that even if tones are spoken incorrectly, listeners will probably still understand. This statement may be true to some extent, but speaking the correct tones is vital to achieving any level of proficiency in Chinese.

Four Basic Tones

In Mandarin Chinese, there are four basic tones plus a neutral tone. A graphic depiction of the four main tones can be displayed as follows:

Figure 1. *Tones represented graphically by pitch level*

Table 3 contains the names of the tones and their written descriptions as they correlate to the pitch changes for each tone.

Table 3. *Tones in Chinese*

Tone	1st	2nd	3rd	4th
Symbol	–	´	ˇ	`
Description	high-level	high-rising	low-dipping or falling-rising	high-falling or falling
Pitch	5-5	3-5	2-1-4	5-1
Chinese Name	第一声 (dì yī shēng)	第二声 (dì èr shēng)	第三声 (dì sān shēng)	第四声 (dì sì shēng)

The Neutral Tone (轻声 qīngshēng)

In addition to the above-mentioned four tones, there is a fifth, neutral tone. There are two types of neutral tones. The first type of neutral tone is used in sentence particles, for example, "ma," the question particle. The second type occurs in many disyllabic words, where the tone on the second syllable is converted to a neutral tone as designated by tone change rules, which you'll learn more about later.

In Depth: The Neutral Tone

Some have the misconception that the neutral tone does not have any pitch at all or is defined as the absence of tone. In fact, the neutral tone's pitch is determined by the tone of the preceding syllable. As your instructor will demonstrate for you, the neutral tone will naturally "land" at the pitch that correlates with the tone of the preceding syllable, and the speaker does not need to consciously aim for a particular pitch (see table 4 below).

The following figure displays the pitch of the neutral tone after each of the four preceding tones:

Figure 2. *The neutral tone (a star [★] represents the position of the neutral tone)*

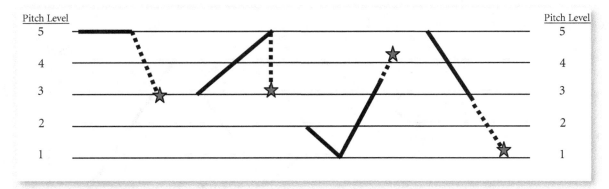

Table 4. *Pronunciation of the neutral tone based on the preceding tone*

Position	After 1st	After 2nd	After 3rd	After 4th
Description	half-low	middle	half-high	low
Example	tā de	lái le	yǒu le	duì le
Meaning	his	coming	have it	correct

In pinyin, the neutral tone does not have a symbolic representation, but in some systems of romanization, the neutral tone is represented by a dot symbol over the vowel, for example, nė.

Example. *How tones affect the meaning of a word*
A classic example of the way different words may sound the same *except for tone* is usually given with the following set of words, which are based on the syllable "ma."

Tone	1st	2nd	3rd	4th	Neutral
Pinyin	mā	má	mǎ	mà	ma
Character	妈	麻	马	骂	吗
Meaning	mother	numb	horse	scold	question particle

In Depth: Tone Sandhi Rules

As stated above, there are rules that dictate how certain tones change when in combination with certain other tones. The term "tone sandhi" is used to describe these tone changes in Chinese. The most important and pervasive of the tone sandhi changes have to do with the third tone. The rules are:

1. A third tone preceding another third tone

This rule states that whenever a third-tone syllable is followed by another third-tone syllable, the first syllable's third tone changes to the second tone. (e.g., nǐ hǎo → ní hǎo, which means "hello"). This rule also applies when more than two third-tone syllables occur in succession. In cases such as this, the third tones that change to second tones depend on the speech rhythm of the speaker and the closeness of their syntactic structure within the sentence. Syntactically close words will change to a second tone, while the others remain the same. (e.g., wǒ yě hěn hǎo → wó yě hén hǎo, "I am also fine"). The yě in the revised instance is actually a half third tone, which is explained in the following section.

Please note that this book follows the general pinyin practice of marking successive third-tone syllables as third tones. Students will soon learn to apply this tone sandhi rule automatically in their spoken Chinese.

2. The half third tone

This rule states that when a third tone is followed by any other tone (first, second, fourth, neutral), it becomes a half third tone, in which the pitch starts at the normal low point (level 2) and descends to the lowest point (level 1) and does not rise to the normal level of a full third tone. Following is a graphic representation:

Figure 3. *The half third tone*

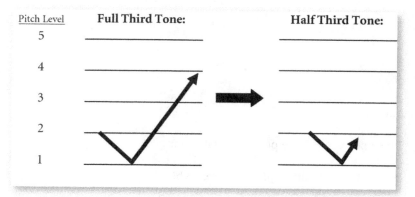

3. Tone shift: 一 yī and 不 bù

一 yī, the pronunciation of the word "one," is yī when it stands alone. However, it shifts from its default first tone to either second or fourth tone depending on the tone of the syllable that follows it. When yī precedes a fourth or neutral tone syllable, its tone becomes a second tone, but when it precedes first, second, or third toned syllables, it takes on a fourth tone. (e.g., yī bǎi → yì bǎi, which means "one hundred.")

不 bù, the negative marker meaning "no" or "not," has a default fourth tone, but when it precedes another syllable with a fourth tone, it switches to a second tone. (e.g., bù duì → bú duì, which means "incorrect.")

Tone Marking Rules

Here are the rules governing where to place the tone when writing pinyin by hand.

1). Simple finals

   The tone mark is placed over the vowel. (e.g., má, shì, wǒ, zhā)

2). Compound finals

   a. Two-vowel syllables: The tone is placed over the first vowel unless the first vowel is "i" or "u," in which case the tone goes over the second vowel. (e.g., dài, chǒu, fèi, qiū, shuō, jué)

   b. Three-vowel syllables or finals with three or more letters: The tone goes over the middle vowel or letter. (e.g., kuài, huái, jiǎo, liào, chuán, zhuāng, jiǎng)

Pronunciation Exercises

Listen to the audio downloads or follow your teacher to practice pronouncing the following syllables.

Simple Finals

	a	o	e	i	u	ü
b-	ba	bo		bi	bu	
p-	pa	po		pi	pu	
m-	ma	mo	me	mi	mu	
f-	fa	fo			fu	

1.

Distinguishing the Sounds:

bā ↔ pā   bó ↔ pó   bǐ ↔ pǐ   bù ↔ pù

mā ↔ bā   bā ↔ fā   mī ↔ pī   mǐ ↔ bǐ

	a	o	e	i	u	ü
d-	da		de	di	du	
t-	ta		te	ti	tu	
n-	na		ne	ni	nu	nü
l-	la		le	li	lu	lü

Distinguishing the sounds:

dā ↔ tā   dē ↔ tē   dí ↔ tí   dú ↔ tú

nà ↔ là   ne ↔ le   nǐ ↔ lǐ   nù ↔ lù   nǚ ↔ lǚ

3.

	a	o	e	i	u	ü
g-	ga		ge		gu	
k-	ka		ke		ku	
h-	ha		he		hu	

Distinguishing the sounds:

gā ↔ kā   gē ↔ kē   gū ↔ kū

kā ↔ hā   kē ↔ hē   kū ↔ hū

4.

	a	o	e	i	u	ü
j-				ji	ju	
q-				qi	qu	
x-				xi	xu	

Distinguishing the sounds:

jī ↔ qī   jù ↔ qù   qī ↔ xī   ——

qū ↔ xū   jī ↔ xī   ——   jù ↔ xù

5.

	a	o	e	i	u	ü
z-	za		ze	zi	zu	
c-	ca		ce	ci	cu	
s-	sa		se	si	su	

Distinguishing the sounds:

zā ↔ cā   zè ↔ cè   zì ↔ cì   zū ↔ cū

cā ↔ sā   cè ↔ sè   cì ↔ sì   cù ↔ sù

zā ↔ sā   zè ↔ sè   zī ↔ sī   zū ↔ sū

6.

	a	o	e	i	u	ü
zh-	zha		zhe	zhi	zhu	
ch-	cha		che	chi	chu	
sh-	sha		she	shi	shu	
r-			re	ri	ru	

Distinguishing the sounds:

zhā ↔ shā	zhé ↔ shé	zhǐ ↔ shǐ	zhù ↔ shù
zhā ↔ chā	zhē ↔ chē	zhí ↔ chí	zhǔ ↔ chǔ
shā ↔ chā	shē ↔ chē	shī ↔ chī	shū ↔ chū
——	shè ↔ rè	shì ↔ rì	shù ↔ rù
——	lè ↔ rè	lì ↔ rì	lù ↔ rù
zā ↔ zhā	——	zī ↔ zhī	——
cā ↔ chā	——	cí ↔ chí	——
sā ↔ shā	——	sì ↔ shì	——

Compound Finals

7.

	ai	ei	ao	ou
b-	bai	bei	bao	
p-	pai	pei	pao	pou
m-	mai	mei	mao	mou
f-		fei		
d-	dai	dei	dao	dou
t-	tai		tao	tou
n-	nai	nei	nao	nou
l-	lai	lei	lao	lou

Distinguishing the sounds:

bái ↔ pái   bēi ↔ pēi   bāo ↔ pāo   méi ↔ féi   dài ↔ tài

8.

	an	en	ang	eng	ong
b-	ban	ben	bang	beng	
p-	pan	pen	pang	peng	
m-	man	men	mang	meng	
f-	fan	fen	fang	feng	
d-	dan	den	dang	deng	dong
t-	tan		tang	teng	tong
n-	nan	nen	nang	neng	nong
l-	lan		lang	leng	long

Distinguishing the sounds:

bān ↔ pān   bēn ↔ pēn   bàng ↔ pàng   bèng ↔ pèng

màn ↔ fàn   mēn ↔ fēn   máng ↔ fáng   mēng ↔ fēng

dān ↔ tān   dēng ↔ tēng   dǎng ↔ tǎng   dǒng ↔ tǒng

nán ↔ lán   néng ↔ léng   náng ↔ láng   nóng ↔ lóng

9.

	ai	ei	ao	ou
g-	gai	gei	gao	gou
k-	kai	kei	kao	kou
h-	hai	hei	hao	hou
z-	zai	zei	zao	zou
c-	cai		cao	cou
s-	sai		sao	sou
zh-	zhai	zhei	zhao	zhou
ch-	chai		chao	chou
sh-	shai	shei	shao	shou
r-			rao	rou

Distinguishing the sounds:

gāi ↔ kāi	——	gǎo ↔ kǎo	gǒu ↔ kǒu
kǎi ↔ hǎi	——	kǎo ↔ hǎo	kǒu ↔ hǒu
gǎi ↔ hǎi	kēi ↔ hēi	gǎo ↔ hǎo	gòu ↔ hòu
zài ↔ cài	——	zǎo ↔ cǎo	zòu ↔ còu
cài ↔ sài	——	cǎo ↔ sǎo	còu ↔ sòu
zài ↔ sài	——	zǎo ↔ sǎo	zǒu ↔ sǒu
zhāi ↔ chāi	——	zhǎo ↔ chǎo	zhōu ↔ chōu
chāi ↔ shāi	——	chǎo ↔ shǎo	chòu ↔ shòu
zhāi ↔ shāi	——	zhǎo ↔ shǎo	zhōu ↔ shōu
——	——	shǎo ↔ rǎo	shòu ↔ ròu

zài ↔ zhài

cāi ↔ chāi

sài ↔ shài

10.

	an	en	ang	eng	ong
g-	gan	gen	gang	geng	gong
k-	kan	ken	kang	keng	kong
h-	han	hen	hang	heng	hong
z-	zan	zen	zang	zeng	zong
c-	can		cang	ceng	cong
s-	san	sen	sang	seng	song
zh-	zhan	zhen	zhang	zheng	zhong
ch-	chan	chen	chang	cheng	chong
sh-	shan	shen	shang	sheng	
r-	ran	ren	rang	reng	rong

Distinguishing the sounds:

gàn ↔ kàn   gěn ↔ kěn   gāng ↔ kāng   gēng ↔ kēng   gòng ↔ kòng   gēn ↔ gēng

kàn ↔ hàn   kěn ↔ hěn   káng ↔ háng   kēng ↔ hēng   kōng ↔ hōng

gān ↔ hān	gěn ↔ hěn	gāng ↔ hāng	gèng ↔ hèng	gòng ↔ hòng	hén ↔ héng
zān ↔ cān	——	zāng ↔ cāng	zēng ↔ cēng	zōng ↔ cōng	zěn ↔ zhěng
cān ↔ sān	——	cāng ↔ sāng	cēng ↔ sēng	cōng ↔ sōng	cān ↔ chān
zān ↔ sān	zēng ↔ sēng	zāng ↔ sāng	zǒng ↔ sǒng	——	sēn ↔ shēng
zhān ↔ chān	zhèn ↔ chèn	zhǎng ↔ chǎng	zhēng ↔ chēng	zhǒng ↔ chǒng	——
chǎn ↔ shǎn	chén ↔ shén	chàng ↔ shàng	chēng ↔ shēng	——	rǎn ↔ rǎng
zhān ↔ shān	zhěn ↔ shěn	zhàng ↔ shàng	zhèng ↔ shèng	——	rén ↔ réng

11.

	ia	ie	iao	iu	ian	in	iang	ing	iong
b-		bie	biao		bian	bin		bing	
p-		pie	piao		pian	pin		ping	
m-		mie	miao	miu	mian	min		ming	
d-		die	diao	diu	dian			ding	
t-		tie	tiao		tian			ting	
n-		nie	niao	niu	nian	nin	niang	ning	
l-	lia	lie	liao	liu	lian	lin	liang	ling	
j-	jia	jie	jiao	jiu	jian	jin	jiang	jing	jiong
q-	qia	qie	qiao	qiu	qian	qin	qiang	qing	qiong
x-	xia	xie	xiao	xiu	xian	xin	xiang	xing	xiong

Distinguishing the sounds:

biē ↔ piē	biāo ↔ piāo	biàn ↔ piàn	bīn ↔ pīn	bīng ↔ pīng	mín ↔ míng
diē ↔ tiē	diào ↔ tiào	diǎn ↔ tiǎn	dīng ↔ tīng	——	——
niè ↔ liè	niǎo ↔ liǎo	niú ↔ liú	niàn ↔ liàn	niáng ↔ liáng	níng ↔ líng
jiā ↔ qiā	jiè ↔ qiè	jiāo ↔ qiāo	jiū ↔ qiū	jiàn ↔ qiàn	jīn ↔ qīn
jiāng ↔ qiāng	jǐng ↔ qǐng	——	——	——	——
qià ↔ xià	qiě ↔ xiě	qiǎo ↔ xiǎo	qiū ↔ xiū	qiān ↔ xiān	qīn ↔ xīn
qiǎng ↔ xiǎng	qìng ↔ xìng	qióng ↔ xióng	——	——	——
jià ↔ xià	jiě ↔ xiě	jiào ↔ xiào	jiù ↔ xiù	jiàn ↔ xiàn	jīn ↔ xīn
jiǎng ↔ xiǎng	jìng ↔ xìng				

12.

	ua	uo	uai	ui	uan	un	uang
d-		duo		dui	duan	dun	
t-		tuo		tui	tuan	tun	
n-		nuo			nuan		
l-		luo			luan	lun	
g-	gua	guo	guai	gui	guan	gun	guang
k-	kua	kuo	kuai	kui	kuan	kun	kuang
h-	hua	huo	huai	hui	huan	hun	huang

Distinguishing the sounds:

duō ↔ tuō   duì ↔ tuì   duàn ↔ tuàn   dūn ↔ tūn   nuó ↔luó   nuǎn ↔ luǎn

guā ↔ kuā   guò ↔ kuò   guài ↔ kuài   guì ↔ kuì   gǔn ↔ kǔn   guāng ↔ kuāng

kuà ↔ huà   kuò ↔ huò   kuài ↔ huài   kuí ↔ huí   kūn ↔ hūn   kuáng ↔ huáng

guà ↔ huà   guó ↔ huó   guài ↔ huài   guì ↔ huì   ——   guāng ↔ huāng

13.

	ua	uo	uai	ui	uan	un	uang
z-		zuo		zui	zuan	zun	
c-		cuo		cui	cuan	cun	
s-		suo		sui	suan	sun	
zh-	zhua	zhuo	zhuai	zhui	zhuan	zhun	zhuang
ch-	chua	chuo	chuai	chui	chuan	chun	chuang
sh-	shua	shuo	shuai	shui	shuan	shun	shuang
r-		ruo		rui	ruan	run	

Distinguishing the sounds:

zuò ↔ cuò   zuì ↔ cuì   zuàn ↔ cuàn   zūn ↔ cūn   ——

cuō ↔ suō   cuì ↔ suì   cuàn ↔ suàn   cūn ↔ sūn   ——

zuǒ ↔ suǒ   zuì ↔ suì   zuàn ↔ suàn   zūn ↔ sūn   ——

zhuā ↔ chuā   zhuō ↔ chuō   zhuǎi ↔ chuǎi   zhuī ↔ chuī   zhuǎn ↔ chuǎn

zhǔn ↔ chǔn	zhuàng ↔ chuàng	——	——	zuān ↔ zhuān
chuā ↔ shuā	chuò ↔ shuò	chuǎi ↔ shuǎi	chuí ↔ shuí	chuàn ↔ shuàn
chǔn ↔ shǔn	chuǎng ↔ shuǎng	cǔn ↔ chǔn	chán ↔ chán	cuì↔ shuì
zhuā ↔ shuā	zhuō ↔ shuō	zhuǎi ↔ shuǎi	zhuì ↔ shuì	zhuān ↔ shuān
zhǔn ↔ shǔn	zhuāng ↔ shuāng	sǔn ↔ shǔn	suō ↔ shuō	suì ↔ shuì

14.

	ü	üe	üan	ün
n-	nü	nüe		
l-	lü	lüe		
j-	ju	jue	juan	jun
q-	qu	que	quan	qun
x-	xu	xue	xuan	xun

Distinguishing the sounds:

nǔ ↔ lǔ	nüè ↔ lüè	nǔ ↔ nǔ	lù ↔ lǔ	lǚ↔ lüè
jù ↔ qù	jué ↔ qué	juān ↔ quān	jūn ↔ juān	——
qū ↔ xū	què ↔ xuè	quán ↔ xuán	qún ↔ xún	qún ↔ quán
jū ↔ xū	jué ↔ xué	juǎn ↔ xuǎn	jùn ↔ xùn	xùn ↔ xuàn

Table 5. *Complete pinyin spelling table*[2]

	a	o	e	i	-i	er	ai	ei	ao	ou	an	en	ang	eng	ong	ia	iao	ie	iou	ian	in	iang	ing	iong	u	ua	uo	uai	uei	uan	uen	uang	ueng	ü	üe	üan	ün
b	ba	bo		bi			bai	bei	bao		ban	ben	bang	beng			biao	bie		bian	bin		bing		bu												
p	pa	po		pi			pai	pei	poa	pou	pan	pen	pang	peng			piao	pie		pian	pin		ping		pu												
m	ma	mo	me	mi			mai	mei	mao	mou	man	men	mang	meng			miao	mie	miu	mian	min		ming		mu												
f	fa	fo						fei		fou	fan	fen	fang	feng											fu												
d	da		de	di			dai	dei	dao	dou	dan	den	dang	deng	dong		daio	die	diu	dian			ding		du		duo		dui	duan	dun						
t	ta		te	ti			tai		tao	tou	tan		tang	teng	tong		tiao	tie		tian			ting		tu		tuo		tui	tuan	tun						
n	na		ne	ni			nai	nei	nao	nou	nan	nen	nang	neng	nong		niao	nie	niu	nian	nin	niang	ning		nu		nuo			nuan				nü	nüe		
l	la		le	li			lai	lei	lao	lou	lan		lang	leng	long	lia	liao	lie	liu	lian	lin	liang	ling		lu		luo			luan	lun			lü	lüe		
z	za		ze		zi		zai	zei	zao	zou	zan	zen	zang	zeng	zong										zu		zuo		zui	zuan	zun						
c	ca		ce		ci		cai		cao	cou	can	cen	cang	ceng	cong										cu		cuo		cui	cuan	cun						
s	sa		se		si		sai		sao	sou	san	sen	sang	seng	song										su		suo		sui	suan	sun						
zh	zha		zhe		zhi		zhai	zhei	zhao	zhou	zhan	zhen	zhang	zheng	zhong										zhu	zhua	zhuo	zhuai	zhui	zhuan	zhun	zhuang					
ch	cha		che		chi		chai		chao	chou	chan	chen	chang	cheng	chong										chu	chua	chuo	chuai	chui	chuan	chun	chuang					
sh	sha		she		shi		shai	shei	shao	shou	shan	shen	shang	sheng											shu	shua	shuo	shuai	shui	shuan	shun	shuang					
r			re		ri				rao	rou	ran	ren	rang	reng	rong										ru	rua	ruo		rui	ruan	run						
j				ji												jia	jiao	jie	jiu	jian	jin	jiang	jing	jiong										ju	jue	juan	jun
q				qi												qia	qiao	qie	qiu	qian	qin	qiang	qing	qiong										qu	que	quan	qun
x				xi												xia	xiao	xie	xiu	xian	xin	xiang	xing	xiong										xu	xue	xuan	xun
g	ga		ge				gai	gei	gao	gou	gan	gen	gang	geng	gong										gu	gua	guo	guai	gui	guan	gun	guang					
k	ka		ke				kai	kei	kao	kou	kan	ken	kang	keng	kong										ku	kua	kuo	kuai	kui	kuan	kun	kuang					
h	ha		he				hai	hei	hao	hou	han	hen	hang	heng	hong										hu	hua	huo	huai	hui	huan	hun	huang					
0	a	o	e	yi		er	ai	ei	ao	ou	an	en	ang	eng		ya	yao	ye	you	yan	yin	yang	ying	yong	wu	wa	wo	wai	wei	wan	wen	wang	weng	yu	yue	yuan	yun

[2] From "The Chinese Outpost", *Initials and Finals Tables 1 - 4*. http://www.chinese-outpost.com/language/pronunciation/pron0045.asp.

The Chinese Writing System

Most languages of the world use phonetic or alphabetic writing systems in which each symbol, or letter, has no inherent meaning aside from the sound it represents. However, unlike alphabetic languages, in the Chinese writing system each character represents both an inherent meaning and an associated pronunciation. Although a "phonetic" element in many characters may give a hint as to the pronunciation of the character, one cannot really know how a character is pronounced until one has learned the meaning and pronunciation of the character or referenced it in a dictionary.

Written Chinese vs. Spoken Chinese

In many languages, there exists a difference between how things are expressed in writing and how they are expressed in speech. In modern Chinese, this differentiation is carried to a higher level than in most modern languages, so much so that written and spoken Chinese are referred to by different terms: 书面语 shūmiànyǔ "literary language" or "written language" vs. 口头语 kǒutóuyǔ "colloquial" or "spoken language." Shūmiànyǔ is more formal and sophisticated than kǒutóuyǔ, but it is based on the spoken language, and all educated Chinese are proficient in it. Various genres of written Chinese, from fiction to journalistic writing, have different styles and different degrees of formality, and the shūmiànyǔ used in business correspondence and contracts tends to be quite formal.

Up until 1920 or so, written and spoken Chinese were even more divergent than they are today, because the written form was classical Chinese (文言文 wényánwén), which has a vocabulary and grammar rooted in ancient Chinese. Around 1920, China's modern intelligentsia launched a movement to replace classical Chinese with a written vernacular (白话文 báihuàwén). The modern written Chinese described in the last paragraph evolved out of this written vernacular, but it retains some elements in common with classical Chinese. For thousands of years, the written language of China, classical Chinese, has functioned as a unifying thread among the Chinese people who spoke various regional dialects.

Two Systems of Writing: Simplified and Traditional

There are two Chinese writing forms in use today. Since early in the twentieth century there had been various efforts to simplify the writing system, and after the founding of the People's Republic of China in 1949, the government officially adopted two lists of simplified forms. These two lists, consisting of certain frequently occurring character components as well as individual characters, resulted in a total of more than 2,000 simplified characters coming into general use. Many of these forms had long been used informally in handwritten materials but not used in printed materials. This new form, referred to as "simplified characters" (简体字 jiǎntǐzì) is now used in mainland China, Singapore, and Malaysia; while the traditional characters (繁体字 fántǐzì) continue to be used in Taiwan, Hong Kong, Macao, and most overseas Chinese communities. The simplification of Chinese characters was initiated as an attempt to increase literacy by making the written language easier to learn. Below are some examples of the traditional and simplified equivalents:

誰 = 谁 (shéi, who)

萬 = 万 (wàn, ten thousand)

錢 = 钱 (qián, money)

豐 = 丰 (fēng, plentiful)

Number of Chinese Characters

Between the above-mentioned Classical and Vernacular styles, experts estimate that there are between fifty and eighty thousand Chinese characters in total. Despite this daunting figure, only five to seven thousand characters are currently in common use. Of even this seemingly formidable number, it is widely accepted that one needs to master only about 2000 basic characters in order to have a fundamental level of literacy in Chinese—a level that would be sufficient for reading a newspaper.

Radicals (部首 bùshǒu)

Chinese characters can be broken down into components known as radicals. There are 214 radicals in use in modern Chinese dictionaries. Some of these radicals were originally pictographs in ancient times, describing everyday phenomena from the physical world. Every Chinese character can be identified and referenced in a dictionary by its primary radical. Some characters are composed entirely of radicals, while some have both radical and non-radical components.

Below is a list of the 40 most common radicals, including their ancient forms, alternate forms, and basic pronunciations.

Table 6. *List of commonly used radicals*

	Radical	Ancient Form(s)	Alternate Forms (if Any)	Pinyin	Meaning	Example
1	人	亻 几	亻	rén	person	余, 他
2	刀	刂 刀	刂	dāo	knife	切, 别
3	力	屌		lì	power	功
4	又	ヨ		yòu	again	友
5	口	凵		kǒu	mouth	中
6	囗			wéi	surround	回
7	土	土		tǔ	earth, land	地
8	夕	?		xī	evening	夜
9	大	大		dà	big, great	天
10	女	女 名 名		nǔ	woman	好
11	子	子 子	孑 孓	zǐ	child	孩
12	寸	ヨ		cùn	inch	对
13	小	小		xiǎo	small	少
14	工	口		gōng	work	巧
15	幺	幺		yāo	one	幻
16	弓	尼		gōng	bow	张

17	心		｜	xīn	heart	忘, 情
18	戈			gē	weapon	战
19	日			rì	sun, day	早
20	月			yuè	moon, month	有
21	木			mù	wood, tree	材
22	水		氵	shuǐ	water	永, 油
23	火		灬	huǒ	fire	炒, 煮
24	田			tián	field	备
25	目			mù	eye, look	盲
26	示		礻	shì	show, indicate	票祝
27	糸		纟 (simplified)	sī	silk	素, 纯
28	耳			ěr	ear	取
29	衣		衤	yī	clothes	表, 袖
30	言		讠 (simplified)	yán	words, speak	讲 (講)
31	貝		贝 (simplified)	bèi	shellfish, shell	财 (財)
32	走			zǒu	go, walk, leave	趋
33	足			zú	foot, enough	跑
34	金		钅 (simplified)	jīn	gold, metal	钉 (釘)
35	門		门 (simplified)	mén	door, gate	开 (開)
36	隹			zhuī	small bird	雀
37	雨			yǔ	rain	雷
38	食		饣 (simplified)	shí	food	饭 (飯)
39	馬		马 (simplified)	mǎ	horse	骂 (罵)
40	羊			yáng	sheep	美

Strokes (笔画 bǐhuà)

Another convenient way to break down and classify Chinese characters is through their individual strokes (lines, dots, etc.), which together comprise any given character. There are only 30 types of strokes in common use. The direction in which a single stroke is written and the order in which the strokes combine to form a character are very important. Both of these must be correct in order for the character to be properly written. Below is a list of the most common strokes, together with their Chinese and English names:

Table 7. *List of the eleven most common strokes used to write a Chinese character*

	Stroke[3]	Chinese Name	Pinyin	English	Examples
1	丶	点	diǎn	dot	立
2	一	横	héng	horizontal	大
3	丨	竖	shù	vertical	田
4	丿	撇	piě	down-left	不
5	乀	捺	nà	down-right	人
6	乀	提	tí	upward	我
7	一	横沟	hénggōu	horizontal with hook	家
8	亅	竖沟	shùgōu	vertical with hook	水
9	㇏	斜沟	xiégōu	slanted hook	钱
10	㇕	横折	héngzhé	horizontal bend	口
11	㇗	竖折	shùzhé	vertical bend	忙

Modern Developments: The Computer Age

Through complex encoding systems, software engineers have been able to create a variety of input and display protocols for using Chinese characters in computer operating systems and applications. These systems allow the user to type Chinese characters by using pinyin (the PRC's official romanized "spelling" system for Chinese syllables), zhùyīn (the Taiwanese phonetic system), a combination of radicals, or a combination of strokes. Typing in Chinese can be very efficient using any of these methods individually or in any combination. The significance of Chinese word processing software is that it makes it much easier for a learner of Chinese as a second language to be able to write and communicate. Typing Chinese on a computer becomes primarily a matter of character recognition, rather than recalling the complex structure of Chinese characters for writing by hand, which must be done with precise stroke order, direction, and proportion. For more information about resources for learning how to write characters by hand, see page xxxix.

Another significant development is the use of the Chinese language on the Internet. Given the vast worldwide population of Chinese speakers and the rapid growth of Internet use among the Chinese-speaking population, Chinese will soon become a very prevalent language on the Internet. Currently, English is the most common language on the Internet, but Chinese may soon catch up or even surpass English in terms of the number of web pages written in that language. Therefore, learning Chinese characters, though challenging, will increasingly become a crucial, integral part of the information society.

[3] Stroke images from "Learn Chinese Online" at www.learn-chinese-language-online.com, http://www.learn-chinese-language-online.com/chinese-writing-tutorial-1.html.

For Further Learning

The goal of this book is to teach students how to communicate effectively in Chinese in everyday business settings, and the primary focus is on listening, speaking, and reading skills. Most students will find that once they have learned pinyin and can recognize Chinese characters, they can easily type in Chinese on a computer by using the pinyin input method. As such, how to handwrite characters with the correct stroke order is not specifically covered in this book. Students who are interested in learning how to handwrite Chinese characters may be interested in the following resources:

250 Essential Chinese Characters for Everyday Use
Vol. 1 and Vol. 2
By Phillip Yungkin Lee
Published by Tuttle Publishing

Cheng & Tsui Chinese Character Dictionary
A Guide to the 2000 Most Frequently Used Characters
Wang Huidi, Editor-in-Chief
ISBN-13: 978-0-88727-314-8
Published by Cheng & Tsui Company

Chinese Characters Primer
Mac CD-ROM
ISBN-13: 978-0-88727-388-9
Published by Cheng & Tsui Company

Chinese Odyssey: Innovative Chinese Courseware
This three-year, multimedia-based course for Chinese contains images, video, audio, text, and exercises to enables students to practice all four language skills (listening, speaking, reading, and writing) in Chinese. The Volume 1 textbook and multimedia CD contain stroke order demonstrations and character-writing exercises.
Published by Cheng & Tsui Company

Integrated Chinese, Revised 2nd Edition
Level 1 Part 1 Character Workbook
ISBN-13: 978-0-88727-438-1
The Integrated Chinese series is a two-year college level introductory course that focuses on listening, speaking, reading, and writing. Textbooks, workbooks, character workbooks, audio CDs, CD-ROMs, and teacher's keys are available. A character writing workbook teaches students how to write Chinese characters using the correct stroke order.
Published by Cheng & Tsui Company

New Practical Chinese Reader
This series covers three years of instruction in beginning Mandarin Chinese, and includes textbooks, workbooks, instructor's manuals, and audio cassettes. Character writing is introduced throughout the textbooks and workbooks.
Published by Beijing Language and Culture Press

Reading and Writing Chinese: Simplified Character Edition
By William McNaughton
Published by Tuttle Publishing

Success with Chinese: A Communicative Approach for Beginners—Reading & Writing
ISBN-13: 978-0-88727-475-6
Published by Cheng & Tsui Company

Wenlin Software for Learning Chinese
Dual platform CD-ROM
Published by Wenlin Institute (www.wenlin.com)

Introduction to Numbers in Chinese

Chinese numbering begins with 一 yī "one," and goes all the way up to 十 shí "ten." Then the number 十 shí "ten" is used in combination with 1 through 9 to form 11 through 19, e.g., 十一 shíyī (11), 十二 shí'èr (12), 十三 shísān (13)…十九 shíjiǔ (19).

The number 20 is a combination of 二 èr (2) and 十 shí (10); 二十 èrshí means "two tens." To count further past 20, you combine 二十 èrshí with 一 yī (1) through 九 jiǔ (9) to make 21 through 29. Likewise, 三十 sānshí becomes (30), 四十 sìshí (40), 五十 wǔshí (50)…九十 jiǔshí (90).

"One hundred" is 一百 yìbǎi. Similarly, "two hundred" is 二百 èrbǎi or 两百 liǎngbǎi. "One thousand" begins the process again with 一千 yìqiān.

In Chinese, 万 wàn, meaning 10,000, is a basic counting unit, while in English 1,000 is a basic counting unit. Hence, 100,000 is 十万 shíwàn in Chinese, 1,000,000 is 一百万 yìbǎiwàn, and 10,000,000 is 一千万 yìqiānwàn. When we reach 100,000,000, Chinese has another unit 亿 yì meaning "a hundred million." A popular example of numbering at the high end is the population of China. In English we would state the population as 1.3 billion people, but in Chinese the number is stated as 13亿 shísānyì. See the tables below for a comprehensive listing of Chinese numbers.

 Table 8. *Chinese numerals*

Characters	Pinyin	Arabic Number
零	ling	0
一	yī	1
二	èr	2
三	sān	3
四	sì	4
五	wǔ	5
六	liù	6
七	qī	7
八	bā	8
九	jiǔ	9
十	shí	10
十一	shíyī	11
十二	shí'èr	12
二十	èrshí	20
二十二	èrshíèr	22

一百	yìbǎi	100
一百零三	yìbǎi líng sān	103
一百一十	yìbǎi yīshí	110
一百一十四	yìbǎi yīshísì	114
二百/两百	èrbǎi/liǎngbǎi	200
二百二十五/两百二十五	èrbǎi èrshíwǔ/liǎngbǎi èrshíwǔ	225
三千	sānqiān	3,000
三千零六	sānqiān líng liù	3,006
三千零七十	sānqiān líng qīshí	3,070
三千八百九十五	sānqiān bābǎi jiǔshíwǔ	3,895
一万	yíwàn	10,000
一万六千九百五十	yíwàn liùqiān jiǔbǎi wǔshí	16,950
一亿	yíyì	100,000,000

 Table 9. *Chinese number units*

Characters	Pinyin	Arabic Number
十	shí	10
百	bǎi	100
千	qiān	1,000
万	wàn	10,000
十万	shíwàn	100,000
百万	bǎiwàn	1,000,000
千万	qiānwàn	10,000,000
亿	yì	100,000,000
十亿	shíyì	1,000,000,000
百亿	bǎiyì	10,000,000,000
千亿	qiānyì	100,000,000,000
兆	zhào	1,000,000,000,000

In Depth: The Number "Two"

Both 二 èr and 两 liǎng mean "two," but they are used under different circumstances. In counting, for example, 一，二，三，四，五…, 二 èr is used. 两 liǎng is usually used with a measure word when counting things less than ten in total; whereas 二 is used in compound numbers such as 12, 22, 32, 122 etc. However, both 二 and 两 can be used in front of the following units: 百，千，万，亿，and 兆.

Useful Expressions in Chinese

Greetings

Nǐ hǎo!	Hello! How are you?
Nǐ zǎo!	Good morning!
Zǎoshang hǎo!	Good morning!
Zǎo'ān!	Good morning!
Wǎnshang hǎo!	Good evening!
Wǎn'ān!	Goodnight!

Goodbyes

Zàijiàn!	Goodbye!
Míngtiān jiàn!	See you tomorrow!
Xià xīngqī jiàn!	See you next week!

Introduction

Nín guì xìng?	What's your last name?
Hěn gāoxìng rènshi nín!	Nice to meet you!
Xìnghuì, xìnghuì!	It's an honor to meet you!
Qǐng duō duō zhǐjiào.	Please feel free to instruct/advise me.

Courtesy

Xièxie!	Thank you!
Bú xiè / bú kèqi!	You're welcome!
Qǐng wèn…	May I ask…; Excuse me…
Láojià…	Excuse me; May I trouble you?
Duìbuqǐ!	I'm sorry!
Méi guānxì.	It doesn't matter; Never mind.
Méi shìr.	It's nothing; Don't mention it.

Welcome

Huānyíng!	Welcome!
Qǐng jìnlai!	Please come in!
Qǐng zuò!	Please sit down!
Qǐng yòng chá!	Please have some tea!

Small Talk

Jīntiān máng bù máng?	Are you busy today?
Nǐ zěnmeyàng?	How's it going?
Mǎma hūhu.	Just fine; so so.
Hǎojiǔ bújiàn!	Long time no see!
Zuìjìn gōngzuò máng bù máng?	Are you busy with work lately?
Hái hǎo/Hái xíng.	I'm fine; not so bad.

Politeness

Tài máfan nín le.	Sorry to bother you.
Nǎli, nǎli.	Nice of you to say so; Thank you.

Concern

Qǐng shāo děng.	Please wait a moment.
Qǐng děng yíxià.	Please wait a moment.
Wǒ mǎshàng lái.	I'll come right away.
Bié zhāojí.	Take it easy; Don't be in a hurry.
Mànman lái!	Take it easy; Take it slowly.

Language Difficulty

Duìbuqǐ, wǒ bù zhīdào.	I'm sorry, I don't know.
Wǒ bù dǒng.	I don't understand.
Qǐng nín shuō màn yìdiǎnr.	Please speak more slowly.
Qǐng nín zài shuō yí biàn.	Please say it again.

Abbreviations

Abbreviations for Parts of Speech	
Adj	*Adjective*
Adv	*Adverb*
AV	*Auxiliary verb*
Conj	*Conjunction*
Exc	*Exclamation*
IP	*Interrogative pronoun*
M	*Measure word*
N	*Noun*
Nu	*Numeral*
O	*Object*
P	*Particle*
Pre	*Prefix*
PN	*Proper noun*
Prep	*Preposition*
S	*Subject*
Spe	*Specifier*
Suf	*Suffix*
TD	*Time duration expression*
TF	*Time frequency expression*
TW	*Time word*
UE	*Useful expression*
V	*Verb*
VC	*Verb plus complement*
VO	*Verb plus object*

UNIT
1

问好
Wènhǎo
Greetings

Unit **1.1**

Exchanging Names

In this lesson we will learn:

* How to greet someone when meeting for the first time.
* How to ask what someone's name is.
* How to distinguish Chinese family names from given names.

Chinese Dialogue

高明： 您好！

白有天： 您好！

高明： 您贵姓？

白有天： 我姓白。

高明： 您叫什么名字？

白有天： 我叫白有天。您呢？

高明： 我姓高，我叫高明。

白有天： 高先生，很高兴认识您。

高明： 很高兴认识您，白先生。

Pinyin Dialogue

Gāo Míng:	Nín hǎo!
Bái Yǒutiān:	Nín hǎo!
Gāo Míng:	Nín guì xìng?
Bái Yǒutiān:	Wǒ xìng Bái.
Gāo Míng:	Nín jiào shénme míngzi?
Bái Yǒutiān:	Wǒ jiào Bái Yǒutiān, nín ne?
Gāo Míng:	Wǒ xìng Gāo. Wǒ jiào Gāo Míng.
Bái Yǒutiān:	Gāo Xiānsheng, hěn gāoxìng rènshi nín.
Gāo Míng:	Hěn gāoxìng rènshi nín, Bái Xiānsheng.

Vocabulary

Chinese	Pinyin	Part of Speech	English Equivalent
1. 问好	wènhǎo	N V	greetings to greet
2. 高明	Gāo Míng	PN	the full name of a fictional person in this text
3. 高	Gāo gāo	PN Adj	a surname tall; high
4. 明	Míng míng	PN Adj	the given name of a fictional character in this text bright
5. 您	nín	Pr	you (the honorific form of "you")
6. 好	hǎo	Adj	fine; good
7. 白有天	Bái Yǒutiān	PN	the full name of a fictional person in this text
8. 白	Bái bái	PN Adj	a surname white
9. 有	yǒu	PN	used as part of a name in this text; (cf. Unit 3.1)
10. 天	tiān	PN N	used as part of a name in this text day; sky
11. 贵姓	guì xìng	UE	an honorific form used to ask a person's surname
12. 贵	guì	Adj	the honorific form of "your;" expensive
13. 姓	xìng	N V	surname to be named (surname)
14. 我	wǒ	Pr	I; me
15. 叫	jiào	V	to be called (first name/full name); to call
16. 什么	shénme	Pr	what
17. 名字	míngzi	N	full name; given name
18. 呢	ne	P	(a particle used to form an elliptical question)
19. 先生	xiānsheng	N	Mr.; husband
20. 很	hěn	Adv	very

| 21. | 高兴 | gāoxìng | Adj | glad; pleased; happy |
| 22. | 认识 | rènshi | V | to know (someone); to be acquainted with (a person) |

Sentence Patterns

1. 我姓高。 **Wǒ xìng Gāo. "My family name (surname) is Gao."**

姓 xìng is both a noun and a verb, but it is often used as a verb. When 姓 is used as a verb it must be followed by a person's family name or an interrogative pronoun such as shénme "what." For example: Tā xìng shénme "What is his family name?" (Also see Sentence Pattern 2).

S + 姓 + Family Name	
1. 我姓白。 Wǒ xìng Bái. My family name is Bai.	**Substitution***
	陈 Chén　　江 Jiāng 胡 Hú　　　马 Mǎ 丁 Dīng　　毛 Máo
2. 他姓张。 Tā xìng Zhāng. His family name is Zhang.	林 Lín　　　王 Wáng 李 Lǐ　　　孙 Sūn

*See the Additional Vocabulary list at the end of the lesson for words that are practiced in the "Substitution" sections of the Sentence Patterns.

2. 您叫什么名字？ **Nín jiào shénme míngzi? "What is your name?"**

什么 shénme is the most frequently used interrogative pronoun in Chinese. It can be used as a nominative to modify a noun that follows it, as in (I) in the examples below, or it can be used as an independent interrogative word without a noun, as in (II) in the examples below. Note that in English, interrogative pronouns like "what" are generally placed at the beginning of the sentence; whereas in Chinese, 什么 and all other interrogative pronouns are placed in the same position as their corresponding words in statements (i.e., the word order is not changed in questions). For example:

S + 叫 + 什么 + 名字			
您	叫	什么	名字?
(I) A: Nín	jiào	**shénme**	míngzi?
You	are called	**what**	name?
我	叫	高明。	
B: Wǒ	jiào	**Gāo Míng.**	
I	am called	**Gao Ming.**	

S + 姓 + Family Name			
他	姓	什么?	
(II) A: Tā	xìng	**shénme?**	
He	is surnamed	**what?**	
他	姓	高。	
B: Tā	xìng	**Gāo.**	
He	is surnamed	**Gao.**	

3. 我<u>叫</u>高明。 **Wǒ <u>jiào</u> Gāo Míng. "My name is Gao Ming."**

叫 jiào means "to call" or "to be called." 叫 can be followed either by a person's full name or his/her given name only. As in the example below, in reply to the question 您叫什么名字 Nín jiào shénme míngzi, "What is your name?" one can give either only the given name or the full name after the surname is introduced.

S + 叫 + Full Name/Given Name

A: 您叫什么名字？

B1: 我姓白，叫有天。 (given name only)

B2: 我姓白，我叫白有天。 (full name)

A: Nín jiào shénme míngzi?
B1: Wǒ xìng Bái, jiào Yǒutiān.
B2: Wǒ xìng Bái, wǒ jiào Bái Yǒutiān.

A: What's your name?
B1: My family name is Bai. My given name is Youtian.
B2: My family name is Bai. My name is Bai, Youtian.

4. 您呢？ Nín ne? "How about you?"

呢 ne is a modal particle and it can be added to a noun or a pronoun to form an elliptical question (a question tagged onto the answer to a preceding question), e.g., "How/What about X?"

Noun/Pronoun + 呢？

1. A: 您贵姓？

   B: 我姓李，您呢？

   A: 我姓吴。

   A: Nín guì xìng?
   B: Wǒ xìng Lǐ, nín ne?
   A: Wǒ xìng Wú.

   A: What's your family name?
   B: My family name is Li. And you?
   A: My family name is Wu.

2. A: 我认识林先生，高明呢？

   B: 他认识。

   A: Wǒ rènshi Lín Xiānsheng, Gāo Míng ne?
   B: Tā rènshi.

   A: I know Mr. Lin, what about Gao Ming?
   B: He knows (Mr. Lin).

Cultural Points

1. 您好！ Nín hǎo! "Hello! How are you?"

A common way of greeting others in Chinese is to say 您/你好 Nín/Nǐ hǎo. This can be used to greet an old friend or make an acquaintance of someone you meet for the first time. The response to this greeting is also 您/你好.

While today it is common to say 你好, traditionally, it is more common amongst Chinese people to greet each other by asking questions such as "Have you eaten yet?" or "Are you going to work?" to convey their concerns about another person's well-being.

2. 您贵姓？ Nín guì xìng? "What is your last name?"

贵姓 guì xìng is an honorific form of "your last name." It is a polite way of asking the last name of the person with whom you are speaking. The answer to this question is 我姓 …… Wǒ xìng… but not *我贵姓 …… To ask a third person's last name, 他/她姓什么 Tā xìng shénme is used, but not *他贵姓. Please note after 姓, you give your family name only, not your full name or given name.

3. 您 nín vs. 你 nǐ

China is a hierarchical society. Though many practices deriving from a hierarchical structure of society have lessened or ceased over the centuries, some old honorific speech forms still exist. When one wishes to show respect to a person, it is customary to use the honorific form of 您 nín for "you." Centuries ago, the archaic "Thou" would have been an English equivalent. The common form of "you" is 你 nǐ, which is used more frequently than 您 and denotes closer social equivalence and familiarity. 您 is generally reserved for formal settings, such as business meetings.

4. Chinese Names

A Chinese surname precedes the given name. For example: in the name 白有天 Bái Yǒutiān, 白 Bái is the surname and 有天 Yǒutiān is the given name. The practice of having the surname

*Throughout this textbook, a * symbol is used to highlight incorrect sentences.

before the given name is characteristic of the Chinese hierarchical structure of society. In China, family is of paramount importance and personal identity is less important. Hence the given name follows the surname.

The vast majority of Chinese family names are one syllable or character, but there are a few exceptions, such as 司马 Sīmǎ and 欧阳 Ōuyáng.

A Chinese given name may be comprised of one or two syllables or characters. After the founding of the People's Republic of China, given names in mainland China were, by and large, changed from having two syllables to only having one syllable. This change only took place in mainland China; among overseas Chinese, Hong Kong, and Taiwan residents, the traditional two-syllable given name is preferred. In recent years, due to the large number of duplicate names in mainland China, there has been a reversion to two-syllable given names.

5. Use of Titles

When addressing an individual in Chinese, you say the family name first and the honorific or title after the family name. Thus, "Mr. Bai" in English is actually spoken as "Bai Mr." in Chinese. A person is formally addressed by his/her family name followed by his/her title, e.g., 高先生 Gāo Xiānsheng "Mr. Gao," or 林老师 Lín Lǎoshī "Teacher Lin."

Unlike in the United States, in China it is generally not acceptable to address your superior by his or her given name only. In some joint venture companies, this cultural aspect has changed; among coworkers it is becoming acceptable to address each other by given names. However, unlike in the West, where a person of any rank can be addressed as either Mr. or by his/her first name, a superior in China is still properly addressed by his or her last name followed by the title of the highest position he or she holds. Complications may arise from this tradition. For example: subordinates may find it is difficult to address a superior who is younger than they are. Although there is no clear answer, it would be safer to address the superior with the formal title to show respect. Showing respect is key and should still supercede most other conventions and customs in China.

Titles are highly valued in Chinese society. When addressing someone by his or her title, make sure that you are using the correct one. If the person is both a manager and a member of a governmental agency, use the highest possible title (in this case, the governmental agency title). If the person has the prefix "vice" in his or her title, the "vice" part is usually omitted in direct address.

Additional Vocabulary

	Chinese	Pinyin	Part of Speech	English Equivalent
1.	你	nǐ	Pr	you
2.	他	tā	Pr	he; him
3.	她	tā	Pr	she; her
4.	老师	lǎoshī	N	teacher

Common Chinese Surnames

1.	安	Ān		16.	吕	Lǚ
2.	包	Bāo		17.	马	Mǎ
3.	陈	Chén		18.	毛	Máo
4.	邓	Dèng		19.	钱	Qián
5.	丁	Dīng		20.	司马	Sīmǎ
6.	方	Fāng		21.	孙	Sūn
7.	郭	Guō		22.	唐	Táng
8.	何	Hé		23.	田	Tián
9.	胡	Hú		24.	吴	Wú
10.	黄	Huáng		25.	王	Wáng
11.	江	Jiāng		26.	谢	Xiè
12.	孔	Kǒng		27.	许	Xǔ
13.	李	Lǐ		28.	杨	Yáng
14.	林	Lín		29.	张	Zhāng
15.	刘	Liú		30.	周	Zhōu

Unit **1.2**

Exchanging Greetings

In this lesson you will learn:

• How to greet someone depending on the time of day.

• How to appropriately say good-bye in a conversation.

🔘 Chinese Dialogue

白有天： 早上好!

高明： 早上好!

白有天： 高先生，您今天忙吗?

高明： 我今天很忙。

白有天： 明天呢? 明天忙不忙?

高明： 明天不忙，您呢?

白有天： 明天我也不忙。

高明： 那我们明天见!

白有天： 好，再见!

Pinyin Dialogue

Bái Yǒutiān:	Zǎoshang hǎo!
Gāo Míng:	Zǎoshang hǎo!
Bái Yǒutiān:	Gāo Xiānsheng, nín jīntiān máng ma?
Gāo Míng:	Wǒ jīntiān hěn máng.
Bái Yǒutiān:	Míngtiān ne? Míngtiān máng bù máng?
Gāo Míng:	Míngtiān bù máng, nín ne?
Bái Yǒutiān:	Míngtiān wǒ yě bù máng.
Gāo Míng:	Nà wǒmen míngtiān jiàn!
Bái Yǒutiān:	Hǎo, zàijiàn!

Vocabulary

Chinese	Pinyin	Part of Speech	English Equivalent
1. 早上好	zǎoshang hǎo	UE	Good morning!
2. 早上	zǎoshang	TW	(early) morning
3. 今天	jīntiān	TW	today
4. 忙	máng	Adj	busy
5. 吗	ma	IP	a particle used to form a question
6. 明天	míngtiān	TW	tomorrow
7. 不	bù	Adv	no; not
8. 也	yě	Adv	also
9. 那	nà	Conj	in that case; then
10. 我们	wǒmen	Pr	we; us
11. 们	men	Suf	pluralizes pronouns and nouns that refer to people
12. 见	jiàn	V	to see
13. 再见	zàijiàn	UE	good-bye; see you again
14. 再	zài	Adv	again

Sentence Patterns

1. 您今天忙<u>吗</u>? **Nín jīntiān máng <u>ma</u>?** "Are you busy today?"

In Chinese, a statement, either affirmative or negative, can be changed into a yes/no type of question simply by adding the interrogative particle 吗 ma to the end of the sentence. For example: 他很高 Tā hěn gāo "He is very tall" (a statement) is turned into a question 他很高吗 "Is he very tall?" when 吗 is added to the end. Please note that the sentence structure remains unchanged in Chinese, aside from the addition of 吗 at the end.

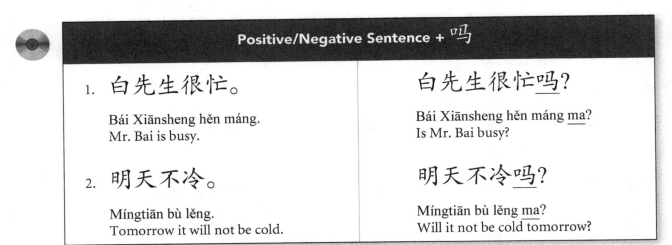

Positive/Negative Sentence + 吗	
1. 白先生很忙。 Bái Xiānsheng hěn máng. Mr. Bai is busy.	白先生很忙<u>吗</u>? Bái Xiānsheng hěn máng <u>ma</u>? Is Mr. Bai busy?
2. 明天不冷。 Míngtiān bù lěng. Tomorrow it will not be cold.	明天不冷<u>吗</u>? Míngtiān bù lěng <u>ma</u>? Will it not be cold tomorrow?

2. 我今天<u>很</u>忙。 **Wǒ jīntiān <u>hěn</u> máng.** "I am busy today."

An adjective in Chinese, such as 好 hǎo "good," 忙 máng "busy," and 高 gāo "tall," can function as the predicate in a sentence describing the state or condition of the subject. Note that no other form of the verb "to be" (am, are, is) is used in the sentence. Because adjectives in Chinese can function as complete predicates, they are sometimes called "stative verbs." However, in an affirmative sentence, 很 hěn, literally meaning "very," is normally used to modify the adjective. Please note that in such a case, 很 does not carry the same degree of intensity as it would in English. In other words, when 很 is used in affirmative sentences, it does not mean "very." Thus, 我很好 Wǒ hěn hǎo means "I am fine." But in negative sentences, it is not necessary to add 很 before the adjective. And if 很 is present in an interrogative sentence, such as 你很忙吗 Nǐ hěn máng ma "Are you very busy?," then 很 does mean "very."

	Substitution	
1. <u>我</u>很<u>好</u>。 Wǒ hěn hǎo. I am fine.	他 她 我们 他们 她们 白先生 司马太太	tā tā wǒmen tāmen tāmen Bái Xiānsheng Sīmǎ Tàitai
2. 他很<u>高</u>。 Tā hěn gāo. He is tall.	好 高兴	hǎo gāoxìng
3. 今天很<u>热</u>。 Jīntiān hěn rè. Today it is hot.	冷 凉	lěng liáng
4. <u>昨天</u>很<u>冷</u>。 Zuótiān hěn lěng. Yesterday it was cold.	今天 今天早上 今天下午 昨天晚上	jīntiān jīntiān zǎoshang jīntiān xiàwǔ zuótiān wǎnshang

3. 明天<u>不</u>忙。 **Míngtiān <u>bù</u> máng. "I'm not busy tomorrow."**

不 bù, a negative marker, is used before an adjective or a non-past verb (present or future tense verb) to negate a sentence. For example: 他不高兴 Tā bù gāoxìng "He is not happy." Note that bù is a fourth tone by itself. But when bù is followed by a fourth tone syllable, bù has to change to bú, a second tone. For example, 不累 bú lèi "not tired."

		Substitution	
1. 我不忙。 Wǒ bù máng. I am not busy.		累 高 饿 高兴	lèi gāo è gāoxìng
2. 今天不冷。 Jīntiān bù lěng. Today it is not cold.		热	rè
3. 昨天不热。 Zuótiān bú rè. Yesterday it was not hot.		今天 明天	jīntiān míngtiān

4. 明天忙不忙? Míngtiān máng bù máng? "Will you be busy tomorrow?"

V/Adj-not-V/Adj is another way to make a question sentence. The question is formed by using a positive verb/adjective and a negative form of the verb/adjective in the same sentence, For example: 你忙不忙 Nǐ máng bù máng means "Are you busy or not busy?" To answer this type of question, you may choose either "V/Adj" or "not V/Adj," which is 我很忙 Wǒ hěn máng "I am busy" or 我不忙 Wǒ bù máng "I am not busy."

When the V/Adj in this pattern is a two-syllable word, it is only necessary to use the first syllable in the first occurrence of the word; but in the second occurrence (after 不) the whole word must be used. For example: 你高不高兴 Nǐ gāo bù gāoxìng can be used instead of 你高兴不高兴 Nǐ gāoxìng bù gāoxìng "Are you happy or not?"

呢 ne, as a modal particle, can also be added to the end of this type of question sentence. It does not add any meaning, but it softens the tone of the question. This usage of 呢 differs from the one mentioned in Unit 1.1 (Sentence Pattern 4). Note that it would be incorrect to use 吗 ma at the end of such questions.

S + Adj/V + bù + Adj/V (呢)		
	Substitution	
1. 他忙不忙(呢)? Tā máng bù máng (ne)? Is he busy?	累 高 饿	lèi gāo è
2. A: 他姓不姓王? B: 他不姓王，他姓陈。 A: Tā xìng bú xìng Wáng? B: Tā bú xìng Wáng, tā xìng Chén. A: Is his family name Wang? B: His family name is not Wang. His family name is Chen.	江 胡 马 毛 林 李	Jiāng Hú Mǎ Máo Lín Lǐ

5. 明天我也不忙。 **Míngtiān wǒ yě bù máng. "I will also not be busy tomorrow."**

也 yě "too, also" is an adverb used to modify a verb or an adjective. It means "likewise; in the same manner," and it must be placed before the word it modifies. Unlike in English, where "also" can appear at the beginning, middle, or end of a sentence, in Chinese 也 can only appear immediately before the verb or adjective, hence *也我很忙 would be incorrect.

A Chinese time word such as 早上 zǎoshang "morning" or 今天 jīntiān "today" can be placed before or after the subject, as long as it precedes the verb in a sentence. Therefore, both 我今天很忙 Wǒ jīntiān hěn máng "I am busy today" and 今天我很忙 Jīntiān wǒ hěn máng are acceptable, but not *我很忙今天 Wǒ hěn máng jīntiān.

1. 我很忙，他也很忙。

   Wǒ hěn máng, tā yě hěn máng.
   I am busy. He is also busy.

2. 昨天不热，今天也不热。

   Zuótiān bú rè, jīntiān yě bú rè.
   Yesterday it was not hot. Today it is also not hot.

3. 我认识丁先生，也认识丁太太。

   Wǒ rènshi Dīng Xiānsheng, yě rènshi Dīng Tàitai.
   I know Mr. Ding. I know Mrs. Ding, too.

6. 那我们明天见。 **Nà wǒmen míngtiān jiàn. "Then, we will meet tomorrow."**

The three primary personal pronouns in Chinese are: 我 wǒ "I; me," 你 nǐ "you," and 他/她 tā "he/she; him/her." Although the pronunciations for "he" and "she" are identical in Chinese, the written forms for these two words are different, e.g., 她 for "she" and 他 for "he." Please also note that the Chinese pronouns do not require case changes as they do in English, thus 我 means both "I" and "me." The same applies to 你 and 他/她.

When 们 men (neutral tone), a plural marker, is attached to a personal pronoun, it pluralizes the pronoun. For example: 我们 wǒmen means "we/us." Likewise, the plural form of 你 nǐ "you" is 你们 nǐmen "you" (plural) and the plural form of 他/她 tā "he/she" is 他们/她们 tāmen "they/them." 们 can also pluralize personal nouns, e.g., 学生们 xuéshengmen "students," 老师们 lǎoshīmen "teachers." This usage, however, is prevalent in directly addressing or referring to groups of people, as in 女士们, 先生们 nǚshìmen, xiānshengmen "ladies and gentlemen."

	Singular			Plual		
1st person	我	wǒ	I; me	我们	wǒmen	we; us
2nd person	你	nǐ	you	你们	nǐmen	you
3rd person	他	tā	he; him	他们	tāmen	they; them
	她	tā	she; her	她们	tāmen	they; them

Cultural Points

1. 早上好! Zǎoshang hǎo! "Good morning!"

In addition to 你好 Nǐ hǎo, 早上好 Zǎoshang hǎo meaning "good morning" is another greeting that is used when people meet each other in the morning. The proper response to this greeting is also 早上好. Other forms of greetings that can be used in the morning are 你早 Nǐ zǎo and simply 早 (less formal but frequently used among acquaintances). The following table presents the various forms of greetings that can be used at different times of the day.

Table 10. Greetings for different times of the day

早!	Zǎo!	Good morning!
你早!	Nǐ zǎo!	
早上好!	Zǎoshang hǎo!	
早安!	Zǎo'ān!	
下午好!	Xiàwǔ hǎo!	Good afternoon!
午安!	Wǔ'ān!	
晚上好!	Wǎnshang hǎo!	Good evening!
晚安!	Wǎn'ān!	Good night!

2. 我们 vs 咱们 Wǒmen vs Zánmen

我们 wǒmen means "we" or "us," which may or may not include the person with whom the speaker is talking, depending on the context of the conversation. In lieu of 我们, 咱们 zánmen is widely used in the northern region of China, especially in Beijing, and 咱们 usually includes the person with whom the speaker is talking.

3. 再见! Zàijiàn! "Good-bye!"

再见 zàijiàn translated contextually means "good-bye," but when translated literally the meaning is closer to "See you again." Many languages have their own version of this phrase. From the simple English "See you later," Spanish *hasta la vista*, Italian *arrivederci*, Russian *Do Svidanya* to German *auf wiedersehen*, each language has an equivalent form of good-bye that translates literally as "until we see each other again."

 # Additional Vocabulary

	Chinese	Pinyin	Part of Speech	English Equivalent
1.	冷	lěng	Adj	cold
2.	热	rè	Adj	hot
3.	凉	liáng	Adj	cool
4.	昨天	zuótiān	TW	yesterday
5.	下午	xiàwǔ	TW	afternoon
6.	晚上	wǎnshang	TW	evening
7.	累	lèi	Adj	tired
8.	饿	è	Adj	hungry
9.	太太	tàitai	N	Mrs.; wife
10.	学生	xuésheng	N	student
11.	学	xué	V	to learn; to study

12.	女士	nǚshì	N	lady
13.	早	zǎo	UE Adj	Good morning! early
14.	早安	zǎo'ān	UE	Good morning!
15.	午安	wǔ'ān	UE	Good afternoon!
16.	晚安	wǎn'ān	UE	Good night!
17.	咱们	zánmen	Pr	we; us

UNIT
2

介绍
Jièshào
Introductions

Unit **2.1**

Meeting the Company Manager

In this lesson we will learn:

- How to address people by their correct title.
- The concept of place of origin and why it's important to Chinese people.

Chinese Dialogue

高明： 这位是马经理。

白有天： 马经理，您好！很高兴见到您。

高明： 这位是我们美国公司的白先生。

马经理： 欢迎您来中国，白先生。

白有天： 马经理是北京人吗？

马经理： 不，我是上海人。

白有天： 我太太也是上海人。上海是个很好的地方。

马经理： 白先生，您的中文很好。

白有天： 哪里，哪里。

Pinyin Dialogue

Gāo Míng:	Zhè wèi shì Mǎ Jīnglǐ.
Bái Yǒutiān:	Mǎ Jīnglǐ, nín hǎo! Hěn gāoxìng jiàndào nín.
Gāo Míng:	Zhè wèi shì wǒmen Měiguó gōngsī de Bái Xiānsheng.
Mǎ Jīnglǐ:	Huānyíng nín lái Zhōngguó, Bái Xiānsheng.
Bái Yǒutiān:	Mǎ Jīnglǐ shì Běijīngrén ma?
Mǎ Jīnglǐ:	Bù, wǒ shì Shànghǎirén.
Bái Yǒutiān:	Wǒ tàitai yě shì Shànghǎirén. Shànghǎi shì ge hěn hǎo de dìfang.
Mǎ Jīnglǐ:	Bái Xiānsheng, nín de Zhōngwén hěn hǎo.
Bái Yǒutiān:	Nǎli, nǎli.

Vocabulary

Chinese	Pinyin	Part of Speech	English Equivalent
1. 介绍	jièshào	N V	introduction to introduce
2. 这	zhè/zhèi	Spe	this
3. 位	wèi	M	(a measure word for addressing people politely)
4. 是	shì	V	to be (am; is; are)
5. 马	Mǎ mǎ	PN N	a surname horse
6. 经理	jīnglǐ	N	manager
7. 见到	jiàndào	VC	to see; to meet
8. 美国	Měiguó	PN	America
9. 美	měi	Adj	beautiful
10. 国	guó	N	country
11. 公司	gōngsī	N	company
12. 的	de	P	(a particle that indicates a possessive or descriptive form)
13. 欢迎	huānyíng	V UE	to welcome; to greet Welcome!
14. 来	lái	V	to come
15. 中国	Zhōngguó	PN	China
16. 中	zhōng	Adj	middle; medium
17. 北京	Běijīng	PN	Beijing
18. 北	běi	N	north
19. 京	jīng	N	(indicates a capital city)
20. 人	rén	N	person; people
21. 上海	Shànghǎi	PN	Shanghai
22. 上	shàng	N	above; on top of

23. 海	hǎi	N	sea
24. 个	gè	M	(a measure word for objects in general)
25. 地方	dìfang	N	place
26. 中文	Zhōngwén	PN	Chinese language
27. 哪里	nǎli	UE	a polite rejection of a compliment

Sentence Patterns

1. 这位是马经理。 Zhè wèi shì Mǎ Jīnglǐ. "This is Manager Ma."

这 zhè or zhèi "this," and 那 nà or nèi "that," are specifiers. Such specifiers can be followed by 位 wèi, an honorific measure word for "person," as a way to introduce someone who is in a higher position or who is older than you. However, 位 is not used if the person being introduced is a family member, your subordinate, and so forth.

A measure word is used between a number and a noun to indicate that the cardinal number applies to that noun. In Chinese (as opposed to in English) measure words are mandatory. Each individual noun or class of nouns has its own specific measure word, such as in the English phrase: "a pair of pants," or "a school of fish." More on measure words will be discussed in Unit 3. For now, note that in formal situations, the measure word for a person or people is 位.

这 (位) 是 + a Person's Name/Title/Relationship

	Substitution	
1. 这位是张经理。 Zhè wèi shì Zhāng Jīnglǐ. This is Manager Zhang.	老师 律师 会计师 大夫	lǎoshī lùshī kuàijìshī dàifu
2. 这是我太太。 Zhè shì wǒ tàitai. This is my wife.	先生 爸爸 妈妈 姐姐 妹妹 哥哥 弟弟	xiānsheng bàba māma jiějie mèimei gēge dìdi

这 (那) + 是 + N

	Substitution	
1. 这是书。 Zhè shì shū. This is a book.	报纸 小说 字典 地图 杂志 学校 公司	bàozhǐ xiǎoshuō zìdiǎn dìtú zázhì xuéxiào gōngsī
2. 那是笔。 Nà shì bǐ. That is a pen.		

2. 这位是我们美国公司的白先生。 **Zhè wèi shì wǒmen Měiguó gōngsī de Bái Xiānsheng. "This is our American company's Mr. Bai."**

The possessive construction in Chinese is formed by placing 的 de (neutral tone) between the "possessor" and a noun. The possessor can be either a noun (公司的经理 gōngsī de jīnglǐ "company's manager") or a pronoun (我的名字 wǒ de míngzi "my name"). When the possessor is a personal pronoun and the noun is a person in a close family relationship, such as 妈妈 māma "mother" or 哥哥 gēge "older brother," 的 can be omitted. For example: 我妈妈 wǒ māma "my mother."

N/PN + 的 + N		
		Substitution
1. 她是白先生的朋友。 Tā shì Bái Xiānsheng de péngyou. She is Mr. Bai's friend.	同学 同事 经理	tóngxué tóngshì jīnglǐ
2. 这是我先生的公司。 Zhè shì wǒ xiānsheng de gōngsī. This is my husband's company.	车子 电脑 电话 地址	chēzi diànnǎo diànhuà dìzhǐ
3. 这是公司的汽车。 Zhè shì gōngsī de qìchē. This is the company's car.		

3. 马经理是北京人吗？ **Mǎ Jīnglǐ shì Běijīngrén ma? "Is Manager Ma from Beijing?"**

是 shì is a verb meaning "to be" (am, is, are). It is used to connect the subject and its nominative, and it identifies or describes the subject. For example: 他是经理 Tā shì jīnglǐ "He is a manager." The negative form of 是 is 不是 bú shì. Note 不 bù is pronounced in the second tone and not the fourth tone here. This was explained in Unit 1.2 (Sentence Pattern 3). The following sentences are examples of how to use 是 to identify a person's place of origin.

	Substitution	
1. 你是<u>北京</u>人吗? Nǐ shì <u>Běijīng</u>rén ma? Are you from Beijing?	天津 上海 南京 西安 广州	Tiānjīn Shànghǎi Nánjīng Xī'ān Guǎngzhōu
2. 我不是<u>美国</u>人。 Wǒ bú shì <u>Měiguó</u>rén. I'm not an <u>American</u>.	英国 法国 德国 俄国 韩国 日本	Yīngguó Fǎguó Déguó Éguó Hánguó Rìběn

4. 上海是个<u>很好</u>的<u>地方</u>。 **Shànghǎi shì ge <u>hěn hǎo</u> de <u>dìfang</u>.**
"Shanghai is a very good place."

In addition to indicating the possessive form, the particle 的 de can be placed between a noun and an adjective to form a descriptive phrase. In this sentence, 的 indicates that 很好 hěn hǎo modifies the noun that follows it. If the adjective is monosyllabic, 很 "very" must be placed before the adjective itself. In other words, 好 "good" cannot be used alone to modify the noun 地方 dìfang "place;" 很 must be placed before 好. This rule does not apply to adjectives made up of two or more syllables.

The character 个 gè in this sentence is a measure word. Though measure words will be discussed in depth in Unit 3, it is worth mentioning here that 个 is the most popular and generic of all measure words.

很 + Adj + 的 + N		
	Substitution	
1. 他是很好的经理。 Tā shì hěn hǎo de jīnglǐ. He is a very good manager.	朋友 老师	péngyou lǎoshī
2. 中国是个很大的国家。 Zhōngguó shì ge hěn dà de guójiā. China is a very big country.	美国 俄国 印度 加拿大	Měiguó Éguó Yìndù Jiānádà

Cultural Points

1. 这位是我们美国公司的白先生。 Zhè wèi shì wǒmen Měiguó gōngsī de Bái Xiānsheng. "This is Mr. Bai from our American company."

It is important to note that in China, as well as other Asian countries, people identify themselves by their organization. This relationship is strong enough to justify the possessive form when talking about an employee of a company.

2. 马经理是北京人吗？ Mǎ Jīnglǐ shì Běijīngrén ma? "Is Manager Ma from Beijing?"

人 rén "person" is placed after a place of origin to convey where an individual is from. In China, people identify strongly with their place of origin. Home cities/provinces are very important because people from a common background and location have a strong bond. This is to some extent universal; no matter the country of origin, people everywhere oftentimes identify strongly with smaller regional areas. This is especially true for Chinese people, particularly overseas Chinese, who may form social groups elsewhere based on their town of origin in China. It is not unusual for the place of origin to be one of the first things that Chinese people will ask of one another.

3. 哪里，哪里。 **Nǎli, nǎli. "Thank you."**

哪里 nǎli in Chinese literally means "where." But it can be used as a polite or modest reply to a compliment. For example: as a response to 你的中文很好 "Nǐ de Zhōngwén hěn hǎo," which means "Your Chinese is very good," 哪里，哪里 can be understood as a discrete "Thank you." When translating the meaning behind the phrase, however, "You're too kind" may be more accurate. This is indicative of how Chinese people typically act humble or show modesty when individually complimented.

In China it is common practice to downplay one's personal abilities and accomplishments. This is not to mislead others, but rather as an expression of humility. The traditional way to acknowledge a compliment is to say 哪里，哪里. In recent years, however, the term 谢谢 xièxie, a term analogous to "Thank you," has become the standard response to a compliment with younger people who have absorbed Western culture; but for the older generation, the traditional acknowledgement of a compliment is still used.

Pronunciation note: Both 哪 and 里 have third tones, but when placed together for 哪里, tone sandhi rules dictate that the 哪 takes a second tone to become ná. In this case 里 is pronounced with the neutral tone. Thus, 哪里 is pronounced as náli.

 # Additional Vocabulary

	Chinese	Pinyin	Part of Speech	English Equivalent
1.	那	nà/nèi	Spe	that
2.	律师	lǜshī	N	lawyer
3.	会计师	kuàijìshī	N	accountant
4.	大夫	dàifu	N	doctor
5.	爸爸	bàba	N	dad
6.	妈妈	māma	N	mom
7.	姐姐	jiějie	N	older sister
8.	妹妹	mèimei	N	younger sister

9.	哥哥	gēge	N	older brother
10.	弟弟	dìdi	N	younger brother
11.	书	shū	N	book
12.	笔	bǐ	N	pen
13.	报纸	bàozhǐ	N	newspaper
14.	小说	xiǎoshuō	N	novel
15.	字典	zìdiǎn	N	dictionary
16.	地图	dìtú	N	map
17.	杂志	zázhì	N	magazine
18.	学校	xuéxiào	N	school; campus
19.	朋友	péngyou	N	friend
20.	同学	tóngxué	N	classmate
21.	同事	tóngshì	N	colleague; co-worker
22.	汽车	qìchē	N	automobile
23.	车子	chēzi	N	car
24.	电脑	diànnǎo	N	computer
25.	电	diàn	N	electricity; electric; electrical
26.	脑	nǎo	N	brain; mind
27.	电话	diànhuà	N	telephone
28.	地址	dìzhǐ	N	address
29.	大	dà	Adj	big; huge; old in age
30.	国家	guójiā	N	country; nation
31.	谢谢	xièxie	UE	thank you

Unit **2.2**

Getting to Know the Company Staff

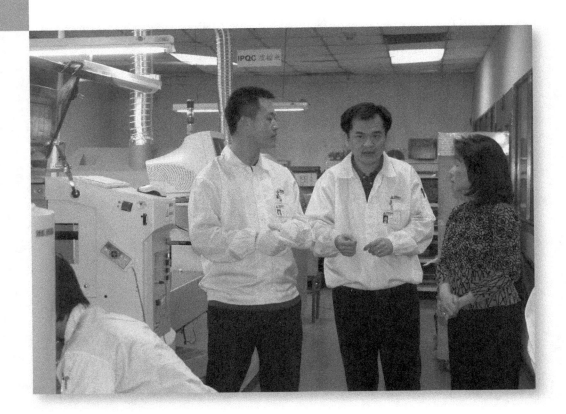

In this lesson we will learn:

• How to inquire about a third person's job functions, nationality, and language abilities.

Chinese Dialogue

白有天： 请问，谁是 Linda？

高明： 她是人事部的经理。

白有天： 她是哪国人？

高明： 她是美国人。

白有天： 她会说普通话吗？

高明： 她会说一点儿。

白有天： 那位小姐是谁？

高明： 那位是公司的秘书，王英小姐。

白有天： 她会说英文吧？

高明： 会，她英文说得很好。

Pinyin Dialogue

Bái Yǒutiān:	Qǐng wèn, shéi shì Linda?
Gāo Míng:	Tā shì rénshìbù de jīnglǐ.
Bái Yǒutiān:	Tā shì nǎ guó rén?
Gāo Míng:	Tā shì Měiguórén.
Bái Yǒutiān:	Tā huì shuō pǔtōnghuà ma?
Gāo Míng:	Tā huì shuō yìdiǎnr.
Bái Yǒutiān:	Nà wèi xiǎojie shì shéi?
Gāo Míng:	Nà wèi shì gōngsī de mìshū, Wáng Yīng Xiǎojie.
Bái Yǒutiān:	Tā huì shuō Yīngwén ba?
Gāo Míng:	Huì, tā Yīngwén shuō de hěn hǎo.

Vocabulary

Chinese	Pinyin	Part of Speech	English Equivalent
1. 请问	qǐng wèn	UE	Excuse me…; May I ask…
2. 请	qǐng	Adv/V	please; to request; to invite
3. 问	wèn	V	to ask (a question)
4. 谁	shéi/shuí	IP	who; whom
5. 人事部	rénshìbù	N	human resources department
6. 人事	rénshì	N	human resource; human concerns
7. 部	bù	N	department
8. 哪	nǎ/něi	IP	which
9. 会	huì	AV / V	can / to know how to
10. 说	shuō	V	to speak; to say
11. 普通话	pǔtōnghuà	N	common speech; a reference to Mandarin Chinese
12. 普通	pǔtōng	Adj	common; ordinary
13. 话	huà	N	spoken language; words; speech
14. 一点	yìdiǎn	Adj	a little
15. 一点儿	yìdiǎnr	Adj	a little (Beijing pronunciation)
16. 小姐	xiǎojie	N	Miss; young lady
17. 秘书	mìshū	N	secretary
18. 王英	Wáng Yīng	PN	the full name of a fictional person in this text
19. 王	Wáng / wáng	PN / N	a surname / king
20. 英	Yīng	PN	the given name of a fictional character in this text
21. 英文	Yīngwén	PN	English
22. 文	wén	N	language; written language

23. 吧	ba	P	(a particle that implies a supposition)
24. 得	de	P	(a particle that indicates a complement of degree)

Sentence Patterns

1. 请问，……? Qǐng wèn, …? "Excuse me; May I ask …?"

请 qǐng, a verb, means "to request; to invite." For example: 请他 qǐng tā means "to ask/invite him." When it precedes another verb, its English equivalent is "please." For example: 请进来 qǐng jìnlái means "please come in," and 请坐 qǐng zuò means "please have a seat." However, when 请 "please" and 问 wèn "ask" are used together, it is a polite expression used to make inquiries or address a stranger, meaning "Excuse me, may I ask…?" 请问 qǐng wèn must be followed by a question.

请问 + Question Sentence

1. **请问，您贵姓？**

   Qǐng wèn, nín guì xìng?
   Excuse me, what is your family name?

2. **请问，您是美国人吗？**

   Qǐng wèn, nín shì Měiguórén ma?
   Excuse me, are you an American?

3. **请问，这是你的报纸吗？**

   Qǐng wèn, zhè shì nǐ de bàozhǐ ma?
   Excuse me, is this your newspaper?

2. 谁是 Linda? Shéi shì Linda? "Who is Linda?"

谁 Shéi (also pronounced as shuí in southern China) is an interrogative pronoun meaning "who" or "whom." For example: the Chinese equivalent of "Who is the manager?" can be 谁是经理 Shéi shì jīnglǐ or 经理是谁 Jīnglǐ shì shéi. Note: as stated in Unit 1.1 (Sentence Pattern 2), the word order in a sentence that uses interrogative pronouns must remain the same in the question and the response.

谁 + 是 + N			
谁	是	你们的	律师?
A: Shéi Who	shì is	nǐmen de your	lǜshī? lawyer?
田先生	是	我们的	律师。
B: Tián Xiānsheng Mr. Tian	shì is	wǒmen de our	lǜshī. lawyer.

谁的 + N		
这是	谁的	杂志?
A: Zhè shì This is	shéi de whose	zázhì? magazine?
这是	我的。	
B: Zhè shì This is	wǒ de. mine.	

Note: The noun (referring to zázhì in this example) can be omitted if it is understood.

S + 是 + 谁		
他	是	谁?
A: Tā He	shì is	shéi? who?
他	是	李大夫。
B: Tā He	shì is	Lǐ Dàifu. Dr. Li.

3. 她是<u>哪国人</u>? Tā shì <u>nǎ guó rén</u>? "What country is she from?"

哪 Nǎ (also pronounced něi) is another interrogative word meaning "which." 国 guó is the short form for 国家 guójiā "country," and it must be used here instead of the full form 国家. 你是哪国人 Nǐ shì nǎ guó rén literally means "You are which country's person?" Note again that interrogative pronouns like 哪, 谁 shéi "who" and 什么 shénme "what," which are explained in Units 1.1 (Sentence Pattern 2), and 2.2 (Sentence Pattern 2), remain in the same word position in the question as they are in the statement.

哪		
她是	哪国	人?
(I) A: Tā shì She is	něi guó which country's	rén? person?
她是	德国	人。
B: Tā shì She is	Déguó Germany	rén. person.

Note: For the purpose of illustrating the sentence structure in Chinese, literal English translations are given for the examples in Sentence Patterns 2-3.

	你	哪天	不忙?
(II) A:	Nǐ	nǎ tiān	bù máng?
	You	which day	not busy?
	我	明天	不忙。
B:	Wǒ	míngtiān	bù máng.
	I	tomorrow	not busy.

	哪位	是	
(III) A:	Nǎ wèi	shì	
	Which person	is	John?
	那位	是	
B:	Nà wèi	shì	
	That person	is	John.

4. 她会说普通话吗? Tā huì shuō pǔtōnghuà ma? "Can she speak Mandarin?"

会 huì "can" is either used as an auxiliary verb when followed by another verb, or as a main verb when followed by a noun. Both usages in this lesson mean that a person has acquired an ability or skill through learning. The negative form of 会 is 不会 bú huì. For example: 我不会说中国话 Wǒ bú huì shuō Zhōngguó huà "I cannot speak Chinese." The interrogative sentence is formed either by adding 吗 at the end of the sentence or by using the affirmative–negative form. See the following examples:

A: 你会不会中文? Nǐ huì bú huì Zhōngwén? Do you know Chinese?

B: 我不会中文，我会英文。 Wǒ bú huì Zhōngwén, wǒ huì Yīngwén.
I don't know Chinese, I know English.

S + (不) + 会 + V + (O)		
	Substitution	
1. 他会说<u>汉语</u>。 Tā huì shuō Hànyǔ. He can speak Chinese.	德语 法语 英语 日语 俄语 西班牙语	Déyǔ Fǎyǔ Yīngyǔ Rìyǔ Éyǔ Xībānyáyǔ
2. 他不会<u>写汉字</u>。 Tā bú huì xiě Hànzì. He cannot write Chinese characters.	开车 打球 做菜	kāi chē dǎ qiú zuò cài

5. 她会说<u>一点儿</u>。 **Tā huì shuō <u>yìdiǎnr</u>. "She can speak a little bit."**

一点儿 yìdiǎnr, meaning "a little," is used as a quantifier to express that the quantity of the noun is minimal. For example: 她会说一点儿普通话 Tā huì shuō yìdiǎnr pǔtōnghuà "She can speak a little Chinese." In northern China, an "r" ending (represented by the character 儿) is often added to nouns and some other specific words like 一点. This is not so in the South. When the "r" ending is added to a syllable that ends in "n," it replaces the "n." So 一点儿 is used in the North, and 一点 in the South.

Another note of importance is that the object of the verb 说 must be the noun 话. If the noun is not modified by an adjective, namely a country, then 说话 simply means "to talk."

6. 她会说英文<u>吧</u>? **Tā huì shuō Yīngwén <u>ba</u>? "She can speak English, can't she?"**

We have already learned that a statement can be changed to a question by adding 吗 ma to the end of the sentence. However, if the speaker is fairly certain about the answer to the question, 吧 ba (neutral tone) can be added to the end of a sentence. By adding 吧 to a statement, it implies that the speaker is making a judgment or a supposition, but is not absolutely certain about it.

Sentence + 吧

1. 你很忙**吧**?

   Nǐ hěn máng ba?
   You are very busy, aren't you?

2. 您是美国人**吧**?

   Nín shì Měiguórén ba?
   You are an American, aren't you?

3. 他不是经理**吧**?

   Tā bú shì jīnglǐ ba?
   He is not the manager, is he?

4. 他不会开车**吧**?

   Tā bú huì kāi chē ba?
   He cannot drive, can he?

---

7. 她英文说<u>得</u>很好。 **Tā Yīngwén shuō <u>de</u> hěn hǎo. "She speaks English well."**

得 de, a structural particle, is used to connect a verb and an adjective. This type of sentence structure describes the manner or degree to which the action is conducted and is known as "complement of degree."

S + V + 得 + Adj

	Substitution	
1. 他<u>说</u>得很好。 Tā shuō de hěn hǎo. He speaks very well.	教 讲 做 写 打	jiāo jiǎng zuò xiě dǎ

	V		Adj	
2. 他<u>说</u>得很<u>快</u>。 Tā shuō de hěn kuài. He speaks very fast.	开 走 做 吃	kāi zǒu zuò chī	快 慢 多 少	kuài màn duō shǎo

Note that if the verb takes an object, then the verb has to be repeated after the object for 得 to follow the repeated verb (after the second instance of the verb).

Example: 他说中文说得很好。

> Tā shuō Zhōngwén shuō de hěn hǎo.
> He speaks Chinese well.

Another variation of the above example is to omit the first instance of the verb.

Example: 他中文说得很好。

> Tā Zhōngwén shuō de hěn hǎo.
> He speaks Chinese well.

S + V + O + V + Adj		
	Substitution	
1. 他说汉语说得很好。 Tā shuō Hànyǔ shuō de hěn hǎo. He speaks Chinese well.	教书 做菜 打球	jiāo shū zuò cài dǎ qiú
	VO	**Adj**
2. 他看书看得很快。 Tā kàn shū kàn de hěn kuài. He reads books fast.	开车 kāi chē 打字 dǎ zì	快 kuài 慢 màn

Cultural Points

1. 普通话 Pǔtōnghuà "Common Speech"

普通话 literally means "common speech," and is a reference to Mandarin Chinese, as it is the most common form of spoken Chinese in mainland China. In Taiwan, the term 国语 guóyǔ, literally translated as the "language of the country," is an equivalent phrase to the mainland pǔtōnghuà.

2. Western Names Used by Chinese Employees

Many multinational corporations have begun adopting Western names for their native employees. It is not uncommon now for Chinese workers to be addressed by American and British first names. Their surnames, being more important, remain in their original Chinese.

3. Country Names and Their Peoples and Languages

In order to state the region or country from which a person originates, one must only take the word for the region/country, and add 人 to designate that they are "a person of…" (cf. note in Sentence Pattern 3, this lesson).

There are three different ways to refer to the language of a region. Each follows the same format as the usage of "country name + 人" to indicate a person's nationality. That is, 文 wén, 语 yǔ, or 话 huà following the name of a country indicates the country from which the language originates. The difference between 文 and 语/话 is that 文 refers to both the written and spoken forms of the language; while 语 and 话 mostly refer to the spoken form of the language.

Table 11. Countries and their languages

Country			People	Language
中国	Zhōngguó	China	中国人	中文, 汉语, 普通话, 中国话
美国	Měiguó	United States	美国人	英文, 英语, 美语, 美国话
英国	Yīngguó	UK	英国人	英文, 英语
法国	Fǎguó	France	法国人	法文, 法语, 法国话
德国	Déguó	Germany	德国人	德文, 德语, 德国话
俄国	Éguó	Russia	俄国人	俄文, 俄语, 俄国话
日本	Rìběn	Japan	日本人	日文, 日语, 日本话
韩国	Hánguó	Korea	韩国人	韩文, 韩语, 韩国话
新加坡	Xīnjiāpō	Singapore	新加坡人	汉语, 英语, 马来语
西班牙	Xībānyá	Spain	西班牙人	西班牙文, 西班牙语, 西班牙话
葡萄牙	Pútáoyá	Portugal	葡萄牙人	葡萄牙文, 葡萄牙语, 葡萄牙话

	墨西哥	Mòxīgē	Mexico	墨西哥人	西班牙文, 西班牙语, 西班牙话
	巴西	Bāxī	Brazil	巴西人	葡萄牙语
	印度	Yìndù	India	印度人	印度语, 英语
	加拿大	Jiānádà	Canada	加拿大人	英语, 法语

Additional Vocabulary

	Chinese	Pinyin	Part of Speech	English Equivalent
1.	进来	jìnlai	VC	to come in
2.	坐	zuò	V	to sit
3.	汉语	Hànyǔ	PN	Chinese language
4.	汉	Hàn	PN	a reference to China; the original tribe from which 97 percent of ethnic Chinese trace their origins
5.	写	xiě	V	to write
6.	汉字	Hànzì	PN	Chinese characters
7.	字	zì	N	Character
8.	开车	kāi chē	VO	to drive a car
9.	开	kāi	V	to drive; to operate; to open
10.	车	chē	N	vehicle
11.	打球	dǎ qiú	VO	to hit a ball; to play a ball game
12.	打	dǎ	V	to hit
13.	球	qiú	N	ball
14.	做菜	zuò cài	VO	to cook (make dishes)
15.	做	zuò	V	to make; to do
16.	菜	cài	N	dish (of food); vegetables

17.	说话	shuō huà	VO	to talk; to speak
18.	教	jiāo	V	to teach
19.	讲	jiǎng	V	to speak; to say
20.	快	kuài	Adj	fast
21.	走	zǒu	V	to walk
22.	慢	màn	Adj	slow
23.	多	duō	Adj	many; much; a lot
24.	吃	chī	V	to eat
25.	少	shǎo	Adj	few; little
26.	教书	jiāo shū	VO	to teach (academic courses)
27.	看书	kàn shū	VO	to read books
28.	看	kàn	V	to read; to watch; to take a look
29.	打字	dǎzì	VO	to type (characters)
30.	国语	guóyǔ	N	Mandarin Chinese (term used in Taiwan); the official national language of a country

UNIT
3

家庭
Jiātíng
Family

Unit **3.1**

Marital Status and Family

In this lesson we will learn:

- About appropriate times and topics for small talk among colleagues or during business negotiations.

- How to ask about someone's marital status and whether they have children.

- How to answer questions about your own family.

⦿ Chinese Dialogue

高明：　白先生，您结婚了吗？

白有天：　我已经结婚了。

高明：　你们有没有孩子？

白有天：　有。

高明：　有几个？

白有天：　有两个。

高明：　男孩儿还是女孩儿？

白有天：　一个男孩儿和一个女孩儿。

高明：　他们几岁了？

白有天：　儿子今年十二岁，是中学生；女儿八岁，上小学了。

高明：　他们会来中国吗？

白有天：　会，他们明年会到中国来。

Pinyin Dialogue

Gāo Míng:	Bái Xiānsheng, nín jié hūn le ma?
Bái Yǒutiān:	Wǒ yǐjīng jié hūn le.
Gāo Míng:	Nǐmen yǒu méiyǒu háizi?
Bái Yǒutiān:	Yǒu.
Gāo Míng:	Yǒu jǐ ge?
Bái Yǒutiān:	Yǒu liǎng ge.
Gāo Míng:	Nánháir háishi nǚháir?
Bái Yǒutiān:	Yí ge nánháir hé yí ge nǚháir.
Gāo Míng:	Tāmen jǐ suì le?
Bái Yǒutiān:	Érzi jīnnián shí'èr suì, shì zhōngxuéshēng; nǚ'ér bā suì, shàng xiǎoxué le.
Gāo Míng:	Tāmen huì lái Zhōngguó ma?
Bái Yǒutiān:	Huì, tāmen míngnián huì dào Zhōngguó lái.

Vocabulary

Chinese	Pinyin	Part of Speech	English Equivalent
1. 家庭	jiātíng	N	family
2. 结婚	jié hūn	VO	to get married
3. 了	le	P	(a particle that indicates completion of an action)
4. 已经	yǐjīng	Adv	already
5. 有	yǒu	V	to have; there is; there are
6. 没有	méiyǒu	V Adv	do not have; there is/are not (negative marker)
7. 孩子	háizi	N	child; children; kids
8. 几	jǐ	IP	how many
9. 男孩儿	nánhái'ér	N	boy
10. 男	nán	N	male
11. 还是	háishi	Conj	or
12. 女孩儿	nǚhái'ér	N	girl
13. 女	nǚ	N	female
14. 和	hé	Conj Prep	and with
15. 岁	suì	M	(a measure word for years of age)
16. 儿子	érzi	N	son
17. 今年	jīnnián	TW	this year
18. 年	nián	N	year
19. 十二	shí'èr	Nu	twelve
20. 中学生	zhōngxuéshēng	N	middle/high school student
21. 中学	zhōngxué	N	middle school
22. 女儿	nǚ'ér	N	daughter

23.	上	shàng	V	to attend a school or class; to go to
24.	小学	xiǎoxué	N	elementary school
25.	小	xiǎo	Adj	small; little; young (used to refer to people only)
26.	会	huì	AV	will
27.	明年	míngnián	TW	next year
28.	到......来	dào...lái	V	to come to (a place)

Sentence Patterns

1. 我结婚了。 Wǒ jié hūn le. "I am married."

了 le is one of the most difficult concepts in the Chinese language for Westerners to understand. 了 is a modal particle that can be used to indicate completion of an action (often in the past), change of status, or pending future action.

In this lesson, 了 is placed at the end of the sentence; it indicates that an action has been completed.

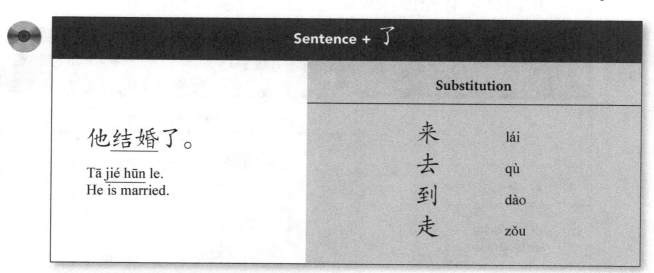

Sentence + 了	
	Substitution
他结婚了。 Tā jié hūn le. He is married.	来 lái 去 qù 到 dào 走 zǒu

The negative counterpart to a sentence involving 了 is formed by adding 没有 méiyǒu before the verb. However, please note that 了 is not needed in a negative sentence that indicates no action has occurred. For example: 他没有来 Tā méiyǒu lái "He didn't come."

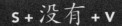

1. 我昨天没有见到他。

   Wǒ zuótiān méiyǒu jiàndào tā.
   I didn't see him yesterday.

2. 他今天早上没有去学校。

   Tā jīntiān zǎoshang méiyǒu qù xuéxiào.
   He didn't go to school this morning.

2. 你们<u>有</u>没有孩子？ **Nǐmen <u>yǒu</u> méiyǒu háizi?** **"Do you have any children?"**

There are two usages of 有 yǒu.

(1) It indicates possession, meaning "to have; to own" when the subject is an animate noun. For example: 他有两个儿子 Tā yǒu liǎng ge érzi "He has two sons."

(2) It also denotes a state of existence when the subject is an inanimate noun: "there is; there are," such as 我们公司有外国人 Wǒmen gōngsī yǒu wàiguórén "There are foreigners in our company."

S + 有 + O		
	Substitution	
1. 他有钱。	哥哥	gēge
Tā yǒu qián.	弟弟	dìdi
He has money.	姐姐	jiějie
	妹妹	mèimei
	儿子	érzi
	女儿	nǚ'ér

2. 我们公司有<u>外国人</u>。 Wǒmen gōngsī yǒu wàiguórén. Our company has foreigners.	美国人 英国人 法国人 德国人 日本人	Měiguórén Yīngguórén Fǎguórén Déguórén Rìběnrén

The negative form of 有 is 没有 méiyǒu. 有 never takes 不 bù for its negative form. 有 can also be dropped in colloquial speech without changing its meaning, for example: 我没钱 Wǒ méi qián "I do not have any money."

s + 没(有) + o

	Substitution	
我没有<u>中文书</u>。 Wǒ méiyǒu Zhōngwénshū. I do not have any Chinese books.	日文书 地图 小说 杂志	Rìwénshū dìtú xiǎoshuō zázhì

The interrogative sentence can either be formed by adding 吗 at the end of the sentence, or by using the affirmative/negative interrogative verb 有没有. See the following examples:

你们公司有外国人吗?

Nǐmen gōngsī yǒu wàiguórén ma?
Are there any foreigners in your company?

Or

你们公司有没有外国人?

Nǐmen gōngsī yǒu méiyǒu wàiguórén?
Are there any foreigners in your company?

s + 有没有 + O		
你今天晚上有没有<u>空</u>？ Nǐ jīntiān wǎnshang yǒu méiyǒu kòng? "Are you free this evening?"	**Substitution**	
	时间	shíjiān
	事	shì

3. 有<u>几</u>个？ Yǒu jǐ ge? "How many (do you have/are there)?"

几 jǐ is a numerical interrogative word used to ask a number that is anticipated to be smaller than ten. Like cardinal numbers, 几 must be followed by a measure word. For more information about measure words, refer to the next grammar point.

Nu + M + N
1. A: 他们有几个孩子？ 　 B: 他们有四个孩子。 　 A: Tāmen yǒu jǐ ge háizi. 　 B: Tāmen yǒu sì ge háizi. 　 A: How many children do they have? 　 B: They have four children. 2. A: 你有几本汉英字典？ 　 B: 我有两本。 　 A: Nǐ yǒu jǐ běn Hàn-Yīng zìdiǎn? 　 B: Wǒ yǒu liǎng běn. 　 A: How many Chinese-English dictionaries do you have? 　 B: I have two. 3. 我有一张上海地图。 　 Wǒ yǒu yì zhāng Shànghǎi dìtú. 　 I have a map of Shanghai.

4. 有两<u>个</u>。 Yǒu liǎng <u>ge</u>. "(I) have two."

When indicating quantity, a number can be placed directly before a noun in English, as in "two books" or "three companies." However, in Chinese, a measure word must be placed between the numeral and the noun, as in 他有两个姐姐 Tā yǒu liǎng ge jiějie "He has two older sisters." 个 in this case follows the number 两 and is used to modify the noun 姐姐.

The appropriate measure word to use varies according to its noun. However, 个 is the most common, generic measure word; it can be used with most nouns, though it is not always the most proper measure word to use.

Another point of interest: There is no subject in the sentence 有两个. In spoken Chinese, the subject can be dropped from a sentence. For example: in the sentence 很高兴认识你 Hěn gāoxìng rènshi nǐ "I am very pleased to meet you," 我 wǒ "I" is omitted from the beginning of the sentence. Unlike English, where subjects are fairly strict and must be present, if the subject is implicit (understood between the speaker and the listener), then it can be dropped in a Chinese sentence.

5. 男孩儿<u>还是</u>女孩儿？ Nánháir <u>háishi</u> nǚháir? "Boy or girl?"

In addition to the interrogative sentences that were introduced in the previous lessons, the "choice-type" question is another kind of question in Chinese. To form this type of interrogative, the conjunction 还是 háishi "or" is used to connect two words, phrases, or sentences. This interrogative form gives the replier an opportunity to choose between two specific alternatives.

X + 还是 + Y

1. A: 你们公司的经理是中国人还是美国人？
   B: 他是中国人。

   A: Nǐmen gōngsī de jīnglǐ shì Zhōngguórén háishi Měiguórén?
   B: Tā shì Zhōngguórén.

   A: Is your company's manager Chinese or American?
   B: He is Chinese.

2. A: 你的秘书还是他的秘书会说日语？

   B: 他的秘书会说日语。

   A: Nǐ de mìshū háishi tā de mìshū huì shuō Rìyǔ?
   B: Tā de mìshū huì shuō Rìyǔ.

   A: Is it your secretary or his secretary who can speak Japanese?
   B: His secretary can speak Japanese.

6. 一个男孩儿和一个女孩儿。 Yí ge nánháir hé yí ge nǚháir. "One boy and one girl."

和 hé is a conjunction meaning "and." It is used to link parallel nouns, pronouns, or noun phrases. It cannot be used to connect verbs or verb phrases (unless the verbs are nominalized). For example: 先生和太太 xiānsheng hé tàitai means "husband and wife," 他和你 tā hé nǐ means "he and you," 看书和写字 kàn shū hé xiě zì means "reading (books) and writing (characters)."

The word "and" in English can be used to link any parts of speech in a sentence, but this is not the case in Chinese. The equivalent of "I am tired and hungry" in Chinese is 我很累, 也很饿 Wǒ hěn lèi, yě hěn è; and *我很累和很饿 is incorrect.

7. 他们几岁了？ Tāmen jǐ suì le? "How old are they (now)?"

As mentioned earlier in the lesson, the Chinese particle 了 has many usages. In this instance, 了 indicates that a passage of time has been noticed. This can be used to state a certain age or time, indicating that a person is one year older or that another hour has passed by. For example:

他的儿子已经十六岁了。

Tā de érzi yǐjīng shíliù suì le.
"His son has already turned sixteen."

几点了？

Jǐ diǎn le.
"What time is it now?"

8. 他们<u>会</u>来中国吗？ **Tāmen <u>huì</u> lái Zhōngguó ma? "Will they come to China?"**

In addition to meaning "can," which indicates a learned or acquired ability and which was introduced in Unit 2.2 (Sentence Pattern 4), 会 huì can also be used to state the probable occurrence of a future event, meaning "It's likely that something will happen." The negative form of 会 is 不会.

S + (不) 会 + V

1. 他今天下午会来公司。

   Tā jīntiān xiàwǔ huì lái gōngsī.
   He will come to the company this afternoon.

2. 我明年不会去上海。

   Wǒ míngnián bú huì qù Shànghǎi
   I will not go to Shanghai next year.

3. 他们会不会结婚？

   Tāmen huì bú huì jié hūn?
   Will they get married?

9. 他们明年会<u>到</u>中国<u>来</u>。 **Tāmen míngnián huì <u>dào</u> Zhōngguó <u>lái</u>. "They will come to China next year."**

The motion verb 来 lái "to come" is used to express that a subject is moving towards the speaker's location. 来 takes a place word designating the destination as its object. For example: 他来中国 Tā lái Zhōngguó "He's coming to China." 到 dào + place word + 来 is a variation of 来 + place word. The same pattern is applied to 去 qù "to go."

来/去 + Place Word *Or* 到 + Place Word + 来/去	
你明天会来/去公司吗？	**Substitution**
Nǐ míngtiān huì lái/qù <u>gōngsī</u> ma?	办公室　　bàngōngshì
Or	图书馆　　túshūguǎn
你明天会到公司来/去吗？	学校　　　xuéxiào
Nǐ míngtiān huì dào <u>gōngsī</u> lái/qù ma?	公园　　　gōngyuán
Will you come/go to the company tomorrow?	

Cultural Points

1. Small Talk

In China, even when discussing official business or matters of the highest importance, Chinese customs dictate that "small talk" be used to open a conversation, before transitioning from pleasant general conversation to the practical point of the meeting. One of the most common subjects of small talk is the family. Questions may include details about your siblings, what your relatives do for a living, and even how much money they earn. Frequently, questions are very personal in nature: e.g., "Are you married?" or "Do you have children?" Asking these questions demonstrates interest in the other person, and is in no way intended to be intrusive or rude. While many of these questions in the United States would be considered impolite for casual acquaintances, in mainland China these introductory questions are considered polite and necessary conversation, although this is becoming less common because of the influence of Western culture.

As opposed to Western societies, where it is not customary to ask a person's age (especially that of women), in China this is an acceptable and common question to ask. It is assumed that with age comes rank and knowledge, and with those characteristics comes respect. The Chinese tradition of respecting and learning from one's elders is still in practice and has not been entirely superceded by a "cult of youth."

2. China's One Child Policy

Concerning the family, it is necessary to understand a piece of Chinese history. In 1978, Deng Xiaoping instituted population control measures to stem a population explosion. To this end, a policy was enacted called the "One Child Policy," meaning that each family could have only one child. This policy, however, has largely been allowed to lapse in recent years. Farming communities, especially, have allowed families multiple children for the purpose of helping on the farms. Presently, city dwellers are among those most restricted by the persistence of the One Child Policy; however, couples that were both single children are now allowed to have a second child. Recent developments in the policy permit city dwellers to have a second child if they pay certain fees.

The One Child Policy has had another indirect result. With only one child to raise, many families dote on that child. This is especially true of the four grandparents of that child. The term 小皇帝 xiǎo huángdì (literally "Little Emperor") has arisen to express the influence that a single child can have over the entire family. For example: these treasured children dictate what the family will eat, where they may go shopping, and what they buy.

 # Additional Vocabulary

Table 12. Basic measure words

Measure Word	Nouns Modified	Further Explanation
个 gè	人 rén, 朋友 péngyou, 汉字 Hànzì	least specific and most commonly used measure word
本 běn	小说 xiǎoshuō, 杂志 zázhì, 字典 zìdiǎn, 画报 huàbào	used with nouns that are "bound together"
支 zhī	笔 bǐ, 毛笔 máobǐ, 香烟 xiāngyān	used with nouns that are stick-like
杯 bēi	水 shuǐ, 茶 chá, 咖啡 kāfēi, 可乐 kělè	used for beverages, referring to "cup" or "glass"
张 zhāng	画 huà, 地图 dìtú	used for flat objects

	Chinese	Pinyin	Part of Speech	English Equivalent
1.	去	qù	V	to go
2.	到	dào	V	to arrive
3.	走	zǒu	V	to leave
4.	钱	qián	N	money
5.	外国人	wàiguórén	N	foreigner
6.	外	wài	N	outside
7.	外国	wàiguó	N	foreign country
8.	空	kòng	N	free time; spare time
9.	时间	shíjiān	N	time
10.	事	shì	N	matter; affair; thing; business
11.	本	běn	M	(a measure word for nouns that are "bound together")
12.	张	zhāng	M	(a measure word for flat objects)
13.	点	diǎn	M	(a measure word for telling time; o'clock)
14.	办公室	bàngōngshì	N	office
15.	图书馆	túshūguǎn	N	library
16.	公园	gōngyuán	N	park
17.	小皇帝	xiǎo huángdì	N	"little emperor"
18.	皇帝	huángdì	N	emperor
19.	画报	huàbào	N	illustrated magazine or newspaper
20.	支	zhī	M	(a measure word for stick-like objects)
21.	毛笔	máobǐ	N	calligraphy brush
22.	香烟	xiāngyān	N	cigarette
23.	杯	bēi	M	(a measure word for cups or glasses)
24.	水	shuǐ	N	water

25.	茶	chá	N	tea
26.	咖啡	kāfēi	N	coffee
27.	可乐	kělè	N	cola
28.	画	huà	N	painting

Unit **3.2**

Family Members and Relatives

In this lesson you will learn:

- About the different ways to ask someone's age in China.

- How to talk about the members of your family: their relationships to you, their health, their work, their ages, and so on.

- How to ask about somebody else's family.

Chinese Dialogue

白有天： 您父亲和母亲身体都好吗？

高明： 都挺好。他们都已经退休了。

白有天： 您父母多大年纪了？

高明： 我父亲六十三岁，母亲五十九岁。

白有天： 您有兄弟姐妹吗？

高明： 有，我有一个哥哥、一个妹妹。

白有天： 他们做什么工作？

高明： 哥哥做生意，妹妹还是学生。

白有天： 您哥哥做什么生意？

高明： 他做进出口贸易。

Pinyin Dialogue

Bái Yǒutiān: Nín fùqin hé mǔqin shēntǐ dōu hǎo ma?

Gāo Míng: Dōu tǐng hǎo. Tāmen dōu yǐjīng tuìxiū le.

Bái Yǒutiān: Nín fùmǔ duō dà niánjì le?

Gāo Míng: Wǒ fùqin liùshísān suì, mǔqin wǔshíjiǔ suì.

Bái Yǒutiān: Nín yǒu xiōngdì jiěmèi ma?

Gāo Míng: Yǒu, wǒ yǒu yí ge gēge, yí ge mèimei.

Bái Yǒutiān: Tāmen zuò shénme gōngzuò?

Gāo Míng: Gēge zuò shēngyì, mèimei hái shì xuéshēng.

Bái Yǒutiān: Nǐ gēge zuò shénme shēngyì?

Gāo Míng: Tā zuò jìnchūkǒu màoyì.

Vocabulary

	Chinese	Pinyin	Part of Speech	English Equivalent
1.	父亲	fùqin	N	father
2.	母亲	mǔqin	N	mother
3.	身体	shēntǐ	N	health; body
4.	都	dōu	Adv	both; all
5.	挺	tǐng	Adv	very; rather; quite
6.	退休	tuìxiū	V	to retire
7.	父母	fùmǔ	N	parents
8.	多	duō	IP	(used to inquire about amount)
9.	年纪	niánjì	N	age
10.	六十三	liùshísān	Nu	63
11.	五十九	wǔshíjiǔ	Nu	59
12.	兄弟姐妹	xiōngdi jiěmèi	N	brothers and sisters; siblings
13.	工作	gōngzuò	N V	job to work
14.	生意	shēngyì	N	business
15.	还	hái	Adv	still; yet
16.	进出口	jìnchūkǒu	N V	import and export to import and export
17.	进口	jìnkǒu	V N	to import import; entrance
18.	进	jìn	V	to enter
19.	口	kǒu	N	mouth; an aperture of a place
20.	出口	chūkǒu	V N	to export export; exit
21.	出	chū	V	to be out; opposite of 进
22.	贸易	màoyì	N	trade

Sentence Patterns

1. 您父亲和母亲身体都好吗？ **Nín fùqin hé mǔqīn shēntǐ dōu hǎo ma? "Are your father and mother in good health?"**

In Unit 3.1 (Sentence Pattern 6) we learned that 和 hé meaning "and" is used to link two nouns. When two or more nouns are connected by 和 and used as a subject, the adjective/verb must be preceded by 都 dōu to indicate totality.

N₁ 和 N₂ + 都 + Adj/V

1. 他和我都很忙。

   Tā hé wǒ dōu hěn máng.
   Both he and I are busy.

2. 中国和美国都很大。

   Zhōngguó hé Měiguó dōu hěn dà.
   Both China and America are big.

3. 王先生和李小姐都会来中国。

   Wáng Xiānsheng hé Lǐ Xiǎojie dōu huì lái Zhōngguó.
   Both Mr. Wang and Miss Li will come to China.

4. 他们都不会说英语。

   Tāmen dōu bú huì shuō Yīngyǔ.
   Neither of them can speak English.

2. 妹妹<u>还</u>是学生。 **Mèimei <u>hái</u> shì xuéshēng. "My younger sister is still a student."**

还 hái is an adverb that means "still/yet." Like other adverbs in Chinese, 还 is used before the verb it modifies, as in 他还是人事部的经理 Tā hái shi rénshìbù de jīnglǐ "He is still the manager of the Department of Human Resources."

还 + Adj/(AV)V

1. 他还很忙。

Tā hái hěn máng.
He is still busy.

2. 上海还很热吗？

Shànghǎi hái hěn rè ma?
Is Shanghai still hot?

3. 他还会来北京吗？

Tā hái huì lái Běijīng ma?
Will he still come to Beijing?

Cultural Points

1. 都挺好。 **Dōu tǐng hǎo. "(Both) are quite well."**

挺 tǐng vs. 很 hěn: We have learned in Unit 1.2 (Sentence Pattern 2) that 很 is used to modify an adjective in affirmative sentences. There are many variations of 很. One such variation used in mainland China is 挺. The usage and definition of 挺 is similar to 很, but it has a bit more substance than 很, so the difference between the two is similar to the difference between "rather; quite" (挺) vs. "very" (很). Of interest to note: in Taiwan, 挺 is not used as often, but is replaced with the word 超 chāo by the younger generation. (超 is increasingly being used in mainland China as well.)

2. 您父母多大年纪了？ Nín fùmǔ duō dà niánjì le? "How old are your parents?"

In Chinese, the sentence pattern used for asking about age varies according to the person's age. 几岁了 Jǐ suì le is used for children under ten. For people in their twenties, thirties, or forties, 多大了 Duō dà le is used. For people older than 60, 多大年纪了 Duō dà niánjì le is more appropriate, as it is considered more respectful.

 ## Additional Vocabulary

Chinese	Pinyin	Part of Speech	English Equivalent
1. 超	chāo	Adv	very; super (mostly Taiwanese usage among youth)

UNIT 4

公司
Gōngsī
The Company

Unit **4.1**

Company Type

In this lesson we will learn:

- About some different forms of companies (such as joint ventures and wholly owned foreign enterprises) operating in China.

- How to introduce and talk briefly about your company: its size, type, location, etc.

⊙ Chinese Dialogue

林小姐:	听说您的公司是电脑公司。
白有天:	是的，是一家电脑公司。
林小姐:	是独资公司吗?
白有天:	不是，是中美合资公司。
林小姐:	公司的总部在什么地方?
白有天:	在北京。
林小姐:	在中国有几家分公司呢?
白有天:	有三家：一家在上海，一家在广州，还有一家在深圳。

Pinyin Dialogue

Lín Xiǎojiě:	Tīngshuō nín de gōngsī shì diànnǎo gōngsī.
Bái Yǒutiān:	Shì de, shì yì jiā diànnǎo gōngsī.
Lín Xiǎojiě:	Shì dúzī gōngsī ma?
Bái Yǒutiān:	Bú shì, shì Zhōng-Měi hézī gōngsī.
Lín Xiǎojiě:	Gōngsī de zǒngbù zài shénme dìfang?
Bái Yǒutiān:	Zài Běijīng.
Lín Xiǎojiě:	Zài Zhōngguó yǒu jǐ jiā fēngōngsī ne?
Bái Yǒutiān:	Yǒu sān jiā: yì jiā zài Shànghǎi, yì jiā zài Guǎngzhōu, hái yǒu yì jiā zài Shēnzhèn.

Vocabulary

Chinese	Pinyin	Part of Speech	English Equivalent
1. 林	Lín	PN	a surname
	lín	N	forest
2. 听说	tīngshuō	V	to have heard it said
3. 听	tīng	V	to hear; to listen
4. 家	jiā	M	(a measure word for business establishments such as companies, stores, or restaurants)
		N	family; home
5. 独资	dúzī	N	wholly owned foreign enterprise (WOFE)
6. 中美	Zhōng-Měi	Adj	Sino-American
7. 合资	hézī	N	joint venture (JV)
8. 总部	zǒngbù	N	headquarters
9. 在	zài	V	to be at (a place)
10. 分公司	fēngōngsī	N	branch office
11. 广州	Guǎngzhōu	PN	Guangzhou
12. 还	hái	Adv	in addition; as well as; also
13. 深圳	Shēnzhèn	PN	Shenzhen

Sentence Patterns

1. <u>听说</u>您的公司是电脑公司。 <u>**Tīngshuō**</u> **nín de gōngsī shì diànnǎo gōngsī. "I heard that your company is a computer company."**

The verb phrase 听说 tīngshuō is composed of two verbs: 听 "to hear," and. 说 "to say," meaning "to have heard it said." This sentence begins with 听说 because the subject is assumed to be "I" (我). When the subject is 我, 听说 is optional; but if it is any other pronoun or noun, it must be stated.

> ### 听说
>
> 1. 我听说他们公司的经理是美国人。
>
>   Wǒ tīngshuō tāmen gōngsī de jīnglǐ shì Měiguórén.
>   I heard that their company's manager is an American.
>
> 2. 听说她已经结婚了。
>
>   Tīngshuō tā yǐjīng jié hūn le.
>   I heard she is already married.
>
> 3. 他听说那是家独资公司。
>
>   Tā tīngshuō nà shì jiā dúzī gōngsī.
>   He heard that that is a wholly owned foreign enterprise.

2. 公司的总部<u>在</u>什么地方？ **Gōngsī de zǒngbù <u>zài</u> shénme dìfang? "Where is the company's headquarters?"**

在 zài, meaning "to be at," is followed by a place word indicating the location of the subject, e.g., 经理在公司 Jīnglǐ zài gōngsi "The manager is at the company." The interrogative sentence is formed by adding 什么地方 shénme dìfang or 哪儿 nǎr "where," after 在. For example: 你在哪儿 Nǐ zài nǎr "Where are you?" Note that the "-r" ending of a word is commonly used in northern China, particularly in Beijing.

	Substitution	

1. 他在<u>家</u>。

Tā zài jiā.
He is at home.

2. 她不在<u>公司</u>。

Tā bú zài gōngsī.
She is not at the company.

办公室	bàngōngshì
图书馆	túshūguǎn
学校	xuéxiào
食堂	shítáng
餐厅	cāntīng

3. 他们的总公司在<u>美国</u>。

Tāmen de zǒnggōngsī zài Měiguó.
Their company's headquarters is in the United States.

英国	Yīngguó
德国	Déguó
法国	Fǎguó
日本	Rìběn

4. 我家在<u>北京</u>。

Wǒ jiā zài Běijīng.
My home is in Beijing.

南京	Nánjīng
东京	Dōngjīng
西安	Xī'ān

5. <u>你</u>在哪儿?

Nǐ zài nǎr?
Where are you?

总经理	zǒngjīnglǐ
李总	Lǐ Zǒng
秘书	mìshū
公园	gōngyuán
餐厅	cāntīng

3. 还有一家在深圳。 **Hái yǒu yì jiā zài Shēnzhèn. "Another one is in Shenzhen."**

The adverb 还 hái is used to modify the verb 有 yǒu, indicating that there are still more things to be mentioned.

还 + 有

1. 他们在广州有一家独资公司，还有一家合资公司。

   Tāmen zài Guǎngzhōu yǒu yì jiā dúzī gōngsī, hái yǒu yì jiā hézī gōngsī.
   In Guangzhou, they have a wholly owned foreign enterprise and a joint venture.

2. 我有一个哥哥，还有三个姐姐。

   Wǒ yǒu yí ge gēge, hái yǒu sān ge jiějie.
   I have an older brother and three older sisters.

3. 你们还有几家分公司？

   Nǐmen hái yǒu jǐ jiā fēngōngsī?
   How many more branch offices do you have?

Cultural Points

1. 是一家电脑公司。 **Shì yì jiā diànnǎo gōngsī. "It is a computer company."**

家 jiā literally means "home," but it is also a measure word for companies, hotels, restaurants, etc. Traditionally, Chinese businesses were family owned and run; thus, the company became an extension of the family unit. In Taiwan and other parts of Southeast Asia, many companies are still family owned and operated. Though this practice has changed over the years on the mainland, the measure word 家 still maintains its original association with "family."

2. Joint Ventures (JVs) and Wholly Owned Foreign Enterprises (WOFEs)

China's economic reform began in the Chinese Special Economic Zones (SEZs). SEZs were originally established in 1980 in relatively few locations in China. Following the establishment of SEZs, the government of the People's Republic of China (PRC) began to allow foreign investment in China through joint venture enterprises. Before the opening of SEZs and the existence of joint venture enterprises, foreign companies were unable to penetrate the Chinese market. Joint venture enterprises enabled foreign companies to acquire experience in the PRC while minimizing exposure risk in this new market. SEZs facilitate operations with concessions and advantages favorable to foreign investment and an environment considered to be familiar or congenial to overseas Chinese.

Following China's accession to the WTO, the strategic importance of SEZs has continually diminished. In addition, many of the initial joint ventures failed and foreign investment in the PRC slowed. In an effort to promote sustained economic growth, the government began allowing the entry of wholly owned foreign enterprises to boost foreign investment. This has been successful. More and more foreign companies are choosing to make large, direct investments in the PRC. Wholly owned foreign enterprises are quickly becoming the favored means of entry for foreign investors.

 ## Additional Vocabulary

	Chinese	Pinyin	Part of Speech	English Equivalent
1.	哪儿	nǎr	IP	where
2.	食堂	shítáng	N	canteen; dining hall
3.	餐厅	cāntīng	N	cafeteria; restaurant
4.	总经理	zǒngjīnglǐ	N	general manager
5.	李总	Lǐ Zǒng	PN	President Li (of a company)

Unit **4.2**

Company Size

In this lesson you will learn:

- How to discuss the size of a company as measured by the number of employees.

- How to describe and compare two or more people or things.

Chinese Dialogue

林小姐： 你们公司有多少人？

白有天： 差不多有一百五十个人。

林小姐： 都是中国人吗？

白有天： 不，有的是中国人，有的是外国人。

林小姐： 中国人多还是外国人多？

白有天： 中国人比外国人多。

林小姐： 你们公司跟方正公司一样大吗？

白有天： 不，方正比我们大多了。

Pinyin Dialogue

Lín Xiǎojiě:	Nǐmen gōngsī yǒu duōshao rén?
Bái Yǒutiān:	Chàbuduō yǒu yìbǎi wǔshí ge rén.
Lín Xiǎojiě:	Dōu shì Zhōngguórén ma?
Bái Yǒutiān:	Bù, yǒude shì Zhōngguórén, yǒude shì wàiguórén.
Lín Xiǎojiě:	Zhōngguórén duō háishi wàiguórén duō?
Bái Yǒutiān:	Zhōngguórén bǐ wàiguórén duō.
Lín Xiǎojiě:	Nǐmen gōngsī gēn Fāngzhèng Gōngsī yíyàng dà ma?
Bái Yǒutiān:	Bù, Fāngzhèng bǐ wǒmen dà duō le.

Vocabulary

Chinese	Pinyin	Part of Speech	English Equivalent
1. 多少	duōshao	IP	how many; how much
2. 差不多	chàbuduō	Adv	about; almost
3. 有的……… 有的………	yǒude…yǒude…	Adj	some…some…
4. 比	bǐ	Prep	a comparison marker; than
5. 跟	gēn	Conj Prep	and with
6. 方正公司	Fāngzhèng Gōngsī	PN	name of a fictional company in this text
7. 一样	yíyàng	Adj	same

Sentence Patterns

1. 你们公司有<u>多少</u>人？ **Nǐmen gōngsī yǒu <u>duōshao</u> rén? "How many people are there in your company?"**

多少 duōshao is a numerical interrogative word which literally combines duō 多 "many" and shǎo 少 "few" to ask "how many; how much." A question can be formed when 多少 is followed by a noun, asking about the quantity of that noun. For example: 多少人 duōshao rén means "how many people?" 多少钱 duōshao qián means "how much money?" Note that 少 is pronounced in a neutral tone when used in the 多少 combination.

Another numerical interrogative word in Chinese is 几 jǐ, which was introduced in Unit 3.1 (Sentence Pattern 3). The differences between 多少 and 几 are:

(1) 几 is used to ask about a number that is estimated to be smaller than ten, whereas 多少 can used for any number;

(2) 几 must take a measure word before the noun; (it is incorrect to say: *你有几书？) whereas 多少 may appear with or without a measure word. When the anticipated number is enormous, the measure word can be omitted. For example: 中国有多少人 Zhōngguó yǒu duōshao rén "How many people are there in China?"

多少 +N

1. 明天有多少人会来？

   Míngtiān yǒu duōshao rén huì lái?
   How many people will come tomorrow?

2. 这本书多少钱？

   Zhè běn shū duōshao qián?
   How much is this book?

3. 你们学校有多少学生？

   Nǐmen xuéxiào yǒu duōshao xuésheng?
   How many students are there in your school?

2. <u>有的</u>是中国人，<u>有的</u>是外国人。 **<u>Yǒude</u> shì Zhōngguórén, <u>yǒude</u> shì wàiguórén. "Some are Chinese, some are foreigners."**

有的 yǒude, an adjective, can be placed before a noun to categorize certain unspecific nouns from within a group. It is usually used in pairs, such as 有的……有的…… meaning "some... some..." For example: 有的公司大，有的公司小 Yǒude gōngsī dà, yǒude gōngsī xiǎo "Some companies are big, some are small." The noun that 有的 modifies can be omitted if its reference is understood or implicit. For example: in the previous example 有的公司大，有的小 the second 公司 can be dropped. Another example is 中国有很多独资公司，有的大，有的小 Zhōngguó yǒu hěn duō dúzī gōngsī, yǒude dà, yǒude xiǎo; in this sentence, both 公司 can be dropped.

有的 …… ……，有的 …… ……

1. 有的人有钱，有的人没有钱。

   Yǒude rén yǒu qián, yǒude rén méiyǒu qián.
   Some people are rich; some people are not rich.

2. 有的工人很努力，有的(工人)不努力。

   Yǒude gōngrén hěn nǔlì, yǒude (gōngrén) bù nǔlì.
   Some workers are very hard-working; some (workers) are not hard-working.

3. 有的小说有意思，有的没有意思。

   Yǒude xiǎoshuō yǒu yìsi, yǒude méiyǒu yìsi.
   Some novels are interesting; some are not interesting.

4. 有的(人)来了，有的(人)没来。

   Yǒude (rén) lái le, yǒude (rén) méi lái.
   Some (people) came; some (people) didn't.

3. 中国人多还是外国人多？ Zhōngguórén duō háishi wàiguórén duō? "Are there more Chinese people or more foreigners?"

还是 háishi is used to form a choice-type question, as explained in Unit 3.1 (Sentence Pattern 5). 还是 can also be used to make a comparison between two clauses (each consisting of a subject and an adjective), thus forming an interrogative sentence. Note that 很 should not be used to modify the adjective in this type of sentence. One can reply to this type of question either by repeating one of the two original sentences or by using the comparison structure, as explained in the next grammar point. See the following example:

X + 还是 +Y

A: 他大还是你大?

B₁: 他大。   *Or*   B₂: 他比我大。

A: Tā dà háishi nǐ dà?
B₁: Tā dà.   *Or*   B₂: Tā bǐ wǒ dà.

A: Is he older or are you older?
B₁: He is older.   *Or*   B₁: He is older than me.

4. 中国人<u>比</u>外国人多。 **Zhōngguórén <u>bǐ</u> wàiguórén duō. "There are more Chinese people than foreigners."**

比 bǐ, a preposition, is used to compare two items with regard to their quality, quantity, or intensity. It is similar to English comparative sentences that use "-er than…" or "more/less… than…"

X + 比 + Y + Adj

1. 他比我高。

   Tā bǐ wǒ gāo.
   He is taller than I am.

2. 我们公司比他们公司小。

   Wǒmen gōngsī bǐ tāmen gōngsī xiǎo.
   Our company is smaller than their company.

3. 中国人比美国人多。

   Zhōngguórén bǐ Měiguórén duō.
   There are more Chinese than Americans.

Please note that 很 hěn should not be used to show intensity in this type of sentence. Instead, an exact amount follows the adjective to show the discrepancy in comparison. To show the degree of the difference, 多了 duō le or 得多 de duō "much, a lot" is used to indicate that the difference between the two items is large or huge. 一点儿 yìdiǎnr "a little" is used to indicate that the difference is small.

X + 比 + Y + Adj + Nu + M

1. 我爸爸比我妈妈大两岁。

   Wǒ bàba bǐ wǒ māma dà liǎng suì.
   My father is two years older than my mother.

X + 比 + Y + Adj + 一点儿

2. 他比我小一点儿。

   Tā bǐ wǒ xiǎo yìdiǎnr.
   He is a little bit younger than I am.

X + 比 + Y + Adj + 得多/多了

3. 她的书比我的书多多了。

   Tā de shū bǐ wǒ de shū duō duō le.
   She has many more books than I have.

4. 日本的电脑比中国的电脑贵得多。

   Rìběn de diànnǎo bǐ Zhōngguó de diànnǎo guì de duō.
   Japanese computers are much more expensive than Chinese computers.

5. 你们公司<u>跟</u>方正公司<u>一样</u>大吗？ **Nǐmen gōngsī <u>gēn</u> Fāngzhèng Gōngsī <u>yíyàng</u> dà ma? "Is your company as big as Fāngzhèng?"**

一 yī means "one" and 样 yàng means "shape; appearance." Thus 一样 yíyàng transliterated means "the same; alike." A sentence using 一样 indicates that two or more entities are either identical or are the same in a certain aspect. The subject can be a plural noun or can be in the form of X 跟 (or 和)Y "X and Y." 都 dōu can precede 一样 to emphasize the degree of similarity. For example: 这三本书都一样 Zhè sān běn shū dōu yíyàng "All three of these books are the same."

X + 跟/和 + Y + 一样

1. 这个电脑跟/和那个电脑一样。

   Zhè ge diànnǎo gēn/hé nà ge diànnǎo yíyàng.
   This computer and that computer are the same.

2. 进口跟出口不一样。

   Jìnkǒu gēn chūkǒu bù yíyàng.
   Importing and exporting are not the same.
   or
   The entrance and the exit are not the same.

3. 小说跟电影不一样。

   Xiǎoshuō gēn diànyǐng bù yíyàng.
   Novels and movies are not the same.
   or
   The novel is different from the movie.

An adjective can be placed at the end of the above pattern to express in what respect the items are identical. For example: 他跟他太太的年纪一样大 Tā gēn tā tàitai de niánjì yíyàng dà means "He and his wife are the same age."

X + 跟 + Y + (差不多) 一样 + Adj

1. 美国跟加拿大(差不多)一样大。

   Měiguó gēn Jiānádà (chàbuduō) yíyàng dà.
   America and Canada are (almost) the same size.

2. 这个和那个一样贵。

   Zhè ge hé nà ge yíyàng guì.
   This one is as expensive as that one.

3. 我哥哥跟我弟弟不一样高。

   Wǒ gēge gēn wǒ dìdi bù yíyàng gāo.
   My older brother and my younger brother are not the same height.

Cultural Points

1. Expatriates in China: An Endangered Species?

The expatriate community in China is large and varied, with individuals and families from all nations of the earth and professionals engaged in everything from business to diplomacy to academic research. After China opened up diplomatically and economically in the late seventies, the floodgates opened for the expatriate community in China. China's largest cities played host to most of the expatriates—Beijing, Shanghai and Guangzhou saw the lion's share of foreign business professionals and diplomatic officials.

In addition to countries establishing diplomatic missions in China, many multinational corporations began sending expatriates to manage many aspects of their business interests in China. Some were sent to oversee China's inexpensive manufacturing operations. Others were sent to manage sales and distribution of foreign products and services in the vast Chinese market. Expatriate assignments arose from the fact that foreign multinational corporations often could not find the middle and upper level management talent they needed amongst the Chinese labor pool.

Many companies are now finding it to be less expensive and more efficient to hire local talent to fill knowledge-based positions and upper-level management positions in Chinese operations. However, for the time being there is still considerable demand for expatriate managers in China, particularly in the upper management positions where fewer Chinese managers are currently prepared to take on those roles. Also, anecdotal evidence suggests that there is more room for expatriate talent in smaller but growing Chinese cities, some of which are regional or emerging national business centers.

Additional Vocabulary

	Chinese	Pinyin	Part of Speech	English Equivalent
1.	有钱	yǒu qián	Adj	rich; wealthy
2.	工人	gōngrén	N	worker
3.	努力	nǔlì	Adj V	diligent to work hard
4.	有意思	yǒu yìsi	Adj	interesting
5.	电影	diànyǐng	N	movie

UNIT
5

询问
Xúnwèn
Inquiries

Unit **5.1**

Inquiring about Someone's Whereabouts

In this lesson we will learn:

- How to inquire about the whereabouts of business contacts.
- How to locate someone.
- How to express the distance between two locations.

🔘 Chinese Dialogue

白有天： 马经理在不在？

王英： 不在，他去电脑城了。

白有天： 马经理下午会回公司来吗？

王英： 对不起，我不太清楚。

白有天： 我能去那儿找他吗？

王英： 当然可以。

白有天： 电脑城在哪儿？

王英： 在中关村。

白有天： 中关村离这儿远吗？

王英： 不太远，很近。只有三公里。

Pinyin Dialogue

Bái Yǒutiān: Mǎ Jīnglǐ zài bú zài?

Wáng Yīng: Bú zài, tā qù Diànnǎochéng le.

Bái Yǒutiān: Mǎ Jīnglǐ xiàwǔ huì huí gōngsī lái ma?

Wáng Yīng: Duìbuqǐ, wǒ bú tài qīngchu.

Bái Yǒutiān: Wǒ néng qù nàr zhǎo tā ma?

Wáng Yīng: Dāngrán kěyǐ.

Bái Yǒutiān: Diànnǎochéng zài nǎr?

Wáng Yīng: Zài Zhōngguāncūn.

Bái Yǒutiān: Zhōngguāncūn lí zhèr yuǎn ma?

Wáng Yīng: Bú tài yuǎn, hěn jìn. Zhǐ yǒu sān gōnglǐ.

Vocabulary

Chinese	Pinyin	Part of Speech	English Equivalent
1. 询问	xúnwèn	V	to ask about; to inquire
2. 在	zài	V	to be present
3. 电脑城	Diànnǎochéng	PN	Computer City (name of a shopping district that specializes in computers and electronics)
4. 城	chéng	N	city; town
5. 回……来	huí...lái	V	to return to (a place)
6. 回	huí	V	to return
7. 对不起	duìbuqǐ	UE	sorry; excuse me (an apology)
8. 太	tài	Adv	too; overly
9. 清楚	qīngchu	Adj	clear; distinct
10. 能	néng	AV	to be able to; can
11. 那儿	nàr	Pr	there
12. 找	zhǎo	V	to look for; to search
13. 当然	dāngrán	Adv	of course
14. 可以	kěyǐ	AV	to allow; may; to be able to; can
15. 中关村	Zhōngguāncūn	PN	name of a district in Beijing
16. 离	lí	Prep	away from (indicates distance between two places)
17. 这儿	zhèr	Pr	here
18. 远	yuǎn	Adj	far; remote
19. 近	jìn	Adj	close; near
20. 只	zhǐ	Adv	only; just
21. 公里	gōnglǐ	M	(a measure word for distance in kilometers)

Sentence Patterns

1. 马经理在吗？ Mǎ Jīnglǐ <u>zài</u> ma? "Is Manager Ma here?"

In addition to the meaning of "to be at (a place)" given in Unit 4.1 (Sentence Pattern 2), 在 zài can also be used as a verb indicating the presence or absence of a person. This usage can be used in making contact by phone or inquiring as to the presence of a person at a specific location.

S + 在
A: 陈先生在吗？
B₁: 在，请问，哪位？
Or
B₂: 他不在。
A:　Chén Xiānsheng zài ma?
B₁: Zài, qǐng wèn, nǎ wèi?
Or
B₂: Tā bú zài.
A:　Is Mr. Chen in?
B₁: Yes, who is calling, please?
Or
B₂: No, he is not in.

2. 马经理下午会<u>回</u>公司<u>来</u>吗？ Mǎ Jīnglǐ xiàwǔ huì <u>huí</u> gōngsī <u>lái</u> ma? "Will Manager Ma be coming back to the office this afternoon?"

回 huí is a verb meaning "to return to an original place." It can be followed by a place word such as 公司 gōngsī or 学校 xuéxiào. The most commonly used compound words involving 回 are 回家 huí jiā "to return home; to go home" and 回国 huí guó "to return to one's own country." 回 can also be followed by a directional complement such as 来 lái or 去 qù to form a verb phrase. For example: 回来 means "to come back," and 回去 means "to go back." If a specific location is indicated, it must be placed between 回 and 来/去. For example: 回公司来/去。

回 + Place Word + 来/去

	Substitution	
1. 他明天回<u>美国</u>来。 Tā míngtiān huí Měiguó lái. He is coming back to the United States tomorrow.	中国 公司 学校 这儿	Zhōngguó gōngsī xuéxiào zhèr

3. 我不<u>太</u>清楚。 **Wǒ bú tài qīngchu. "I'm not too sure."**

太 tài, an adverb, is used to modify an adjective in order to indicate an intensive degree. The negative marker 不 can be placed before 太 to indicate that the adjective is not too intensive or not too strong.

(不) + 太 + Adj

	Substitution	
1. 他太<u>小</u>。 Tā tài xiǎo. He is too young (small).	高 矮 忙 累	gāo ǎi máng lèi
2. 我不太<u>高兴</u>。 Wǒ bú tài gāoxìng. I am not too happy.	忙 累 懂 会	máng lèi dǒng huì
3. 今天太<u>热</u>。 Jīntiān tài rè. Today it is too hot.	冷 凉 闷	lěng liáng mēn

		S		Adj	
4.	电脑太贵。 Diànnǎo tài guì. Computers are too expensive.	公司 孩子 美国	gōngsī háizi Měiguó	大 小 远	dà xiǎo yuǎn

4. 我**能**去那儿找他吗？ Wǒ **néng** qù nàr zhǎo tā ma? "May I go there to look for him?"

能 néng is an auxiliary verb meaning "can; to be able to." Both 能 and 会 huì can be translated as "can," and they are sometimes used interchangeably. For example: both 他能说中文 Tā néng shuō Zhōngwén and 他会说中文 Tā huì shuō Zhōngwén mean "He can speak Chinese." However, 会 means having a skill or an ability which is obtained through learning, as we learned in Unit 2.2 (Sentence Pattern 4); whereas 能 shows physical capabilities that are not acquired through learning but rather predetermined by nature, such as 人能走，不能飞 Rén néng zǒu, bù néng fēi "Human beings can walk, but cannot fly" and 他很能吃 Tā hěn néng chī "He eats a lot (literally, he really can eat)."

S + 能 + V	
	Substitution
他能说英文。 Tā néng shuō Yīngwén. He can speak English.	看中文 kàn Zhōngwén 写汉字 xiě Hànzì 开车 kāi chē

In addition, 能 also indicates whether the circumstance or condition allows one to do something. It is usually used in the negative or interrogative form. For example:

A: 你明天能不能来？

Nǐ míngtiān néng bù néng lái?
"Can you come tomorrow or not?"

B:　我明天会很忙，不能来。

Wǒ míngtiān huì hěn máng, bù néng lái.
"I'll be busy tomorrow; I won't be able to come."

The negative form of 能 is either "不能" bù néng (for present and future tenses), or "没能" méi néng (for past tense). For example: 对不起，我昨天有事，没能来看你
Duìbuqǐ, wǒ zuótiān yǒu shì, méi néng lái kàn nǐ "Sorry, I had things to do yesterday; I was unable to come to see you."

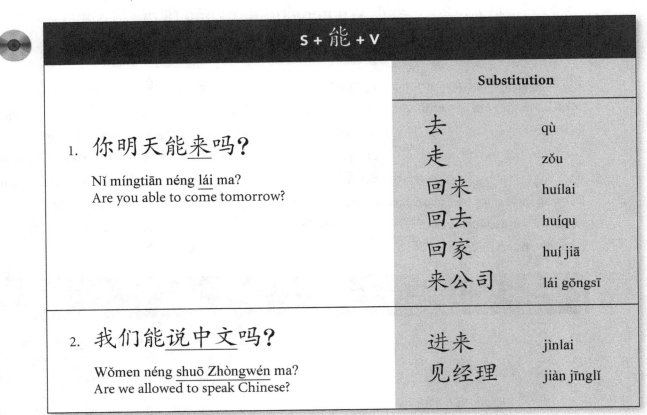

S + 能 + V		
	Substitution	
1. 你明天能<u>来</u>吗？ Nǐ míngtiān néng <u>lái</u> ma? Are you able to come tomorrow?	去 走 回来 回去 回家 来公司	qù zǒu huílai huíqu huí jiā lái gōngsī
2. 我们能<u>说中文</u>吗？ Wǒmen néng <u>shuō Zhòngwén</u> ma? Are we allowed to speak Chinese?	进来 见经理	jìnlai jiàn jīnglǐ

5. 当然<u>可以</u>。 Dāngrán <u>kěyǐ</u>. "Of course you can."

可以 kěyǐ is another auxiliary verb, meaning "may; can; to be allowed to," which expresses permission, possibility, or ability like 能 néng, and therefore can be interchangeable with 能 in most cases. However, when asking for permission, 可以 is preferred over 能. When referring to ability, both 能 and 可以 may be used in the positive, but only 能 can be used in the negative (i.e., 不可以 may not be used in referring to negative ability). For example:

你可以/能去，我没有钱不能去 Nǐ kěyǐ/néng qù, wǒ méiyǒu qián bù néng qù "You can go, but I don't have money, I can't." But when referring to permission, 不可以 is an acceptable negative form of 可以.

S + 可以 + V		Substitution
1. 你明天可以/能来吗？ Nǐ míngtiān kěyǐ/néng lái ma? Are you able to come tomorrow?	去 走 回家 来公司	qù zǒu huí jiā lái gōngsī
2. 我可以进来吗？ Wǒ kěyǐ jìnlai ma? May I come in?	进去 问经理 说英文 请他来 吸烟	jìnqu wèn jīnglǐ shuō Yīngwén qǐng tā lái xī yān

6. 中关村离这儿远吗？ Zhōngguāncūn lí zhèr yuǎn ma? "Is Zhongguancun far from here?"

The meaning of the verb 离 lí is "to depart, to leave," when used in the combination 离开 líkāi. For example: 你们几点离开 Nǐmen jǐ diǎn líkāi means "What time do you leave?" 离 can also be used as a preposition to indicate the distance between two places, which can be expressed using adjectives such as 远 yuǎn or 近 jìn, or using numbers to indicate the actual distance.

X + 离 + Y + 很远/近

1. 公司离这儿很远。

   Gōngsī lí zhèr hěn yuǎn.
   The company is far from here.

X + 离 + Y + 不(是) + 很远/近

1. 那个公园离我家不是很近。

   Nà ge gōngyuán lí wǒ jiā bú shì hěn jìn.
   That park is not very close to my house.

2. 公寓离车站不太远。

   Gōngyù lí chēzhàn bú tài yuǎn.
   It is not too far from the apartment to the station.

X + 离 + Y + (有) + Nu 公里

1. 他家离那儿差不多有五公里。

   Tā jiā lí nàr chàbuduō yǒu wǔ gōnglǐ.
   It is about five kilometers from his home to there.

X + 离 + Y + 有多远

1. 你家离公司有多远?

   Nǐ jiā lí gōngsī yǒu duō yuǎn?
   How far is it from your home to the company?

7. <u>只</u>有三公里。 <u>**Zhǐ**</u> **yǒu sān gōnglǐ.** **"It is only three kilometers."**

只 zhǐ is an adverb meaning "only; just; merely" and is used to delimit a specified amount or quantity and nothing more. However, note that unlike the English word "only," 只 is an adverb, and therefore must be followed by a verb.

S + 只 + (AV)V

1. 我只有一个妹妹。

   Wǒ zhǐ yǒu yí ge mèimei.
   I have only one younger sister.

2. 郭总只会说中文。

   Guō Zǒng zhǐ huì shuō Zhōngwén.
   President Guo can only speak Chinese.

Cultural Points

1. 我不太清楚 Wǒ bú tài qīngchu "I'm not too sure."

It is considered somewhat impolite to state another person's opinions or to volunteer personal information about another person. While this is qualitatively true in Western culture as well as in Chinese, such indiscretions are even worse faux pas in mainland China. In point of fact, the word for secretary, 秘书 mìshū, means "secret keeper," one who knows the secret, but keeps it a secret. Secretaries in particular are very loyal to their superiors, and will refrain from divulging any aspects of their superiors' lives more than absolutely necessary. When speaking on behalf of other people, therefore, do not assume that information communicated to you was intended for general knowledge. You should be cautious and avoid expressing another person's opinions, or sharing personal information about another person, even if no special measure of secrecy was imposed when that person shared the information with you.

2. 中关村 Zhōngguāncūn "Computer City"

For the last ten years, China has been a major manufacturing center for everything from textiles to technology-based products. In the city of Beijing, a spirit of cooperation among technology manufacturers and designers has led to the creation of Zhōngguāncūn , a one-stop shopping and information center for electronics and high technology products. One can not only buy individual computer components and the latest software for personal use, but can also arrange for the purchase of components to be assembled in another location, all while collaborating with the country's best hardware and software designers. Located just off the west gate of Beijing University, this center has been particularly successful in part because of its location. It has also become a major recruitment center for local talent for both domestic and international companies. It is rumored that the taskforce employed by the Chinese government to oversee the country's internet usage makes widespread use of the technology and the talent of this center.

 ## Additional Vocabulary

	Chinese	Pinyin	Part of Speech	English Equivalent
1.	回家	huí jiā	VO	to return home
2.	回国	huí guó	VO	to return to one's own country
3.	回来	huílai	VC	to come back
4.	回去	huíqu	VC	to go back
5.	矮	ǎi	Adj	short; low
6.	懂	dǒng	V	to understand
7.	闷	mēn	Adj	humid; stifling
8.	飞	fēi	V	to fly
9.	进去	jìnqu	VC	to go in
10.	吸烟	xī yān	VO	to smoke
11.	离开	líkāi	VC	to leave
12.	公寓	gōngyù	N	apartment
13.	车站	chēzhàn	N	station (usually for a bus or train)

Unit **5.2**

Inquiring after Someone's Profession

In this lesson you will learn:

- Numbers.
- How to express the time of day and the days of the week.
- How to describe the location of an activity.

Chinese Dialogue

白有天： 林小姐，你在哪里工作？

林小姐： 我在中国银行工作。

白有天： 你们几点上班？

林小姐： 我们上午九点上班，下午五点半下班。

白有天： 现在几点钟？

林小姐： 现在九点一刻。

白有天： 那你为什么还没去上班呢？

林小姐： 今天是星期六，我们周末休息。

Pinyin Dialogue

Bái Yǒutiān: Lín Xiǎojie, nǐ zài nǎli gōngzuò?

Lín Xiǎojie: Wǒ zài Zhōngguó Yínháng gōngzuò.

Bái Yǒutiān: Nǐmen jǐ diǎn shàng bān?

Lín Xiǎojie: Wǒmen shàngwǔ jiǔ diǎn shàng bān, xiàwǔ wǔ diǎn bàn xià bān.

Bái Yǒutiān: Xiànzài jǐ diǎn zhōng?

Lín Xiǎojie: Xiànzài jiǔ diǎn yí kè.

Bái Yǒutiān: Nà nǐ wèishénme hái méi qù shàng bān ne?

Lín Xiǎojie: Jīntiān shì xīngqīliù, wǒmen zhōumò xiūxi.

Vocabulary

	Chinese	Pinyin	Part of Speech	English Equivalent
1.	在	zài	Prep	at; in; on
2.	哪里	nǎli	IP	where
3.	银行	yínháng	N	bank
4.	上班	shàng bān	VO	to go to work
5.	上午	shàngwǔ	TW	morning
6.	半	bàn	Nu	half (an hour)
7.	下班	xià bān	VO	to get off work
8.	现在	xiànzài	TW	now; at present
9.	钟	zhōng	N	o'clock; time as measured in minutes or seconds; clock
10.	刻	kè	M	(a measure word meaning a quarter of an hour; fifteen minutes)
11.	为什么	wèishénme	IP	why
12.	还没(有)	hái méi(yǒu)	Adv	not yet
13.	星期六	xīngqīliù	TW	Saturday
14.	星期	xīngqī	N	week
15.	周末	zhōumò	TW	weekend
16.	休息	xiūxi	V	to rest; to take a break

Sentence Patterns

1. 你在哪里工作? Nǐ zài nǎli gōngzuò? "Where do you work?"

In Units 4.1 (Sentence Pattern 2) and 5.1 (Sentence Pattern 1), we introduced 在 zài as a verb meaning "to be at (a certain place); to be present." In this unit, we will introduce another usage of 在, as a preposition to specify the location of an activity. In this type of structure, the verb indicating the action is the main verb of the sentence. For example: 你在哪儿工作 Nǐ zài nǎr gōngzuò means "Where do you work?"

In English, the action word precedes the location; but in Chinese, the location, constructed by 在 + place word, must be placed before the action verb. The negative marker 不 is usually placed before 在, not before the main verb. But if the negation applies specifically to what a person *doesn't* do at a certain location, then 不 is placed before the verb. For example: 他在家不工作 Tā zài jiā bù gōngzuò means that this person draws a line between work and home life, and doesn't bring his or her work home.

S + (不) 在 + Place Word + V		
	Substitution	
1. 他在人事部工作。 Tā zài rénshìbù gōngzuò. He works in the Department of Human Resources.	**Place**	**V**
	餐厅 cāntīng	吃午饭 chī wǔfàn
	公司 gōngsī	上班 shàng bān
2. 她(不)在公司的食堂吃饭。 Tā (bú) zài gōngsī de shítáng chī fàn. She doesn't eat at the company's cafeteria.	银行 yínháng	工作 gōngzuò
	学校 xuéxiào	上课 shàng kè
	公园 gōngyuán	打球 dǎ qiú
	图书馆 túshūguǎn	看书 kàn shū

3. 他们在<u>这儿</u>做什么？ Tāmen zài <u>zhèr</u> zuò shénme? What are they doing here?	东京　　Dōngjīng 纽约　　Niǔyuē 伦敦　　Lúndūn 巴黎　　Bālí 莫斯科　Mòsīkē
4. 你在<u>哪儿</u><u>念书</u>？ Nǐ zài <u>nǎr</u> <u>niàn shū</u>? Where do you go to school?	教书　　jiāo shū 学习　　xuéxí 上班　　shàng bān 打网球　dǎ wǎngqiú

哪儿 nǎr meaning "where" is a regional variation of 哪里 nǎli and 什么地方 shénme dìfang. Note that the "-r" ending of a word is commonly used in northern China, particularly in Beijing, as explained in Unit 4.1 (Sentence Pattern 2). When 里 or 儿 is added to 这, 那, or 哪, the meaning will change. The following are examples of this phenomenon.

这	那	哪
zhè this	nà that	nǎ which
这儿/这里	那儿/那里	哪儿/哪里/什么地方
zhèr/zhèli here	nàr/nàli there	nǎr/nǎli/shénme dìfang where

2. 你们几点上班？ Nǐmen jǐ diǎn shàng bān? "What time do you go to work?"

In Chinese, time is expressed through the use of different time words. Unlike English, where adverbial phrases of time can be placed relatively freely in a sentence, a time word (TW) in Chinese has to be placed before the main verb of the sentence, either before or after the subject. For example: 我九点上班 Wǒ jiǔ diǎn shàng bān (and not *我上班九点) means "I go to work at nine." 今天我很忙 jīntiān wǒ hěn máng (and not *我很忙今天) means "I am very busy today."

In Unit 3.1 (Sentence Pattern 3), we learned that 几 jǐ, a numerical interrogative word, is used to ask about a number that is smaller than ten. In this lesson, 几, followed by a relevant time unit as introduced in the example table, is used to ask the time. Please note that 是 shì is optional in forming either a positive or interrogative sentence. However, in a negative sentence, 是 is required. For example:

几 + 点/分/刻

1. A: 现在几点？
   B: 现在九点十分。

   A: Xiànzài jǐ diǎn?
   B: Xiànzài jiǔ diǎn shí fēn.

   A: What time is it now?
   B: It is 9:10.

2. A: 现在九点十分吗？
   B: 现在不是九点十分，现在是九点一刻。

   A: Xiànzài jiǔ diǎn shí fēn ma?
   B: Xiànzài búshì jiǔ diǎn shí fēn, xiànzài shì jiǔ diǎn yí kè.

   A: Is it 9:10 right now?
   B: It is not 9:10 right now, it is 9:15.

This section explains how to tell time in Chinese. 点 diǎn "o'clock," 分 fēn "minute," and 刻 kè "quarter of an hour," which are all measure words *per se*, are basic units used to tell time, and they are listed in the following table.

Please note that 钟 zhōng can be added to the time phrase only when the listed time does not contain minutes. It can be equated to the English phrase "sharp" or "on the dot," which are added to the end of a time phrase to indicate exactness.

Table 13. Basic units of time

	点 + 分	diǎn + fēn	刻	kè
1:00	一点(钟)	yī diǎn (zhōng)		
1:01	一点一分	yī diǎn yì fēn		
2:02	两点零二分	liǎng diǎn líng èr fēn		
3:05	三点五分	sān diǎn wǔ fēn		
4:10	四点十分	sì diǎn shí fēn		
5:12	五点十二分	wǔ diǎn shí'èr fēn		
6:15	六点十五分	liù diǎn shíwǔ fēn	六点一刻	liù diǎn yí kè
7:20	七点二十分	qī diǎn èrshí fēn		
8:22	八点二十二分	bā diǎn èrshí'èr fēn		
9:30	九点三十分	jiǔ diǎn sānshí fēn		
10:45	十点四十五分	shí diǎn sìshíwǔ fēn	十点三刻	shí diǎn sān kè
			差一刻十一点	chà yí kè shíyī diǎn
11:55	十一点五十五分	shíyī diǎn wǔshíwǔ fēn		
	差五分十二点	chà wǔ fēn shí'èr diǎn		
12:00	十二点(钟)	shí'èr diǎn (zhōng)		

3. 现在几点钟？ **Xiànzài jǐ diǎn zhōng?** "What time is it now?"

现在 xiànzài is a time word meaning "right now." 现在 can appear at the beginning of a sentence, as in 现在几点？Xiànzài jǐ diǎn? "What time is it now?" When 现在 is used as a time word, it can be placed before or after the subject, so long as it precedes the main verb in the sentence. When both a time word and a place word (such as 在) are used in the sentence, the time word appears before the place word. See the examples below:

现在 + 在 + Place Word

1. 现在你在中国吗？

   Xiànzài nǐ zài Zhōngguó ma?
   Are you in China now?

   Or

   你现在在中国吗？

   Nǐ xiànzài zài Zhōngguó ma?
   Are you in China now?

2. 你现在在中国工作吗？

   Nǐ xiànzài zài Zhōngguó gōngzuò ma?
   Are you working in China now?

4. 你为什么还没去上班呢？ **Nǐ wèishénme hái méi qù shàng bān ne? "Why haven't you gone to work yet?"**

还没 or 还没有 is used to negate a verb, indicating that an action has not yet taken place or been completed, but is expected to take place soon. 呢 can be added at the end of the sentence to confirm the statement.

S + 还没(有) + V

	Substitution
来	lái
去	qù
走	zǒu
到	dào
上班	shàng bān
下班	xià bān
退休	tuìxiū
上大学	shàng dàxué
买车子	mǎi chēzi
卖房子	mài fángzi
吃午饭	chī wǔfàn

1. 他们还没结婚(呢)。

Tāmen hái méi jié hūn (ne).
They haven't gotten married yet.

5. 今天是星期六。 **Jīntiān shì xīngqīliù. "Today is Saturday."**

To indicate days of the week, use 星期 + a number (see below for more detail). In Taiwan, 礼拜 lǐbài is another variation of "week." The following table shows the days of the week.

Table 14. Days of the week

星期一/礼拜一	xīngqīyī/lǐbàiyī	Monday
星期二/礼拜二	Xīngqī'èr/lǐbài'èr	Tuesday
星期三/礼拜三	Xīngqīsān/lǐbàisān	Wednesday
星期四/礼拜四	xīngqīsì/lǐbàisì	Thursday
星期五/礼拜五	xīngqīwǔ/lǐbàiwǔ	Friday
星期六/礼拜六	xīngqīliù/lǐbàiliù	Saturday
星期日/礼拜日	xīngqīrì/lǐbàirì	Sunday
星期天/礼拜天	xīngqītiān/lǐbàitiān	Sunday

The following tables list additional time expressions involving references to days or years in the past or future.

Table 15. Time expressions involving days in the past or future

大前天	dà qiántiān	three days ago
前天	qiántiān	the day before yesterday
昨天	zuótiān	yesterday
今天	jīntiān	today
明天	míngtiān	tomorrow
后天	hòutiān	the day after tomorrow
大后天	dà hòutiān	three days from today

Table 16. Time expressions involving years in the past or future

大前年	dà qiánnián	three years ago
前年	qiánnián	the year before last
去年	qùnián	last year
今年	jīnnián	this year
明年	míngnián	next year
后年	hòunián	the year after next
大后年	dà hòunián	three years from this year

Cultural Points

1. Business Hours

Usual business hours in larger Chinese cities are from 9:00 a.m. until 6:00 p.m., Monday through Saturday. In some Chinese companies, employees are expected to work six days a week, although there is a movement directed by China's government to ensure a two day weekend for all workers. Government offices often keep their own schedules and may close unexpectedly and without published reasons, particularly embassies. Those governmental offices that oversee specific businesses might hypothetically share the same hours as the businesses in their respective areas of responsibility. In practice, they seem susceptible to unscheduled and unpublished changes in their operational hours.

Many Chinese businesses and government offices will take a two-hour afternoon break on workdays, particularly in the summer. Many workers will use this time to eat and take an afternoon nap. However, this practice is becoming less common.

2. The Chinese Concept of Time

Chinese society is more long-term oriented than many other societies, especially those in the Western world. For this reason, many foreign businesspeople going to China may be frustrated at what they consider to be the slow pace set by their Chinese counterparts. Chinese beliefs, however, preclude the rapid implementation of any long-term plans. There are many well-known and oft-repeated ancient Chinese phrases that support this viewpoint, including Confucius's philosophy, "Think three times before action is taken."

Furthermore, because of the long-term orientation of Chinese society, the order in which Chinese people state their time measurement units flows from longest term to shortest. One would start out, then, with millennium, or decade, or year, and proceed to month, day, and time when telling the date.

 # Additional Vocabulary

	Chinese	Pinyin	Part of Speech	English Equivalent
1.	吃饭	chī fàn	VO	to eat a meal
2.	午饭	wǔfàn	N	lunch
3.	上课	shàng kè	VO	to go to class; to begin class
4.	念书	niàn shū	VO	to read books; to study
5.	学习	xuéxí	V	to study (mainland China usage)
6.	网球	wǎngqiú	N	tennis
7.	这里	zhèli	Pr	here
8.	那里	nàli	Pr	there
9.	分	fēn	M	(a measure word for minutes when stating a specific time)
10.	差	chà	V Adj	to be short by lack; inferior
11.	买	mǎi	V	to buy
12.	卖	mài	V	to sell
13.	房子	fángzi	N	house
14.	礼拜	lǐbài	N	week (same as 星期, but more colloquial and more commonly used in Taiwan)

UNIT 6

约见

Yuējiàn

Making Appointments

Unit **6.1**

Setting up an Appointment

In this lesson we will learn:

- About culturally appropriate interaction between superior and subordinate in a Chinese business.

- How to set up appointments.

- How to obtain someone's contact information.

- How to express time in terms of the days, weeks, months, and years.

Chinese Dialogue

白有天： 小王，你能帮我联系方正公司吗？

王英： 是方正电脑公司吗？

白有天： 是的。

王英： 您要找哪位？

白有天： 我想见市场部的张经理。

王英： 什么时间呢？

白有天： 下星期一。

王英： 下星期一是六月三号，您上下午都要开会。

白有天： 那么星期二吧！

王英： 好，我马上帮您联系。

Pinyin Dialogue

Bái Yǒutiān:　Xiǎo Wáng, nǐ néng bāng wǒ liánxì Fāngzhèng Gōngsī ma?

Wáng Yīng:　Shì Fāngzhèng Diànnǎo Gōngsī ma?

Bái Yǒutiān:　Shì de.

Wáng Yīng:　Nín yào zhǎo nǎ wèi?

Bái Yǒutiān:　Wǒ xiǎng jiàn shìchǎngbù de Zhāng Jīnglǐ.

Wáng Yīng:　Shénme shíjiān ne?

Bái Yǒutiān:　Xià xīngqīyī.

Wáng Yīng:　Xià xīngqīyī shì liùyuè sān hào, nín shàngxiàwǔ dōu yào kāi huì.

Bái Yǒutiān:　Nàme xīngqī'èr ba!

Wáng Yīng:　Hǎo, wǒ mǎshàng bāng nín liánxì.

Vocabulary

Chinese	Pinyin	Part of Speech	English Equivalent
1. 约见	yuējiàn	V	to make an appointment
2. 小王	Xiǎo Wáng	PN	Little Wang
3. 小	xiǎo	Adj	a title used to address one who is younger than you
4. 帮	bāng	V	to help
5. 联系	liánxì	V	to contact
6. 要	yào	AV	must; to have to; to need to
		V	to want to; to desire to have (something)
7. 想	xiǎng	AV	would like to; to think of (doing something)
		V	to think; to miss
8. 市场	shìchǎng	N	market
9. 张	Zhāng	PN	a surname
10. 下星期	xià xīngqī	TW	next week
11. 下	xià	Adj	next; below
12. 星期一	xīngqīyī	TW	Monday
13. 月	yuè	N	month
14. 号	hào	N	day of the month; number
15. 上下午	shàngxiàwǔ	TW	morning and afternoon
16. 开会	kāi huì	VO	to attend (or have) a meeting
17. 开	kāi	V	to hold (a meeting/party, etc.)
18. 那么	nàme	Conj	then; in that case
19. 星期二	xīngqī'èr	TW	Tuesday
20. 吧	ba	P	(a particle that implies suggestion or advice)
21. 马上	mǎshàng	Adv	immediately; right away

Sentence Patterns

1. 你能<u>帮</u>我联系方正公司吗？ **Nǐ néng <u>bāng</u> wǒ liánxì Fāngzhèng Gōngsī ma?** "Can you help me contact the Fangzheng Company?"

帮 bāng "to help" is a verb that is usually followed by an indirect object (person) and a direct object (an action). 帮忙 bāng máng is a frequently used verb phrase that cannot have an indirect object. For example: 请你帮忙 Qǐng nǐ bāng máng "Please help" and 谢谢你帮忙 Xièxie nǐ bāng máng "Thank you for your help." When making a request, 请 is used to make the request more polite.

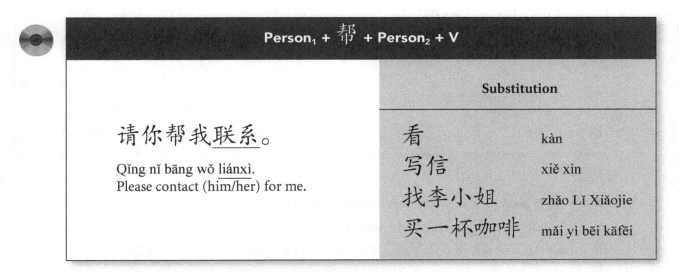

Person₁ + 帮 + Person₂ + V		
	Substitution	
请你帮我<u>联系</u>。 Qǐng nǐ bāng wǒ liánxì. Please contact (him/her) for me.	看 写信 找李小姐 买一杯咖啡	kàn xiě xìn zhǎo Lǐ Xiǎojie mǎi yì bēi kāfēi

2. 您<u>要</u>找哪位？ **Nín <u>yào</u> zhǎo nǎ wèi?** "Whom are you looking for?"

The word 要 can be used as a verb or an auxiliary verb. When it is used as a verb, it must be followed by a noun meaning "to want; to desire to have (something)." This usage is often associated with ordering or buying items. For example: 我们要啤酒 Wǒmen yào píjiǔ "We want beer" or 我不要咖啡，我要茶 Wǒ búyào kāfēi, wǒ yào chá "I do not want coffee; I want tea."

	Substitution
A: 你们要什么？	啤酒　píjiǔ
B: 我们要<u>米饭</u>。	白酒　báijiǔ
	红酒　hóngjiǔ
A: Nǐmen yào shénme?	咖啡　kāfēi
B: Wǒmen yào <u>mǐfàn</u>.	茶　chá
	红茶　hóngchá
A: What do you want?	绿茶　lǜchá
B: We want rice.	冰水　bīngshuǐ
	果汁　guǒzhī
	可乐　kělè

When 要 is used as an auxiliary verb and is followed by a main verb, it has several meanings, depending on the context. One of the meanings is to express one's intention or determination to do something, e.g., 我要学中文 Wǒ yào xué Zhōngwén "I want to learn Chinese" or 您要去哪儿 Nín yào qù nǎr "Where do you want to go?"

	Substitution	
我们要见胡经理。 Wǒmen yào jiàn Hú Jīnglǐ. We want to meet with Manager Hu.	找王先生	zhǎo Wáng Xiānsheng
	联系分公司	liánxì fēngōngsī
	做生意	zuò shēngyì
	学汉语	xué Hànyǔ
	去中国	qù Zhōngguó
	喝茶	hē chá
	吃中国菜	chī Zhōngguócài
	去买饮料	qù mǎi yǐnliào

3. 我想见市场部的经理。 **Wǒ xiǎng jiàn shìchǎngbù de jīnglǐ.**
"I would like to see (meet with) the manager of the marketing department."

Similar to 要 yào, 想 xiǎng can be used as a verb and an auxiliary verb and has the following different usages and meanings: When used as a verb, it means "to miss someone," e.g., 他很想家 Tā hěn xiǎng jiā "He is very homesick" or 你想你的女儿吧 Nǐ xiǎng nǐ de nǚ'ér ba "You miss your daughter, right?" 想 also means "to think; to ponder something," e.g., 我会想办法 Wǒ huì xiǎng bànfǎ "I'll come up with (literally: think of) a solution."

S + (很)想 + O

我(很)想<u>家人</u>。

Wǒ (hěn) xiǎng jiārén.
I miss my family (very much).

Substitution	
你(们)	nǐ(men)
他(们)	tā(men)
她(们)	tā(men)
孩子(们)	háizi(men)

When used as an auxiliary verb, 想 means "would like to; to plan to; to think of (doing something); to feel like (doing something)," and is followed by a main verb to express one's desires, intentions, and wishes to do something. In this case, the meaning of 想 is similar to 要, but the expression of the desire or intention is weaker than 要. Please also note that the negative form 不要 búyào is rarely used because it is too strong, whereas 不想 bù xiǎng is used frequently, particularly when the degree of desire or wish is moderate. In fact, 不要 + verb has another usage, which is to form a negative imperative sentence, such as 你不要喝太多酒 Nǐ búyào hē tài duō jiǔ "You shouldn't drink too much." See more examples in Unit 8.2 (Sentence Pattern 6).

S + 想 + V

我(不)想<u>学习</u>。

Wǒ (bù)xiǎng xuéxí.
I (don't) want to study.

Substitution	
做贸易	zuò màoyì
学汉语	xué Hànyǔ
退休	tuìxiū
喝咖啡	hē kāfēi
吃日本菜	chī Rìběncài
去买东西	qù mǎi dōngxi
去公园玩儿	qù gōngyuán wánr

When 想 is followed by what can be considered a sentence by itself, it means "to think; to believe; to consider." For example: in 我想这个问题很大 Wǒ xiǎng zhè ge wèntí hěn dà "I think this is a big problem," the phrase 这个问题很大 "This is a big problem" can be a sentence by itself. Please note that "I don't think this is a big problem" in Chinese is 我想这个问题不大 Wǒ xiǎng zhè ge wèntí bú dà and not *我不想这个问题很大. Both 想 and 要 have multiple meanings, but context and sentence structure will tell you which meaning is intended in each occurrence.

S + 想 + (Positive/Negative/Interrogative) Sentence

1. 我想他明天会来。

   Wǒ xiǎng tā míngtiān huì lái.
   I think he will come tomorrow.

2. 我想他不是我们的律师。

   Wǒ xiǎng tā bú shì wǒmen de lùshī.
   I don't think he is our lawyer.

3. 你想他会不会帮我们想个办法？

   Nǐ xiǎng tā huì bú huì bāng wǒmen xiǎng ge bànfǎ?
   Do you think he will help us find a solution?

4. 你想他明天能来上班吗？

   Nǐ xiǎng tā míngtiān néng lái shàng bān ma?
   Do you think he'll be able to make it to work tomorrow?

4. 您上下午都要开会。 Nín shàngxiàwǔ dōu yào kāi huì. "You have (must attend) meetings all day."

In addition to the meanings mentioned above, 要 yào can also be used to indicate a necessity or obligation, meaning "to need to; must; to have to." 要 here is actually the shortened version of 需要 xūyào. See more examples in Unit 11.2 (Sentence Pattern 2). Please note that the negative form of 要 in this context is not 不要 búyào, but rather 不必 búbì or 不用 búyòng, both of which mean "need not."

S + 要 + V

1. A: 你们星期六也要上班吗?

   B: 不，我们周末不必上班。

   A: Nǐmen xīngqīliù yě yào shàng bān ma?
   B: Bù, wǒmen zhōumò búbì shàng bān.

   A: Do you also have to work on Saturdays?
   B: No, we don't have to work on weekends.

2. A: 你下个月还要出差吗?

   B: 我下个月不用出差，下下个月需要出差。

   A: Nǐ xià ge yuè hái yào chū chāi ma?
   B: Wǒ xià ge yuè búyòng chū chāi, xià xià ge yuè xūyào chū chāi.

   A: Will you have to make another business trip next month?
   B: I won't need to travel for business next month; but I'll have to the month after next.

3. 你要小心开车。

   Nǐ yào xiǎoxīn kāi chē.
   You have to drive carefully.

---

5. 下星期一是<u>六月三号</u>。**Xià xīngqīyī shì <u>liùyuè sān hào</u>. "Next Monday is June 3."**

When telling the date, the month precedes the day, and is written as 几月几号 jǐ yuè jǐ hào if spoken, or 几月几日 jǐ yuè jǐ rì if written. For example: 八月十五号 bāyuè shíwǔ hào or 十月一日 shíyuè yī rì.

Table 17. Months of the year

一月	yīyuè	January
二月	èryuè	February
三月	sānyuè	March
四月	sìyuè	April
五月	wǔyuè	May
六月	liùyuè	June
七月	qīyuè	July
八月	bāyuè	August
九月	jiǔyuè	September
十月	shíyuè	October
十一月	shíyīyuè	November
十二月	shí'èryuè	December

Table 18. Time expressions for weeks

(Note: the measure word 个 gè is optional with 星期 xīngqī.)

上上(个)星期	shàng shàng (ge) xīngqī	two weeks ago
上(个)星期	shàng (ge) xīngqī	last week
这(个)星期	zhè (ge) xīngqī	this week
下(个)星期	xià (ge) xīngqī	next week
下下(个)星期	xià xià (ge) xīngqī	two weeks from now

Table 19. Time expressions for months

上上个月	shàng shàng ge yuè	two months ago
上个月	shàng ge yuè	last month
这个月	zhè ge yuè	this month
下个月	xià ge yuè	next month
下下个月	xià xià ge yuè	two months from now

The year is simply stated as a succession of four numbers. It is not proper to state the date as "two thousand and X." It is simply stated as "2, 0, 0, X." For example: the year 1949 is stated as yī jiǔ sì jiǔ; and the year 2008 is stated as èr líng líng bā.

6. <u>那么</u>星期二<u>吧</u>!   <u>Nàme</u> xīngqī èr <u>ba</u>! "Then make it Tuesday!"

那么 nàme is used at the beginning of a sentence and serves as a transitional conjunction. It introduces a clause or sentence that expresses the logical result, suggestion, or judgment drawn from the previous sentence. 那么 can be shortened to 那 nà and is often followed by a pause.

吧 ba is often added to the end of this type of sentence to reinforce the expression, the idea, or notion of suggestion. Please note that the usage of 吧 is different from what was introduced in Unit 2.2 (Sentence Pattern 6).

那么 + Sentence/Noun Phrase + 吧

1. 你不想喝红酒，那我们要啤酒吧!

   Nǐ bù xiǎng hē hóngjiǔ, nà wǒmen yào píjiǔ ba!
   You don't want to drink red wine; then let's have beer!

2. A: 我今天没有时间。
   B: 那么明天见吧!

   A: Wǒ jīntiān méiyǒu shíjiān.
   B: Nàme míngtiān jiàn ba!

   A: I don't have time today.
   B: In that case, let's meet tomorrow!

7. 我<u>马上</u>帮您联系。 Wǒ <u>mǎshàng</u> bāng nín liánxì. **"I will help you get in touch immediately."**

马上 mǎshàng is an adverb meaning "immediately; right away," which must appear before the verb. In English, adverbs are relatively flexible in terms of their placement within a sentence. All Chinese adverbs, however, must appear before the verb and most of them must follow the subject.

S + (AV) 马上 + V

1. 我会马上到你们公司去。

   Wǒ huì mǎshàng dào nǐmen gōngsī qù.
   I'll go to your company immediately.

2. A: 你能马上来我的办公室吗?
   B: 好,我马上来。

   A: Nǐ néng mǎshàng lái wǒ de bàngōngshì ma?
   B: Hǎo, wǒ mǎshàng lái.

   A: Can you come to my office immediately?
   B: Yes, I will come immediately.

Cultural Points

1. Addressing Superiors and Subordinates at Work

When addressing coworkers in China, one should generally adhere to the guidelines explained in Unit 1.1 (Cultural Point 5). To reiterate, these guidelines suggest that it is always safe to use proper titles when addressing coworkers, especially superiors. However, to express a closer relationship between coworkers, the affectionate terms 老 lǎo + family name can be used for superiors or coworkers who are older than you, and 小 xiǎo + family name can be used for subordinates or coworkers who are younger than you. This is roughly equivalent to referring to someone as "Old So-and-So" or "Little So-and-So," which may sound strange to Westerners, but it is an appropriate and good-natured form of address when used for coworkers with whom you have a long working history or a friendly relationship. This is a way of expressing closeness, whereas use of titles, though polite, usually indicates a degree of distance between two people. To ensure you are using this informal style of address appropriately, it is always safe to ask the other party how they would like to be addressed.

Additional Vocabulary

	Chinese	Pinyin	Part of Speech	English Equivalent
1.	帮忙	bāng máng	VO	to help
2.	信	xìn	N	letter
3.	啤酒	píjiǔ	N	beer
4.	酒	jiǔ	N	alcohol; wine
5.	米饭	mǐfàn	N	rice
6.	米	mǐ	N	(uncooked) rice
7.	饭	fàn	N	(cooked) rice; meal
8.	白酒	báijiǔ	N	white wine; a strong Chinese liquor
9.	红酒	hóngjiǔ	N	red wine
10.	红	hóng	Adj	red
11.	红茶	hóngchá	N	black tea
12.	绿茶	lǜchá	N	green tea
13.	绿	lǜ	Adj	green
14.	冰水	bīngshuǐ	N	ice water
15.	冰	bīng	N	ice
16.	果汁	guǒzhī	N	fruit juice
17.	喝	hē	V	to drink

18.	菜	cài	N	cuisine of a particular place (e.g., 中国菜 Zhōngguócài = Chinese cuisine/food)
19.	饮料	yǐnliào	N	drinks; beverage (usually non-alcoholic drinks)
20.	想家	xiǎng jiā	VO Adj	to miss home homesick
21.	办法	bànfǎ	N	way to handle things; solution
22.	家人	jiārén	N	family member(s)
23.	东西	dōngxi	N	stuff; things
24.	玩/玩儿	wán/wánr	V	to have fun; to play
25.	问题	wèntí	N	problem; question
26.	需要	xūyào	V	to need
27.	不必	búbì	AV	need not; not necessary
28.	不用	búyòng	AV	need not; not necessary
29.	出差	chū chāi	VO	to be on a business trip
30.	下个月	xià ge yuè	TW	next month
31.	小心	xiǎoxīn	Adj Adv	careful to do something carefully
32.	日	rì	N	day; the sun
33.	上(个)星期	shàng (ge) xīngqī	TW	last week
34.	上	shàng	Adj	last; previous
35.	上个月	shàng ge yuè	TW	last month

Unit **6.2**

Rescheduling an Appointment

In this lesson you will learn:

- How to reschedule an existing appointment.
- How to coordinate schedules with others in order to arrange a mutually agreeable meeting time.

Chinese Dialogue

白有天： 小王，你给方正公司打电话了吗？

王英： 打了，可是张经理出差去了。

白有天： 你知道他什么时候回来吗？

王英： 他下周三才会回来。

白有天： 那么能不能安排下周四见面呢？

王英： 我试试看，您下周四几点方便呢？

白有天： 下午两点半。

王英： 好的，我现在就给他的秘书打个电话。

Pinyin Dialogue

Bái Yǒutiān: Xiǎo Wáng, nǐ gěi Fāngzhèng Gōngsī dǎ diànhuà le ma?

Wáng Yīng: Dǎ le, kěshì Zhāng Jīnglǐ chū chāi qù le.

Bái Yǒutiān: Nǐ zhīdào tā shénme shíhou huílai ma?

Wáng Yīng: Tā xià zhōusān cái huì huílai.

Bái Yǒutiān: Nàme néng bù néng ānpái xià zhōusì jiàn miàn ne?

Wáng Yīng: Wǒ shìshi kàn, nín xià zhōusì jǐdiǎn fāngbiàn ne?

Bái Yǒutiān: Xiàwǔ liǎng diǎn bàn.

Wáng Yīng: Hǎo de, wǒ xiànzài jiù gěi tā de mìshū dǎ ge diànhuà.

Vocabulary

Chinese	Pinyin	Part of Speech	English Equivalent
1. 给	gěi	Prep V	to; for to give
2. 打电话	dǎ diànhuà	VO	to call; to make a phone call
3. 可是	kěshì	Conj	but
4. 知道	zhīdào	V	to know; to have the knowledge of; to be aware of
5. 时候	shíhou	N	(a point of) time
6. 周	zhōu	N	week (= 星期, but more formal)
7. 才	cái	Adv	not until; as late as
8. 安排	ānpái	V N	to arrange arrangement; plans
9. 见面	jiàn miàn	VO	to meet; to see
10. 试	shì	V	to try; to attempt
11. 方便	fāngbiàn	Adj	available; convenient
12. 就	jiù	Adv	right away; as early as

Sentence Patterns

1. 你给方正公司打电话了吗？ Nǐ gěi Fāngzhèng Gōngsī dǎ diànhuà le ma? "Did you give Fangzheng Company a call?"

给 gěi can function as a verb or as a preposition. When it is used as a verb, it means "to give." See the examples below:

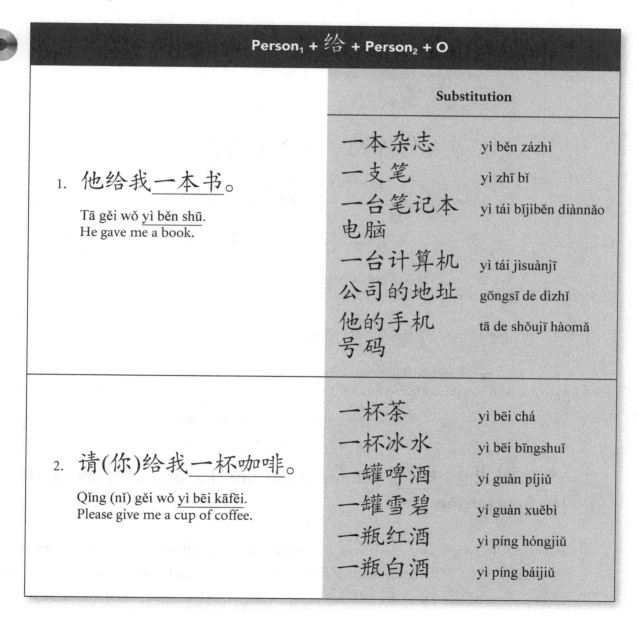

Person₁ + 给 + Person₂ + O

	Substitution
1. 他给我<u>一本书</u>。 Tā gěi wǒ yì běn shū. He gave me a book.	一本杂志 yì běn zázhì 一支笔 yì zhī bǐ 一台笔记本 电脑 yì tái bǐjìběn diànnǎo 一台计算机 yì tái jìsuànjī 公司的地址 gōngsī de dìzhǐ 他的手机 号码 tā de shǒujī hàomǎ
2. 请(你)给我<u>一杯咖啡</u>。 Qǐng (nǐ) gěi wǒ yì bēi kāfēi. Please give me a cup of coffee.	一杯茶 yì bēi chá 一杯冰水 yì bēi bīngshuǐ 一罐啤酒 yí guàn píjiǔ 一罐雪碧 yí guàn xuěbì 一瓶红酒 yì píng hóngjiǔ 一瓶白酒 yì píng báijiǔ

The following sentences are examples where 给 is used as a preposition. The pattern means someone does something "to" or "for" another party.

Person₁ + 给 + Person₂ + V

1. 他给公司打了一个电话。

   Tā gěi gōngsī dǎ le yí ge diànhuà.
   He made a phone call to the company.

2. 请你给我写信。

   Qǐng nǐ gěi wǒ xiě xìn.
   Please write me a letter.

3. 你要我给你介绍一个医生吗?

   Nǐ yào wǒ gěi nǐ jièshào yí ge yīshēng ma?
   Do you want me to introduce a doctor to you?

4. 我需要给他发一个电子邮件。

   Wǒ xūyào gěi tā fā yí ge diànzǐ yóujiàn.
   I need to send him an e-mail.

5. 你给公司发传真了吗?

   Nǐ gěi gōngsī fā chuánzhēn le ma?
   Did you send a fax to the company?

2. 张经理出差去了。 **Zhāng Jīnglǐ chū chāi qù le. "Manager Zhang left for a business trip."**

When 去了 qù le is used after a verb, it shows the action has already occurred or happened. The meaning of V + 去了 is the same as 去 + verb + 了, but it is a more colloquial way of saying that someone has gone to do something.

	Substitution	
他开会去了。	上班	shàng bān
Tā kāi huì qù le.	吃饭	chī fàn
He went to a meeting.	买东西	mǎi dōngxi
	听报告	tīng bàogào
	回国	huí guó
	回家	huí jiā
	回公司上班	huí gōngsī shàng bān
	回学校上课	huí xuéxiào shàng kè

3. 你知道他什么时候回来吗？ Nǐ zhīdào tā shénme shíhou huílai ma? "Do you know when he will be back?"

知道 zhīdào and 认识 rènshi both mean "to know," but they have different connotations. 知道 means "to know (a fact); to have the knowledge about; to be aware of." 认识 means "to be acquainted with; to be familiar with; to recognize." 认识 is more closely associated with cognitive awareness and recognition, while 知道 shows knowledge about a fact or truth. For example: 我不知道他 means "I don't know of him;" while 我不认识他 means "I'm not acquainted with him," or "I don't personally know him."

1. 我知道他明天能来。

   Wǒ zhīdào tā míngtiān néng lái.
   I know he is able to come tomorrow.

2. 你知道昨天谁打电话给我吗?

   Nǐ zhīdào zuótiān shéi dǎ diànhuà gěi wǒ ma?
   Do you know who called me yesterday?

3. 你知道市场部的经理叫什么名字吗?

   Nǐ zhīdào shìchǎngbù de jīnglǐ jiào shénme míngzi ma?
   Do you know the name of the manager of the marketing department?

4. 我不知道他今天下午会不会来?

   Wǒ bù zhīdào tā jīntiān xiàwǔ huì bú huì lái?
   I don't know if he'll come this afternoon or not.

4. 他下周三<u>才</u>会回来。 **Tā xià zhōusān cái huì huílai. "He won't be back until next Wednesday."**

When 才 cái, meaning "not until; as late as" is used with a specific time, it indicates that something occurs later than expected or wished. Please note that there is already a negative connotation with 才; therefore, it is incorrect to make a negative structure (*不才 is incorrect).

1. 他昨天晚上一点才睡。

   Tā zuótiān wǎnshang yì diǎn cái shuì.
   He did not go to bed until 1:00 a.m. last night.

2. 我今天早上十点才起来。

   Wǒ jīntiān zǎoshang shí diǎn cái qǐlái.
   I did not get up until 10:00 a.m. this morning.

3. 她这个星期不作报告，她下星期才作。

   Tā zhè ge xīngqī bú zuò bàogào, tā xià xīngqī cái zuò.
   She isn't doing the presentation this week; she won't do it until next week.

4. 他四十岁才结婚。

   Tā sìshí suì cái jié hūn.
   He did not get married until he was 40 years old.

5. 我<u>试试</u>看。 **Wǒ <u>shìshi</u> kàn. "I will see what I can do."**

Some Chinese verbs can be reduplicated, resulting in an A + A form. Verb reduplication conveys the sense of doing something casually or for a brief time. The reduplication of 试 means "to try out (something)." 看 kàn is often added to a reduplicated verb to convey the idea of "doing something and seeing what happens." For example:

你想想看 Nǐ xiǎngxiang kàn "You think it over (and see what you come up with)."

我找找看 Wǒ zhǎozhao kàn "I'll look for it (and see if it turns up)."

The second syllable in the duplicated verb is always pronounced with a neutral tone. See more examples in 8.2 (Sentence Pattern 4).

6. 我现在<u>就</u>给他的秘书打个电话。**Wǒ xiànzài <u>jiù</u> gěi tā de mìshū dǎ ge diànhuà. "I will give his secretary a call right now."**

Contrary to 才 cái, 就 jiù, meaning "as early as," when used with a specific time, indicates that an action occurs or occurred earlier than expected. 就 is not always preceded by a specific time; when not preceded by a specific time, 就 takes on the meaning of "immediately; at once." For example: 他就来，请稍等 Tā jiù lái, qǐng shāo děng "He will come right away. Please wait for a moment" or 我马上就到 Wǒ mǎshàng jiù dào "I'll be there immediately."

S + TW + 就 + V

1. 我现在就去公司找他。

   Wǒ xiànzài jiù qù gōngsī zhǎo tā.
   I'll go to the company to look for him right now.

2. 九点半开会，有的人九点就到了，有的人十点才到。

   Jiǔ diǎn bàn kāi huì, yǒude rén jiǔ diǎn jiù dào le, yǒude rén shí diǎn cái dào.
   The meeting started at 9:30; some people arrived as early as 9:00, while some people did not arrive until 10:00.

3. 他昨天晚上两点才睡，可是今天早上六点就起来了。

   Tā zuótiān wǎnshang liǎng diǎn cái shuì, kěshì jīntiān zǎoshang liù diǎn jiù qǐlái le.
   He did not go to sleep until 2:00 a.m. last night; but this morning he was already up at 6:00 a.m.

4. A: 她下星期回国吗？

   B: 不，她这个星期就回国。

   A: Tā xià xīngqī huí guó ma?
   B: Bù, tā zhè ge xīngqī jiù huí guó.

   A: Is she going back to her country next week?
   B: No, she will be going back this week.

Cultural Points

1. Appointments

Appointments are necessary prerequisites to meetings in the People's Republic of China and Taiwan. Chinese business firms are typically strongly hierarchical. It is necessary to make a specific appointment for a specific meeting. Secretaries are usually delegated the responsibility of setting up and planning for these meetings. Once an appointment has been made, it is extremely rude and inconsiderate to fail to appear on time. Breaking an appointment without adequate advance warning can be disastrous. This scenario is generally true when you are the client, however, Chinese business people may cancel appointments at the last moment if more important issues arise.

 ## Additional Vocabulary

	Chinese	Pinyin	Part of Speech	English Equivalent
1	台	tái	M	(a measure word for certain machinery, apparatuses, etc.)
2.	笔记本电脑	bǐjìběn diànnǎo	N	laptop
3.	笔记本	bǐjìběn	N	notebook
4.	计算机	jìsuànjī	N	computer (mainland China usage); calculator (Taiwan usage)
5.	手机	shǒujī	N	cellular phone
6.	号码	hàomǎ	N	number
7.	罐	guàn	M	(a measure word for cans or jars)
8.	雪碧	xuěbì	N	Sprite
9.	瓶	píng	M	(a measure word for bottles)
10.	医生	yīshēng	N	doctor
11.	发	fā	V	to send; to dispatch; to distribute

12.	电子邮件	diànzǐ yóujiàn	N	e-mail
13.	传真	chuánzhēn	N	fax
14.	报告	bàogào	N	report; presentation
15.	睡	shuì	V	to sleep
16.	起来	qǐlái	VC	to get up
17.	作	zuò	V	to do
18.	稍等	shāo děng	UE	to wait for a moment
19.	稍	shāo	Adv	slightly; for a moment
20.	等	děng	V	to wait

UNIT
7

访问
Fǎngwèn
Visiting

Unit **7.1**

Visiting a Company for the First Time

In this lesson we will learn:

- About company or plant visits, and what etiquette to use when first meeting a business counterpart.

- How to exchange business cards.

- How to express the duration and frequency of an activity.

Chinese Dialogue

白有天： 您好，我是蓝星电脑公司的经理，白有天。

张国强： 您好，白经理，我叫张国强，欢迎您来方正公司。

白有天： 谢谢。张经理，这是我的名片。

张国强： 这是我的名片，请多多指教。请坐！请坐！

白有天： 张经理，听说您刚出差回来。

张国强： 是的，我前天刚从四川回来。对不起，上个星期没能见您。

白有天： 没关系，我知道您忙。

张国强： 您是第一次来中国吗？

白有天： 不，我常来，我一年来两、三次。

张国强： 您这次会待多久？

白有天： 大概一个月左右。

Pinyin Dialogue

Bái Yǒutiān:	Nín hǎo, wǒ shì Lánxīng Diànnǎo Gōngsī de jīnglǐ, Bái Yǒutiān.
Zhāng Guóqiáng:	Nín hǎo, Bái Jīnglǐ, wǒ jiào Zhāng Guóqiáng, huānyíng nín lái Fāngzhèng Gōngsī.
Bái Yǒutiān:	Xièxie. Zhāng Jīnglǐ, zhè shì wǒ de míngpiàn.
Zhāng Guóqiáng:	Zhè shì wǒ de míngpiàn, qǐng duō duō zhǐjiào. Qǐng zuò! qǐng zuò!
Bái Yǒutiān:	Zhāng Jīnglǐ, tīngshuō nín gāng chū chāi huílai.
Zhāng Guóqiáng:	Shì de, wǒ qiántiān gāng cóng Sìchuān huílai. Duìbuqǐ, shàng ge xīngqī méi néng jiàn nín.
Bái Yǒutiān:	Méiguānxi, wǒ zhīdào nín máng.
Zhāng Guóqiáng:	Nín shì dì yí cì lái Zhōngguó ma?
Bái Yǒutiān:	Bù, wǒ cháng lái, wǒ yì nián lái liǎng, sān cì.
Zhāng Guóqiáng:	Nín zhè cì huì dāi duō jiǔ?
Bái Yǒutiān:	Dàgài yí ge yuè zuǒyòu.

Vocabulary

Chinese	Pinyin	Part of Speech	English Equivalent
1. 访问	fǎngwèn	V	to visit
2. 蓝星	Lánxīng	PN	the name of a fictional company in this text
3. 蓝	lán	Adj	blue
4. 星	xīng	N	star
5. 张国强	Zhāng Guóqiáng	PN	the full name of a fictional person in this text
6. 名片	míngpiàn	N	name card; business card
7. 指教	zhǐjiào	V	to give advice (a polite expression used when meeting for the first time)
8. 刚	gāng	Adv	just now; a short while ago
9. 前天	qiántiān	TW	the day before yesterday
10. 从	cóng	Prep	from
11. 四川	Sìchuān	PN	Sichuan province
12. 没关系	méiguānxi	UE	It doesn't matter; never mind
13. 第	dì	Pre	(prefix for ordinal numbers); -th/-nd/-rd
14. 次	cì	M	(a measure word for frequency)
15. 常	cháng	Adv	often
16. 这次	zhè cì	TW	this time
17. 待	dāi	V	to stay
18. 久	jiǔ	Adj/TD	long; for a long time
19. 大概	dàgài	Adv	probably; most likely
20. 左右	zuǒyòu	Adv	about; around; approximately
21. 左	zuǒ	N/Adj	left
22. 右	yòu	N/Adj	right

Sentence Patterns

1. 您刚出差回来吗？ Nín gāng chū chāi huílai ma? "Did you just come back from a business trip?"

The adverb 刚 gāng or 刚刚 gānggāng, meaning "just now; a short while ago," is used to modify an action that has taken place either a moment ago, or at least, very recently.

S + 刚/刚刚 + V		
	Substitution	
他刚回家。 Tā gāng huí jiā. He has just returned home.	回国	huí guó
	回去	huíqu
	回来	huílai
	来	lái
	去	qù
	走	zǒu
	结婚	jié hūn
	下班	xià bān
	上大学	shàng dàxué
	到银行去	dào yínháng qù

2. 我前天刚从四川回来。 Wǒ qiántiān gāng cóng Sìchuān huílai. "I just came back from Sichuan the day before yesterday."

从 cóng, a preposition meaning "from," indicates a place of origin or departure, which is followed by a main verb such as 来 lái "to come," 去 qù "to go," 回来 huílai "to come back," or 回去 huíqu "to go back." Please note that if a personal noun or a pronoun is used, 这儿 zhèr "here" or 那儿 nàr "there" has to appear after the personal noun/pronoun in order to denote a location. For example: 你从高明那儿去吗 Nǐ cóng Gāomíng nàr qù ma "Are you going from Gaoming's place?" or 你从他那儿来吗 Nǐ cóng tā nàr lái ma "Are you coming from his place?"

S + 从 + Place Word + 回来/回去

	Substitution

他刚从<u>四川</u>回来/回去。

Tā gāng cóng <u>Sìchuān</u> huílai/huíqu.
He just came back/went back from Sichuan.

广东/西	Guǎngdōng/xī
浙江	Zhèjiāng
江苏	Jiāngsū
湖北/南	Húběi/nán
山东/西	Shāndōng/xī
河北/南	Héběi/nán

S + 从 + Place Word + 来/去

	Substitution

我会从<u>北京</u>来/去。

Wǒ huì cóng <u>Běijīng</u> lái/qù.
I will be coming/going from Beijing.

东京	Dōngjīng
首尔	Shǒu'ěr
莫斯科	Mòsīkē
华盛顿	Huáshèngdùn
伦敦	Lúndūn
巴黎	Bālí
柏林	Bólín
罗马	Luómǎ

The above examples can be expanded by adding a place of arrival. For example: 他会从我这儿去你那儿 Tā huì cóng wǒ zhèr qù nǐ nàr "He'll be coming from my place to your place."

S + 从 + Place₁ + 来/去 + Place₂

我从公司来/去机场。

Wǒ cóng gōngsī lái/qù jīchǎng.
I will come/go to the airport from
the company.

Substitution

车站	饭店	chēzhàn	fàndiàn
宾馆	中关村	bīnguǎn	Zhōngguāncūn
学校	办公室	xuéxiào	bàngōngshì

3. 这是您第一次来中国吗? **Zhè shì nín dì yí cì lái Zhōngguó ma?**
"Is this your first trip to China?"

第 dì is a prefix used before cardinal numbers to form ordinal numbers. For example, 第一次 dì yí cì means "the first time," 第二次 dì èr cì means "the second time," 第三个人 dì sān ge rén means "the third person," 第四个星期 dì sì ge xīngqī means "the fourth week," etc. Please note that the proper measure word should precede the noun and follow the cardinal number.

4. 我常来。 **Wǒ cháng lái.** **"I come often."**

常 cháng, 常常 chángcháng, and 经常 jīngcháng are all forms of "often" in Chinese. This is an adverb and must be placed before the verb that it modifies, e.g., 我常/常常来中国 Wǒ cháng/chángcháng lái Zhōngguó or 我经常来中国 Wǒ jīngcháng lái Zhōngguó "I often come to China." The negative form can be either 不常 bù cháng or 不经常 bù jīngcháng, but never *不常常 bù chángcháng. Please note that 常 can be placed either before or after 不, the negative marker, but there is a difference in nuance. Examples:

他不常吃早饭。

Tā bù cháng chī zǎofàn.
He does not often have breakfast.

他常不吃早饭。

Tā cháng bù chī zǎofàn.
Quite often, he does not have breakfast.

	Substitution	
	运动	yùndòng
	打网球	dǎ wǎngqiú
	看电影	kàn diànyǐng
我常/常常/经常出差。	看电视	kàn diànshì
Wǒ cháng/chángcháng/jīng cháng chū chāi.	吃广东菜	chī Guǎngdōngcài
I often go on business trips.	去分公司	qù fēngōngsī
	到香港来	dào Xiānggǎng lái
	见到他	jiàndào tā
	给女儿打电话	gěi nǚ'ér dǎ diànhuà

Please also note that 常 alone is not a correct answer to the question 你常来中国吗
Nǐ cháng lái Zhōngguó ma "Do you come to China often?" The response should include an action
verb, e.g., 常来 cháng lái or 不常来 bù cháng lái. If 常 is used with a string of adverbs such as
也 yě, 都 dōu, and 不 bù, they should be listed in this order: 也都不常 yě dōu bù cháng.
Example:

我们不常开会，他们也都不常开会。

Wǒmen bù cháng kāi huì, tāmen yě dōu bù cháng kāi huì.
We do not have meetings often; they also all do not have meetings often.

5. 我一年来两、三次。 Wǒ yì nián lái liǎng, sān cì. "I come about two or three times a year."

次 cì is a measure word used to denote the number of occurrences or frequency of an action
(e.g., 一次) or a specific occurrence (e.g., 第一次). Unlike English, in Chinese this phrase,
which is called a time frequency (TF) expression, precedes a time duration (TD) expression.

For example, to say "once a day" in Chinese you must reverse the order of time frequency and time duration from the English, and state 一天一次 yì tiān yí cì, literally "one day once." Below is a table of common time duration expressions with possible time frequency phrases. See Sentence Pattern 6 of this lesson for more information about time duration expressions.

Table 20. Common time duration expressions

Time Duration	Time Frequency
一分钟 yì fēnzhōng one minute	一次 yí cì once
一(个)小时 yí (ge) xiǎoshí one hour	两次 liǎng cì twice
一天 yì tiān one day	三次 sān cì three times
一(个)星期 yí (ge) xīngqī one week	四次 sì cì four times
一个月 yí ge yuè one month	五次 wǔ cì five times
一年 yì nián one year	几次？ jǐ cì? How many times?

Please note that normal grammatical rules do not apply to days or years. These two nouns do not take measure words to modify them because they are measure word themselves. It would therefore be incorrect to state *一个天 yí ge tiān or *一个年 yí ge nián.

The frequency of an action is expressed in the following pattern:

S + TD + V + TF + (O)

1. 他一天送两次信。

   Tā yì tiān sòng liǎng cì xìn.
   He delivers mail twice a day.

2. 经理两星期去一次分公司。

   Jīnglǐ liǎng xīngqī qù yí cì fēngōngsī.
   The manager goes to the branch office once every two weeks.

3. 他一个星期买一、两次菜。

   Tā yí ge xīngqī mǎi yì, liǎng cì cài.
   He buys groceries one or two times each week.

4. 我一个月打三次网球。

   Wǒ yí ge yuè dǎ sān cì wǎngqiú.
   I play tennis three times a month.

5. A: 你一年去中国几次？
   B: 我一年大概去两次。

   A: Nǐ yì nián qù Zhōngguó jǐ cì?
   B: Wǒ yì nián dàgài qù liǎng cì.

   A: How many times do you go to China each year?
   B: I go about twice a year.

6. A: 你们多久去一次卡拉OK?

   B: 我们差不多一个月去两次。

   A: Nǐmen duō jiǔ qù yí cì kǎlā OK?
   B: Wǒmen chàbuduō yí ge yuè qù liǎng cì.

   A: How often do you go to karaoke?
   B: We go about twice a month.

6. 您这次会待多久? Nín zhè cì huì dāi duō jiǔ? "How long will you stay this time?"

We learned in Unit 5.2 (Sentence Pattern 2) that a time word (TW) referring to a specific point in time must appear before the verb in Chinese. In this lesson, we learn about another type of time expression, called time duration (TD). Similar to English, a Chinese time duration phrase follows a verb to indicate the duration of the action. For example: 我每天睡八个小时 Wǒ měitiān shuì bā ge xiǎoshí "I sleep eight hours every day."

If the verb takes an object, however, then the verb must be repeated after the object, and the time duration phrase has to follow the repeated verb. For example: 他学中文学了三年 Tā xué Zhōngwén xué le sān nián "He studied Chinese for three years." The time duration phrase can also be placed between the verb and the object, if the object is not a personal pronoun, without changing the meaning of the sentence. In this case, the time duration phrase is followed by 的, and is used as an adjective modifier. For example: 他学了三年的中文 Tā xué le sān nián de Zhōngwén.

The following are examples of present and future tense sentences that use TD phrases and signify habitual actions.

S + (TW) + V + TD (Without Object)	S + (TW) + V + O + V + TD *Or* S + (TW) + V + TD + 的 + O (With Object)
1. 我每天上一个小时。 Wǒ měitiān shàng yí ge xiǎoshí. I attend (class) for one hour every day.	我每天上课上一个小时。 Wǒ měitiān shàng kè shàng yí ge xiǎoshí. *Or* 我每天上一个小时的课。 Wǒ měitiān shàng yí ge xiǎoshí de kè.
2. 我要学两年。 Wǒ yào xué liǎng nián. I want to study (Chinese) for two years.	我要学中文学两年。 Wǒ yào xué Zhōngwén xué liǎng nián. *Or* 我要学两年的中文。 Wǒ yào xué liǎng nián de Zhōngwén.
3. 他经常打三、四个 小时。 Tā jīngcháng dǎ sān, sì ge xiǎoshí. He often plays (ball) for three or four hours.	他经常打球打三、四个 小时。 Tā jīngcháng dǎ qiú dǎ sān, sì ge xiǎoshí. *Or* 他经常打三、四个小时 的球。 Tā jīngcháng dǎ sān, sì ge xiǎoshí de qiú.

The following are examples of past tense sentences that use time duration phrases. Please note that 了 must follow the verb in order to indicate past tense. For example: 我们去年在上海待了一个月。 Wǒmen qùnián zài Shànghǎi dāi le yí ge yuè. Last year we stayed in Shanghai for a month.

S + (TW) + V + 了 + TD (Without Object)	S + (TW) + V + O + V + 了 + TD S + (TW) + V + 了 + TD + 的 + O (With Object)
1. 我哥哥做了六年。 Wǒ gēge zuò le liù nián. My brother did (import and export business) for six years.	我哥哥做进出口生意做了六年。 Wǒ gēge zuò jìnchūkǒu shēngyì zuò le liù nián. *Or* 我哥哥做了六年的进出口生意。 Wǒ gēge zuò le liù nián de jìnchūkǒu shēngyì.
2. 我教了三十年。 Wǒ jiāo le sānshí nián. I taught (English) for 30 years.	我教英文教了三十年。 Wǒ jiào Yīngwén jiào le sānshí nián. *Or* 我教了三十年的英文。 Wǒ jiāo le sānshí nián de Yīngwén.
3. 你们昨天开了多长时间？ Nǐmen zuótiān kāi le duō cháng shíjiān? How long did you attend (the meeting) yesterday?	你们昨天开会开了多长时间？ Nǐmen zuótiān kāi huì kāi le duō cháng shíjiān? *Or* 你们昨天开了多长时间的会？ Nǐmen zuótiān kāi le duō cháng shíjiān de huì?

The following are examples of present perfect tense sentences that use time duration phrases. By adding another 了 at the end of the sentence, it indicates that the action started some time ago, is ongoing, and will continue into the future. Please note that in this case, the first 了 can be omitted.

S + V + (了) + TD + 了 (Without Object)	S + V + O + V + (了) + TD + 了 S + V + (了) + TD + 的 + O + 了 (With Object)
1. 我做了十年了。 Wǒ zuò le shínián le. I have been working (as an accountant) for ten years.	我做会计做了十年了。 Wǒ zuò kuàijì zuò le shínián le. *Or* 我做了十年的会计了。 Wǒ zuò le shínián de kuàijì le.
2. 他找三个月了。 Tā zhǎo sān ge yuè le. He has been looking for (a job) for three months.	他找工作找了三个月了。 Tā zhǎo gōngzuò zhǎo le sān ge yuè le. *Or* 他找了三个月的工作了。 Tā zhǎo le sān ge yuè de gōngzuò le.

Please note that the forms on the left hand side of the tables above, describing a sentence pattern without an object, are used only when the object of the verb is understood, as in a reply to a question.

7. 多久? Duō jiǔ? "How long?"

多 can be used as an interrogative word when followed by an adjective. It is used to ask about the extent of the adjective following 多. It is usually used with an adjective in a positive sense (much like in English), such as 大 dà "big," 高 gāo "tall," 远 yuǎn "far," or 长 cháng "long," etc.

1. A: 他(有)多高？
   B: 他有一米七。

   A: Tā (yǒu) duō gāo?
   B: Tā yǒu yì mǐ qī.

   A: How tall is he?
   B: He is 170 cm.

2. A: 你要去多长时间？
   B: 一个月左右。

   A: Nǐ yào qù duō cháng shíjiān?
   B: Yí ge yuè zuǒyòu.

   A: How long will you be gone?
   B: About one month.

3. 你会在上海住多久？

   Nǐ huì zài Shànghǎi zhù duō jiǔ?
   How long will you live in Shanghai?

4. 你们公司有多大？

   Nǐmen gōngsī yǒu duō dà?
   How big is your company?

5. 这本书有多贵？

   Zhè běn shū yǒu duō guì?
   How expensive is this book?

8. 大概一个月左右。 **Dàgài yí ge yuè zuǒyòu. "About one month."**

When 左右 appears after a numeral/measure word combination, it indicates that the number mentioned is only a rough estimate, not an exact number.

	Substitution	
1. A: 你会在中国待多久？ B: <u>两年</u>左右。	十五天 两个星期 半个月	shíwǔ tiān liǎng ge xīngqī bàn ge yuè
A: Nǐ huì zài Zhōngguó dāi duō jiǔ? B: <u>Liǎng nián</u> zuǒyòu.		
A: How long will you stay in China? B: About two years.		
2. A: 林经理什么时候回来？ B: <u>中午十二点</u>左右。	下午三点 明天上午十点 下星期三	xiàwǔ sān diǎn míngtiān shàngwǔ shí diǎn xià xīngqīsān
A: Lín Jīnglǐ shénme shíhou huílai? B: <u>Zhōngwǔ shí'èr diǎn</u> zuǒyòu.		
A: When will Manager Lin be back? B: Around noon.		
3. A: 他多大年纪了？ B: 大概六十左右。		
A: Tā duō dà niánjì le? B: Dàgài liùshí zuǒyòu.		
A: How old is he? B: Probably around 60.		

Cultural Points

1. Business Cards

The exchange of business cards is important in Chinese society. Chinese business cards are different in format compared with those of the United States. In the United States, business cards show the name and title of the person. Because Chinese people are more conscious of titles and rank, Chinese business cards might state all the academic, social, governmental, and commercial positions that an individual holds. The position listed first is the most prestigious, followed by the others in order of prestige. Furthermore, business cards in China are commonly two-sided, English on one side and Chinese on the other. The English side is generally the same format as an American card may have.

Presentation of business cards to a person of higher rank or social status is a very formal procedure. It is an introductory gambit. The presentation is not only an exchange of information, but also a way of showing mutual respect and putting your best foot forward. Business cards should be offered with both hands, with the wording on the card facing the recipient. Feet should be side by side, and there should be a slight bow of the head. Cards should be received in a similar respectful posture. This protocol does not necessarily hold true when presenting a business card to one who is not of a higher status.

2. Mentoring

The phrase 请多多指教 Qǐng duō duō zhǐjiào is perhaps best expressed as "please instruct me in many areas," though this is not an exact translation. This is a polite expression used when meeting someone for the first time, and it indicates a willingness to learn from or be mentored by the other person. Frequently, younger members will be mentored by senior members, and it is polite and respectful for someone in a junior position to ask a senior member to teach him/her the ins and outs of their field while they are working together. This is a further demonstration of the hierarchical structure of Chinese society and business.

 # Additional Vocabulary

	Chinese	Pinyin	Part of Speech	English Equivalent
1.	大学	dàxué	N	university; college
2.	机场	jīchǎng	N	airport
3.	饭店	fàndiàn	N	restaurant; hotel
4.	宾馆	bīnguǎn	N	hotel
5.	常常	chángcháng	Adv	often; frequently

6.	经常	jīngcháng	Adv	often; frequently; constantly
7.	早饭	zǎofàn	N	breakfast
8.	运动	yùndòng	V	to exercise; to work out
9.	电视	diànshì	N	television
10.	香港	Xiānggǎng	PN	Hong Kong
11.	分钟	fēnzhōng	TD	duration or period of minutes
12.	小时	xiǎoshí	TD	hour
13.	送信	sòng xìn	VO	to deliver mail
14.	送	sòng	V	to deliver
15.	买菜	mǎi cài	VO	to buy groceries
16.	卡拉OK	kǎlā OK	N	karaoke
17.	每天	měitiān	TW	every day
18.	每	měi	Pr	every; each
19.	长	cháng	Adj	long
20.	会计	kuàijì	N	accounting
21.	米	mǐ	M	(a measure word for length in meters)

Unit **7.2**

Introducing Products and Plants

In this lesson you will learn:

- Additional words and structures to discuss companies and manufacturing plants.

- How to comment on the product offerings, the location of company headquarters or plants, and the number of employees in a company.

Chinese Dialogue

白有天：　我这次来是介绍我们的新产品。

张国强：　太好了，我们对你们的产品非常感兴趣。

白有天：　这种产品是我们在江苏的工厂生产的。

张国强：　是吗？在江苏哪一个城市？

白有天：　在苏州，我们在那儿建了一个分厂。

张国强：　是什么时候建的？

白有天：　去年建的。

张国强：　有多少员工？

白有天：　一共有一千三百人。

张国强：　那很大呀！

白有天：　还可以。有空，欢迎您来参观我们的工厂。

张国强：　谢谢，有机会我一定来。

Pinyin Dialogue

Bái Yǒutiān:	Wǒ zhè cì lái shì jièshào wǒmen de xīn chǎnpǐn.
Zhāng Guóqiáng:	Tài hǎo le, wǒmen duì nǐmen de chǎnpǐn fēicháng gǎn xìngqù.
Bái Yǒutiān:	Zhè zhǒng chǎnpǐn shì wǒmen zài Jiāngsū de gōngchǎng shēngchǎn de.
Zhāng Guóqiáng:	Shì ma? Zài Jiāngsū nǎ yí ge chéngshì?
Bái Yǒutiān:	Zài Sūzhōu, wǒmen zài nàr jiàn le yí ge fēnchǎng.
Zhāng Guóqiáng:	Shì shénme shíhou jiàn de?
Bái Yǒutiān:	Qù nián jiàn de.
Zhāng Guóqiáng:	Yǒu duōshao yuángōng?
Bái Yǒutiān:	Yígòng yǒu yìqiān sānbǎi rén.
Zhāng Guóqiáng:	Nà hěn dà ya!
Bái Yǒutiān:	Hái kěyǐ. Yǒu kòng, huānyíng nín lái cānguān wǒmen de gōngchǎng.
Zhāng Guóqiáng:	Xièxiè, yǒu jīhuì wǒ yídìng lái.

Vocabulary

Chinese	Pinyin	Part of Speech	English Equivalent
1. 新	xīn	Adj	new
2. 产品	chǎnpǐn	N	product
3. 对	duì	Prep	in; (signifies the object of an interest or action)
4. 非常	fēicháng	Adv.	very; extremely; highly
5. 感	gǎn	V	to feel; to sense
6. 兴趣	xìngqù	N	interest
7. 种	zhǒng	M	(a measure word for types/kinds/sorts)
8. 江苏	Jiāngsū	PN	Jiangsu province
9. 工厂	gōngchǎng	N	factory
10. 生产	shēngchǎn	V	to manufacture; to produce
11. 城市	chéngshì	N	city
12. 苏州	Sūzhōu	PN	Suzhou
13. 建	jiàn	V	to build
14. 分厂	fēnchǎng	N	branch factory
15. 去年	qùnián	TW	last year
16. 员工	yuángōng	N	employee; staff; personnel
17. 一共	yígòng	Adv	all together; totally
18. 呀	ya	P	(used in place of 啊 when the preceding word ends with the sound of *a, o, e, i,* or *ü*)
19. 参观	cānguān	V	to visit; to observe; to tour (a company/factory, etc.)
20. 还可以	hái kěyǐ	UE	it's OK; not bad (a humble expression)
21. 机会	jīhuì	N	opportunity; chance
22. 一定	yídìng	Adv	definitely; for sure

Sentence Patterns

1. 我们<u>对</u>你们的产品非常<u>感兴趣</u>。 **Wǒmen <u>duì</u> nǐmen de chǎnpǐn fēicháng <u>gǎn xìngqù</u>. "We are very interested in your products."**

This pattern is used to express that one is interested in something. 对 duì, used in this lesson, is a preposition. It is followed by a noun that serves as an object of interest. In this case, the verb can be either 感兴趣 gǎn xìngqù or 有兴趣 yǒu xìngqù, signifying interest in the aforementioned noun. 非常 or 很 is used before the verb phrase to intensify the degree of interest.

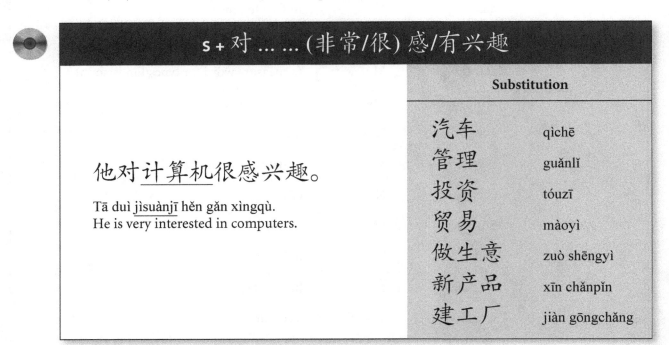

s + 对 ... ... (非常/很) 感/有兴趣	
	Substitution
他对<u>计算机</u>很感兴趣。 Tā duì jìsuànjī hěn gǎn xìngqù. He is very interested in computers.	汽车 qìchē 管理 guǎnlǐ 投资 tóuzī 贸易 màoyì 做生意 zuò shēngyì 新产品 xīn chǎnpǐn 建工厂 jiàn gōngchǎng

2. <u>太</u>好<u>了</u>。 **<u>Tài</u> hǎo <u>le</u>. "Great."**

In Unit 5.1 (Sentence Pattern 3), we learned that 太 tài is used to signify an excessive or extreme degree of an adjective. This meaning is changed somewhat when the modal particle 了 is added at the end of the sentence. The new pattern expresses more subjective or personal opinions than when the more objective 太 and 很 are used. However, when the sentence is negative, 了 is not added. For example: 这本书不太贵 Zhè běn shū bú tài guì "This book is not too expensive."

太 + SV + 了

	Substitution	
累		lèi
紧张		jǐnzhāng
高兴		gāoxìng
兴奋		xīngfèn
开心		kāixīn

1. 他今天太忙了。

Tā jīntiān tài máng le.
He's too busy today.

2. 你能来，太好了。

Nǐ néng lái, tài hǎo le.
You are able to come; that's great.

3. 这家公司太大了。

Zhè jiā gōngsī tài dà le.
This company is too big.

4. 那种手机太旧了。

Nà zhǒng shǒujī tài jiù le.
That kind of cellular phone is too old.

5. 她的东西太多了。

Tā de dōngxi tài duō le.
She has too many things.

3. 这种产品是我们在江苏的工厂生产的。 **Zhè zhǒng chǎnpǐn shì wǒmen zài Jiāngsū de gōngchǎng shēngchǎn de.** "It is our factory in Jiangsu that produced this type of product."

The 是 ... ... 的 construction is used to focus on a specific bit of information about a given fact. Most of the time, the 是 ... ... 的 construction is used to emphasize information about a past event in terms of time, place, person, or means of transportation. 是 appears before the emphasized component, but can be omitted without changing the meaning. 的 is placed at the end of the sentence. The negative form is 不是 ... ... 的; in the negative sentence the 是 cannot be omitted.

---

s (是) ... ... 的

1. A: 马经理是什么时候回来的？
   B: 是昨天回来的。

   A: Mǎ Jīnglǐ shì shénme shíhou huílai de?
   B: Shì zuótiān huílai de.

   A: When did Manager Ma come back?
   B: It was yesterday.

2. A: 这个产品是在哪儿生产的？
   B: 是在中国生产的。

   A: Zhè ge chǎnpǐn shì zài nǎr shēngchǎn de?
   B: Shì zài Zhōngguó shēngchǎn de.

   A: Where was this product manufactured?
   B: It was in China that this was manufactured.

3. A: 这本字典是谁买的？
   B: 是王小姐买的。

   A: Zhè běn zìdiǎn shì shéi mǎi de?
   B: Shì Wáng Xiǎojie mǎi de.

   A: Who bought this dictionary?
   B: It was Miss Wang who bought it.

> 4. A: 他开车去苏州的吗？
>
>   B: 他不是开车去的，他是坐火车去的。
>
>   A: Tā kāi chē qù Sūzhōu de ma?
>   B: Tā bú shì kāi chē qù de, tā shì zuò huǒchē qù de.
>
>   A: Did he drive to Suzhou?
>   B: He didn't drive. He took the train.

Cultural Points

1. The Growth of Manufacturing across China

The concept of Special Economic Zones as the sole regions for foreign investment in China is changing. In years past, foreign enterprises were limited to these specific geographic areas. As such, with this inflow of foreign capital, Special Economic Zones have had better infrastructure than other less-developed regions. Even preceding China's entry into the WTO, restrictions on when and where a foreign company may invest had already been lessening. Now, other regions are becoming specialized in manufacturing certain products.

2. Specialization in Manufacturing

Piracy in China is pervasive. This piracy is not limited to movies and music, but extends into manufacturing designs and even management techniques. In China, this is not considered stealing. Instead, friends and family "help" one another by passing on such information and products as needed. As many of the factories are located in close proximity to one another, people who have known one another for their entire lives and work in separate factories share information and technology within a region. Thus, an entire region may become known for a particular product. For instance, the Pearl River Delta and lower Yangtze River areas are well-known for their manufacturing of textiles and technology components. Their high rate of success and inflow of capital have induced other regions to compete for investment in the same way that Shanghai competed with Hong Kong several years ago.

Additional Vocabulary

Chinese	Pinyin	Part of Speech	English Equivalent
1. 管理	guǎnlǐ	N	management
2. 投资	tóuzī	N	investment
3. 紧张	jǐnzhāng	Adj	nervous
4. 兴奋	xīngfèn	Adj	excited
5. 开心	kāixīn	Adj	happy
6. 旧	jiù	Adj	old (opposite of 新 xīn)
7. 坐火车	zuò huǒchē	VO	to take a train
8. 坐	zuò	V	to travel by; to take (a means of transportation)
9. 火车	huǒchē	N	train

UNIT
8

晚餐
Wǎncān
Dining

Unit **8.1**

Dining Invitations

In this lesson we will learn:

- Some words and phrases related to dining invitations.

- How to arrange when and where to meet for a meal, and how to discuss which type of food to eat.

Chinese Dialogue

张国强： 白先生，今天晚上我请您吃饭。

白有天： 谢谢，您太客气了！

张国强： 您吃过北京烤鸭吗？

白有天： 没吃过，不过听说北京烤鸭是北京的名菜。

张国强： 对，那我们就去全聚德吃北京烤鸭吧！您住在哪家宾馆？

白有天： 我住在王府饭店。

张国强： 今天晚上六点钟我去饭店接您，好吗？

白有天： 好的，我在饭店大堂等您。

Pinyin Dialogue

Zhāng Guóqiáng:	Bái Xiānsheng, jīntiān wǎnshang wǒ qǐng nín chī fàn.
Bái Yǒutiān:	Xièxie, nín tài kèqi le!
Zhāng Guóqiáng:	Nín chī guò Běijīng kǎoyā ma?
Bái Yǒutiān:	Méi chī guò, búguò tīngshuō Běijīng kǎoyā shì Běijīng de míngcài.
Zhāng Guóqiáng:	Duì, nà wǒmen jiù qù Quánjùdé chī Běijīng kǎoyā ba! Nín zhù zài nǎ jiā bīnguǎn?
Bái Yǒutiān:	Wǒ zhù zài Wángfǔ Fàndiàn.
Zhāng Guóqiáng:	Jīntiān wǎnshang liù diǎn zhōng wǒ qù fàndiàn jiē nín, hǎo ma?
Bái Yǒutiān:	Hǎo de, wǒ zài fàndiàn dàtáng děng nín.

Vocabulary

Chinese	Part of Pinyin	Part of Speech	English Equivalent
1. 晚餐	wǎncān	N	dinner
2. 客气	kèqi	Adj	polite; courteous
3. 过	guò	P	(a particle that indicates a past action or state)
4. 烤鸭	kǎoyā	N	roast duck
5. 不过	búguò	Conj	but
6. 名菜	míngcài	N	signature dish
7. 对	duì	Adj	right; correct
8. 全聚德	Quánjùdé	PN	a famous roast duck restaurant in Beijing
9. 住	zhù	V	to reside; to stay (at a hotel)
10. 王府饭店	Wángfǔ Fàndiàn	PN	Wangfu Hotel
11. 接	jiē	V	to pick up (people); to answer (the telephone)
12. 大堂	dàtáng	N	lobby

Sentence Patterns

1. 今天晚上我请您吃饭。 **Jīntiān wǎnshang wǒ qǐng nín chī fàn.
"I would like to invite you for dinner tonight."**

The meaning of 请 qǐng in this lesson is "to treat or to invite someone (for meal)," as in the following examples:

P₁ + 请 + P₂ + V

	Substitution	
	吃午饭	chī wǔfàn
	吃晚饭	chī wǎnfàn
我请你吃饭!	喝咖啡	hē kāfēi
Wǒ qǐng nǐ chī fàn!	喝酒	hē jiǔ
I would like to invite you for dinner!	喝茶	hē chá
	去唱卡拉 OK	qù chàng kǎlā OK
	看电影	kàn diànyǐng

请 was briefly introduced in Unit 2.2 (Sentence Pattern 1) as a way to make a request in semi-formal or formal settings. Here are more examples of this usage of 请.

请 + V

	Substitution	
1. 请进!	进来	jìnlai
	进去	jìnqu
Qǐng jìn!	坐	zuò
Please come in!	站起来	zhàn qǐlái
	吸烟	xī yān
2. 请喝茶!	指教	zhǐjiào
	稍等	shāo děng
Qǐng hē chá!	接电话	jiē diànhuà
Please drink some tea!	讲	jiǎng

When asking someone who is your superior to do something, 请 is used to show a respectful attitude. The meaning of 请 in the following examples is "to ask or invite someone to do something."

(N₁) + 请 + N₂ + V		
		Substitution
1. 我想请江经理来分公司。 Wǒ xiǎng qǐng Jiāng Jīnglǐ lái fēngōngsī. I would like to ask (invite) Manager Jiang to come to the branch office.	去工厂 到总公司来 参观子公司	qù gōngchǎng dào zǒnggōngsī lái cānguān zǐgōngsī
2. 请吴经理介绍。 Qǐng Wú Jīnglǐ jièshào. Manager Wu, please make the introductions.	报告 说明 说几句话	bàogào shuōmíng shuō jǐ jù huà

2. 您吃过北京烤鸭吗? Nín chī guò Běijīng kǎoyā ma? "Have you ever had Peking duck?"

过 guò, an aspect particle, is used after a verb to indicate a person's past experience throughout his or her lifetime. The negative of this statement is formed by 没(有) méi(yǒu) + V + 过. The following table shows structures of positive, negative, and interrogative forms of such past experience phrases. The object in the sentences may be dropped if it is understood.

Table 21. Interrogative forms of past experience phrases

Interrogative V + 过 + (O) + 吗? V + 过 + (O) + 没有?	Positive V + 过 + (O)	Negative 没(有) + V + 过 + (O)
1. 你来过这个饭店吗? Nǐ lái guò zhè ge fàndiàn ma? Have you been to this restaurant?	我来过。 Wǒ lái guò. Yes, I've been here.	我没来过。 Wǒ méi lái guò. No, I've never been here.
2. 他去过长城吗? Tā qù guò Chángchéng ma? Has he been to the Great Wall?	他去过(长城)。 Tā qù guò (Chángchéng). He has been.	他没去过(长城)。 Tā méi qù guò (Chángchéng). He has never been.
3. 他看过中文报吗? Tā kàn guò Zhōngwén bào ma? Has he ever read a Chinese newspaper?	他看过(中文报)。 Tā kàn guò (Zhōngwén bào). He has read Chinese newspapers.	他没看过(中文报)。 Tā méi kàn guò (Zhōngwén bào). He has never read a Chinese newspaper.
4. 你见过王经理没有? Nǐ jiàn guò Wáng Jīnglǐ méiyǒu? Have you met Manager Wang?	我见过(王经理)。 Wǒ jiàn guò (Wáng Jīnglǐ). I have met Manager Wang.	我还没见过(王经理)。 Wǒ hái méi jiàn guò (Wáng Jīnglǐ). I haven't met Manager Wang yet.

3. 那我们就去全聚德吃北京烤鸭吧！ **Nà wǒmen jiù qù Quánjùdé chī Běijīng kǎoyā ba!** "In that case, let's go to Quánjùdé for Peking duck!"

In Unit 6.1 (Sentence Pattern 6), we learned 那 nà or 那么 nàme is used to make an observation or suggestion that is logically concluded from the previous statement. Following are extra examples to review this usage. Please note that the adverb 就 jiù, meaning "then," can also be used before the verb to stress the positive tone, making the suggestion or conclusion stronger. 吧 is usually added at the end of this type of sentence to reinforce the tone of the suggestion made.

那 + S + (就) + V + 吧

1. 已经六点半了，那我们下班吧！

Yǐjīng liù diǎn bàn le, nà wǒmen xià bān ba!
It's 6:30 already, so let's leave work!

2. 大家都到了，那么我们就开始吧！

Dàjiā dōu dào le, nàma wǒmen jiù kāishǐ ba!
Everybody is here. Let's begin!

3. A: 我还没吃午饭呢。
   B: 那我们就一起去吃吧！

A: Wǒ hái méi chī wǔfàn ne.
B: Nà wǒmen jiù yìqǐ qù chī ba!

A: I haven't eaten lunch yet.
B: In that case, let's go to eat together!

4. 您住在哪家宾馆？ **Nín zhù zài nǎ jiā bīnguǎn?** "Which hotel are you living (staying) at?"

We learned in Unit 5.2 (Sentence Pattern 1) that in Chinese a place word or locative expression (在 zài + place word) has to precede the verb, e.g., 你在哪里工作 Nǐ zài nǎli gōngzuò "Where do you work?" However, there are several verbs, such as 住 zhù, 坐 zuò "to sit," 站 zhàn "to stand," 建 jiàn "to build," 放 fàng "to put," or 睡 shuì "to sleep," which are followed by the "在 + place word" phrase.

1. 您住在哪儿?

   Nín zhù zài nǎr?
   Where do you live?

2. 谁坐在这儿?

   Shéi zuò zài zhèr?
   Who is sitting here?

3. 李小姐站在那儿。

   Lǐ Xiǎojie zhàn zài nàr.
   Ms. Li is standing over there.

4. 我刚到这儿，我昨天晚上睡在朋友的家。

   Wǒ gāng dào zhèr, wǒ zuótiān wǎnshang shuì zài péngyou de jiā.
   I just arrived here; I slept (stayed) at my friend's house last night.

5. 今天的报纸你放在哪儿?

   Jīntiān de bàozhǐ nǐ fàng zài nǎr?
   Where did you put today's newspaper?

6. 你们的新工厂建在哪儿?

   Nǐmen de xīn gōngchǎng jiàn zài nǎr?
   Where did you build your new factory?

5. 今天晚上六点钟我去饭店接您，<u>好吗</u>? **Jīntiān wǎnshang liù diǎn zhōng wǒ qù fàndiàn jiē nín, <u>hǎo ma</u>? "I'll go to the hotel to pick you up tonight at 6:00. Is that alright?"**

好吗 hǎo ma is used after the speaker makes a suggestion or proposal to find out if the addressee agrees or not, and may be considered the equivalent of the English phrase "All right?" If the addressee agrees, he or she may respond by saying 好 hǎo, 好吧 hǎo ba or 好啊 hǎo a. If the addressee disagrees, he or she should give other suggestions, instead of replying with 不好 bù hǎo.

Cultural Points

1. Accepting and Extending Dining Invitations

When you are invited out to meals, it is important to listen to the wording of the invitation. If the word used in the invitation was 请 qǐng, then your host has already expressed the desire to take you out to eat and also intends to pay for it. In Western cultures, a person invited to a meal may make a polite gesture of offering to pay, but would not persistently insist on it. In China, when invited as a non-paying guest, it is customary to insist on offering to pay the bill. It would be considered rude and impolite not to offer to pay, especially if you have dined together multiple times and you have not paid an equal number of the checks. If the other party uses 请 when asking you out, you should know that they expect to pick up the tab, so you may want to show a little hesitation while accepting the invitation to express politeness. But do not completely decline the invitation, because that would be considered even ruder (i.e., would be a loss of face for the person inviting you).

2. Regional Cuisine and China's Signature Dishes

Several regions throughout China are known for their signature dishes. 西安 Xī'ān, the city of the Terracotta Warriors, is known for its famous lamb kebab and dumpling dishes. Shanghai and its surrounding areas are known for their seafood dishes. Beijing is famous for a favorite dish known as roast duck (or Peking duck), 北京烤鸭 Běijīng kǎoyā. This dish has a history of over 300 years, and some of the best restaurants in Beijing that serve this dish are nearly that old. 全聚德 Quánjùdé, the restaurant mentioned earlier in this lesson, is one of the most famous of these. The restaurant itself is a testament to Chinese hierarchical structure, as it is a multilevel building. The higher in rank and salary one is, the higher the level one may sit in the restaurant.

Additional Vocabulary

	Chinese	Pinyin	Part of Speech	English Equivalent
1.	晚饭	wǎnfàn	N	dinner; supper
2.	唱	chàng	V	to sing
3.	站起来	zhàn qǐlái	VC	to stand up
4.	站	zhàn	V	to stand
5.	子公司	zǐgōngsī	N	subsidiary company
6.	说明	shuōmíng	V	to explain
7.	句	jù	M	(a measure word for sentences)
8.	长城	Chángchéng	PN	The Great Wall
9.	大家	dàjiā	Pr	everybody
10.	开始	kāishǐ	V	to begin; to start
11.	放	fàng	V	to put
12.	啊	a	P	(a particle used after 好/是 to indicate agreement)

Unit **8.2**

Dining Etiquette

In this lesson you will learn:

- Dining etiquette and protocol for meals with business associates.
- How to accept offers of food and drink from the host.
- How to ask about or comment on a particular dish.

Chinese Dialogue

张国强： 白先生，您喝点儿什么？

白有天： 随便，什么都行。

张国强： 想不想尝一尝中国的茅台酒？

白有天： 中国的白酒很厉害，我怕会喝醉！

张国强： 那我们喝啤酒，好吗？

白有天： 好。

张国强： 您喜欢喝青岛啤酒还是燕京啤酒？

白有天： 青岛啤酒吧。这道菜是什么？

张国强： 这是宫保鸡丁。会不会太辣？

白有天： 不会，不会，我不怕辣。

张国强： 那就多吃一点吧！别客气。

Pinyin Dialogue

Zhāng Guóqiáng: Bái Xiānsheng, nín hē diǎnr shénme?

Bái Yǒutiān: Suíbiàn, shénme dōu xíng.

Zhāng Guóqiáng: Xiǎng bù xiǎng cháng yi cháng Zhōngguó de Máotáijiǔ?

Bái Yǒutiān: Zhōngguó de báijiǔ hěn lìhai, wǒ pà huì hēzuì.

Zhāng Guóqiáng: Nà wǒmen hē píjiǔ, hǎo ma?

Bái Yǒutiān: Hǎo.

Zhāng Guóqiáng: Nín xǐhuan hē Qīngdǎo píjiǔ háishi Yànjīng píjiǔ?

Bái Yǒutiān: Qīngdǎo píjiǔ ba. Zhè dào cài shì shénme?

Zhāng Guóqiáng: Zhè shì gōngbǎo jīdīng. Huì bú huì tài là?

Bái Yǒutiān: Bú huì, bú huì, wǒ bú pà là.

Zhāng Guóqiáng: Nà jiù duō chī yìdiǎn ba! Bié kèqi.

Vocabulary

	Chinese	Pinyin	Part of Speech	English Equivalent
1.	随便	suíbiàn	UE	as one pleases
2.	行	xíng	Adj/V	all right; OK
3.	尝	cháng	V	to taste; to try the flavor of
4.	茅台酒	Máotáijiǔ	PN	Maotai (a Chinese liquor)
5.	厉害	lìhai	Adj	strong; severe
6.	怕	pà	V	to be afraid; to fear
7.	喝醉	hēzuì	VC	to drink to excess
8.	醉	zuì	V Adj	to get drunk drunk
9.	喜欢	xǐhuan	V	to like; to love; to be fond of
10.	青岛啤酒	Qīngdǎo Píjiǔ	PN	Tsingtao beer
11.	燕京啤酒	Yànjīng Píjiǔ	PN	Yanjing beer
12.	道	dào	M	(a measure word for courses of meals)
13.	宫保鸡丁	gōngbǎo jīdīng	N	Kung Pao Chicken
14.	辣	là	Adj	spicy; hot; peppery
15.	别	bié	Adv	don't

Sentence Patterns

1. 您喝点儿什么？ **Nín hē diǎnr shénme?** "What would you like to drink?"

In Unit 2.2 (Sentence Pattern 5) we learned 一点儿 yìdiǎnr is a quantity modifier to describe that the quantity of the noun is minimal. The character 一 yī can usually be omitted in spoken Chinese. In this instance, the phrase 喝点儿 hē diǎnr literally translates as "a little something to drink."

2. 随便。 **Suíbiàn.** "As you please; as you like."

随便 suíbiàn means "As one pleases; as one wishes." Literally, it means "to follow convenience." When used in response to a question asking your preference, 随便 is a marker for politeness, signifying that you do not wish to impose your own will or desires upon another. It can be used as an adverb to modify the verb, or it can be used alone in a sentence.

随便

1. 我们有茶、咖啡、还有酒，请大家别客气，随便喝。

   Wǒmen yǒu chá, kāfēi, hái yǒu jiǔ, qǐng dàjiā bié kèqi, suíbiàn hē.
   We have tea, coffee, as well as alcohol; please help yourself; drink whatever you like.

2. A: 咱们吃什么呢？
   B: 随便。

   A: Zánmen chī shénme ne?
   B: Suíbiàn.

   A: What should we eat?
   B: Whatever.

If a specific person is indicated, a noun or a pronoun can be placed between 随便, such as 随你便 Suí nǐ biàn to mean "As you like."

3. 什么都行。 **Shénme dōu xíng. "Whatever is OK."**

When an interrogative pronoun such as 什么/谁/哪儿 shénme/shéi/nǎr is followed by either 都 dōu or 也 yě, it changes the meaning from "what/who/where" to "everything/everyone/everywhere." The pattern indicates "all are included," with no limitations. For example: 我什么都吃 Wǒ shénme dōu chī means "I eat everything." 谁都喜欢吃中国菜 Shéi dōu xǐhuan chī Zhōngguócài means "Everyone likes to eat Chinese food."

什么/谁/哪儿 + 都 + v		Substitution	
1. 我什么都<u>做</u>。 Wǒ shénme dōu zuò. I do everything.		买 卖 吃 学 怕 喜欢 感兴趣	mǎi mài chī xué pà xǐhuan gǎn xìngqù
2. 谁都<u>知道</u>。 Shéi dōu zhīdào. Everyone knows.		来 去 行 喜欢 感兴趣	lái qù xíng xǐhuan gǎn xìngqù
3. 哪儿都<u>有中国人</u>。 Nǎr dōu yǒu Zhōngguórén. Chinese people are everywhere.		行 可以	xíng kěyǐ
4. 她哪儿都<u>不想去</u>。 Tā nǎr dōu bù xiǎng qù. She doesn't want to go anywhere.		去过	qù guò

If a specific noun is mentioned, it should be placed after 什么 shénme in the sentence.

For example: 他什么电影都喜欢看 Tā shénme diànyǐng dōu xǐhuan kàn

"He likes to watch all kinds of movies."

什么(O) + 都 + V		
	Substitution	
	O	V
我什么菜都喜欢。 Wǒ shénme cài dōu xǐhuan. I like all kinds of food.	书　　shū 生意　shēngyì 地方　dìfang 产品　chǎnpǐn 事　　shì	看　　kàn 做　　zuò 去　　qù 有　　yǒu 知道　zhīdào

4. 想不想尝一尝中国的茅台酒？ Xiǎng bù xiǎng cháng yi cháng Zhōngguó de Máotáijiǔ? "Would you like to try Chinese Maotai?"

As introduced in Unit 6.2 (Sentence Pattern 5), certain monosyllabic verbs can be reduplicated to indicate that an act is done casually. The repeated verbs can also be used to make the expression more casual. 一 yī can be inserted into monosyllabic reduplicated verbs to construct the "A 一 A" form, e.g., 我想听一听他要说什么 Wǒ xiǎng tīng yi tīng tā yào shuō shénme "I would like to listen to what he is going to say." A disyllabic verb such as 介绍 jièshào or 认识 rènshi can also be reduplicated to form an "ABAB" form; for example, 介绍介绍 jièshào jièshao, or 认识认识 rènshi rènshi. However, 一 cannot be inserted in between the disyllabic reduplicated verbs.

V (一) V + O			
		Substitution	
1. 你想不想<u>尝</u>一<u>尝</u>这道菜? Nǐ xiǎng bù xiǎng <u>cháng</u> yi <u>cháng</u> zhè dào cài? Would you like to try this dish?	看 kàn 学 xué 试 shì	这本小说 zhè běn xiǎoshuō 普通话 pǔtōnghuà 新产品 xīn chǎnpǐn	
2. 请大家<u>休息</u>休息。 Qǐng dàjiā <u>xiūxi</u> xiūxi. Please, everyone relax a little.	等 děng 看 kàn 介绍 jièshào 参观 cānguān		

5. 那就<u>多吃</u>一点吧! **Nà jiù <u>duō chī</u> yìdiǎn ba!** "In that case, have some more!"

When 多 duō, meaning "more," or 少 shǎo, meaning "less," appears before a verb, it is used to advise or recommend someone to do something more or less. 一点 yìdiǎn can follow the verb to form the pattern 多/少 + V + 一点. The object may be omitted when it is understood.

多 + V + 一点 + (O)				
	Substitution			
	V		**O**	
请多<u>喝</u>一点<u>水</u>。 Qǐng duō <u>hē</u> yìdiǎn <u>shuǐ</u>. Please drink more water.	看 kàn 学 xué 做 zuò 睡 shuì 吃 chī		书 shū 东西 dōngxi 事 shì 觉 jiào 菜 cài	

少 + V + 一点 + (O)

要少<u>喝</u>一点<u>酒</u>。

Yào shǎo <u>hē</u> yìdiǎn <u>jiǔ</u>.
(You) should drink less alcohol.

Substitution			
吸	xī	烟	yān
花	huā	钱	qián
看	kàn	电视	diànshì
买	mǎi	东西	dōngxi

6. <u>别</u>客气。 **Bié kèqi. "Don't be shy."**

别 bié, meaning "don't," is a negative imperative marker used in a command or advice to prohibit (or dissuade) someone from doing something. 不要 búyào is a variant form of 别, and these two can be used interchangeably. As in English, the subject of an imperative sentence is usually omitted.

别/不要 + V

请<u>别</u><u>点太多菜</u>。

Qǐng bié <u>diǎn tài duō cài</u>.
Please don't order too much food.

Substitution	
走	zǒu
等我	děng wǒ
喝醉	hēzuì
跟他去	gēn tā qù
开得太快	kāi de tài kuài
安排开会	ānpái kāi huì
打电话给他	dǎ diànhuà gěi tā

Cultural Points

1. Meals

Chinese business associates generally like to invite guests to dinner. This is a very common social practice. By and large, however, these dinners will take place in restaurants. To be invited to a house for dinner is rare. This is usually reserved for close relatives and personal friends.

Business meetings are generally followed by dinner invitations. These dinners generally consist of multiple courses and can serve both as a surreptitious show of power for the one hosting the dinner and as a sign of respect for the one invited.

Meals themselves are eaten in a communal fashion. The host will order several dishes for the group, and these dishes, when delivered to the table, will be placed on a food carousel in the middle. The dishes are then rotated so everyone can try each dish.

Many Chinese, especially the older generation, have been raised to not look greedy. They will not ask for anything, even when it is offered. As such, hosts will generally offer their guests food or drinks many times over the course of the meal to show hospitality. This may reach the extent of a host placing food on your plate, or ordering drinks on your behalf, even without your asking. However, the younger generation is more open and honest. Guests may politely decline what they are offered if the food or drink does not coincide with their religious beliefs or personal preferences.

2. Drinking

Drinking alcoholic beverages is a widespread social activity in business and may be necessary in order to close a specific deal. Rounds of drinks will be brought in, and a series of toasts will be made by various people. The phrase 干杯 gānbēi, literally translated as "dry glass," means that you are expected to drink the entire contents of the glass in one gulp. The purpose of drinking in this setting is for "male bonding."(It is becoming more and more acceptable for women to drink in business settings). In this situation, it is necessary to observe the people in the group around you. After a while, 干杯 may be meant as a toast, not as an order to drain the glass. At this point, 干杯 is an invitation to sip your drink.

There is generally a round of drinks after each dish is served (but before eating). In addition, it is always polite when you request another drink to offer to get drinks for the rest of the party at the same time.

If you prefer not to drink alcohol in these social settings, you can politely refuse and cite religious or health reasons. Similarly, if you are offered a cigarette, you can politely refuse for the same reasons. In China, offering a cigarette to a guest is also considered good social etiquette, and Chinese people may smoke in your presence without asking you, "Do you mind if I smoke?"

 ## Additional Vocabulary

	Chinese	Pinyin	Part of Speech	English Equivalent
1.	睡觉	shuì jiào	VO	to sleep
2.	花钱	huā qián	VO	to spend money
3.	点	diǎn	V	to order (food)
4.	干杯	gān bēi	UE VO	Cheers! to make a toast

应酬
Yìngchou
Social Events

Unit **9.1**

Nightlife

In this lesson we will learn:

• How to arrange meetings and social activities.

• About some major landmarks in China.

⊙ Chinese Dialogue

高明： 对不起，打扰一下，您现在忙吗？

白有天： 请进！请进！我正在看一份报告。

高明： 您晚上有安排了吗？

白有天： 还没有，有什么事吗？

高明： 我约了几个朋友去酒吧，您跟我们一块儿去吧！

白有天： 好啊！听说后海开了几家新的酒吧，我一直想去看看。

高明： 我们就是打算到那儿去的。

白有天： 太好了，去哪一家呢？

高明： 我们到了那儿再决定吧！

白有天： 好，那我们一下班就走。

Pinyin Dialogue

Gāomíng: Duìbuqǐ, dǎrǎo yíxià, nín xiànzài máng ma?

Bái yǒu tiān: Qǐng jìn! Qǐng jìn! Wǒ zhèngzài kàn yí fèn bàogào.

Gāo Míng: Nín wǎnshang yǒu ānpái le ma?

Bái Yǒutiān: Hái méiyǒu, yǒu shénme shì ma?

Gāo Míng: Wǒ yuē le jǐ ge péngyou qù jiǔbā, nín gēn wǒmen yíkuàir qù ba!

Bái Yǒutiān: Hǎo a! Tīngshuō Hòuhǎi kāi le jǐ jiā xīn de jiǔbā, wǒ yìzhí xiǎng qù kànkan.

Gāo Míng: Wǒmen jiù shì dǎsuàn dào nàr qù de.

Bái Yǒutiān: Tài hǎo le, qù nǎ yì jiā ne?

Gāo Míng: Wǒmen dào le nàr zài juédìng ba!

Bái Yǒutiān: Hǎo, nà wǒmen yí xià bān jiù zǒu.

Vocabulary

	Chinese	Pinyin	Part of Speech	English Equivalent
1.	应酬	yìngchou	N V	to engage in social activities (when off duty) (work-related) social activities
2.	打扰一下	dǎrǎo yíxià	UE	(May I) disturb/interrupt you a bit
3.	打扰	dǎrǎo	V	to disturb
4.	一下	yíxià	TD	(used after a verb to indicate that an action is only for a moment); a short while
5.	正在	zhèngzài	Adv	in the midst of; in the middle of
6.	份	fèn	M	(a measure word for things that come in a set or pile, such as reports, newspapers, etc.)
7.	约	yuē	V	to make a date or appointment in advance; to invite
8.	几	jǐ	Nu	several; a few
9.	酒吧	jiǔbā	N	pub; bar
10.	一块儿	yíkuàir	Adv	together
11.	后海	Hòuhǎi	PN	name of a park-like area in Beijing
12.	一直	yìzhí	Adv	always; all along; straight through
13.	就	jiù	Adv	exactly; precisely; just
14.	打算	dǎsuàn	V	to plan (to do something)
15.	再	zài	Adv	then
16.	决定	juédìng	V N	to decide decision; resolution

Sentence Patterns

1. 对不起，打扰<u>一下</u>。 **Duìbuqǐ, dǎrǎo yíxià. "Sorry to disturb you."**

When 一下 yíxià or 一下儿 yíxiàr, meaning "for awhile," follows a verb, it indicates that the action is a brief one. For example, 请等一下 qǐng děng yíxià means "Wait a moment, please." The pattern V + 一下 can also be used to soften the tone of the expression or to make the statement more causal, as in 大家认识一下吧 Dàjiā rènshi yíxià ba "Let everyone get to know each other a little bit."

V + 一下

1. 这个报告我不懂，请你说明一下。

   Zhè ge bàogào wǒ bù dǒng, qǐng nǐ shuōmíng yíxià.
   I do not understand this report; please explain it, will you?

2. 这个问题很重要，我想一下，好吗？

   Zhè ge wèntí hěn zhòngyào, wǒ xiǎng yíxià, hǎo ma?
   This issue is very important; I'll think about it, OK?

3. 你们第一次见面，我给你们介绍一下。

   Nǐmen dì yí cì jiàn miàn, wǒ gěi nǐmen jièshào yíxià.
   This is your first time meeting; let me introduce you two.

4. 我们工作一天了，休息一下吧！

   Wǒmen gōngzuò yì tiān le, xiūxi yíxià ba!
   We've been working the whole day; let's rest for a while!

5. 请您坐一下，经理马上就出来。

   Qǐng nín zuò yíxià, jīnglǐ mǎshàng jiù chūlai.
   Please have a seat; the manager will come out immediately.

2. 我<u>正在</u>看一份报告。 **Wǒ <u>zhèngzài</u> kàn yí fèn bàogào. "I'm reading a report."**

When the adverb 正在 zhèngzài or 在 zài precedes a verb or a verb phrase, it marks the progressive aspect of an action, indicating that the action is occurring at this very moment. 呢 ne can be added at the end of the sentence without changing the meaning, but the tone of the sentence becomes more confirmative, rather than expressive. For example: 她正在睡觉呢 Tā zhèngzài shuì jiào ne "She is sleeping" or 他在看报呢 Tā zài kàn bào ne "He is reading the newspaper."

正在 + V + 呢	
	Substitution
他现在正在<u>谈生意</u>。 Tā xiànzài zhèng zài <u>tán shēngyì</u>. He is talking about business.	开会　　　　　　　　kāi huì 打电话　　　　　　　dǎ diànhuà 帮你联系　　　　　　bāng nǐ liánxì 给客户介绍新产品　gěi kèhù jièshào xīn chǎnpǐn 跟经理讨论问题　　gēn jīnglǐ tǎolùn wèntí

3. 我<u>约</u>了<u>几</u>个朋友去酒吧。 **Wǒ <u>yuē</u> le jǐ ge péngyou qù jiǔbā. "I made plans with a few friends to go out to a bar."**

约 yuē is a verb, and is followed by a personal noun or pronoun, indicating that the person is setting up an appointment or date with someone to do something. For example: 我想约她去看电影 Wǒ xiǎng yuē tā qù kàn diànyǐng "I would like to ask her (out on a date) to go see a movie."

Person₁ + 约 + Person₂ + V	
	Substitution
他约我去看<u>电影</u>。 Tā yuē wǒ <u>qù kàn diànyǐng</u>. He asked me out for a movie.	去吃日本菜 qù chī Rìběncài 去酒吧喝酒 qù jiǔba hē jiǔ 一块儿去打网球 yíkuàir qù dǎ wǎngqiú 下周四见面 xià zhōusì jiàn miàn 谈生意 tán shēngyì

In addition, 约 can also be followed by a time or place that pertains to an appointment or meeting arrangement set by two parties. For example: 咱们约约下星期见面的时间和地方吧 Zánmen yuēyue xià xīngqī jiàn miàn de shíjiān hé dìfang ba "Let's set up (arrange) a time and place for our next week's appointment" or 你们约去哪儿吃饭呢 Nǐmen yuē qù nǎr chī fàn ne "Where did you arrange to go for dinner?"

S + 约 + Time + V		
	Substitution	
	TW	**V**
我们约(一)个时间打 高尔夫球。 Wǒmen yuē (yí) ge shíjiān dǎ gāo'ěrfūqiú. Let's set up a time to play golf.	今天晚上 jīntiān wǎnshang	去后海 qù Hòuhǎi
	明天下午三点 míngtiān xiàwǔ sān diǎn	见面 jiàn miàn
	这个周末 zhè ge zhōumò	去唱卡拉OK qù chàng kǎlā OK
	下周 xià zhōu	去参观新工厂 qù cānguān xīn gōngchǎng

In Unit 3.1 (Sentence Pattern 3), we introduced the interrogative word 几, which refers to a number smaller than ten. The usage of 几 in this lesson is not interrogative, but is in a statement meaning "several" or "a few." It is used when the subject being discussed has an indefinite quantity. For example: 我昨天在那家书店买了几本中文书 Wǒ zuótiān zài nà jiā shūdiàn mǎi le jǐ běn Zhōngwén shū "I bought several books at that bookstore yesterday."

几 + M + N

1. 他在中国交了几个朋友。

   Tā zài Zhōngguó jiāo le jǐ ge péngyou.
   He has made a few friends in China.

2. 请你点几个菜。

   Qǐng nǐ diǎn jǐ ge cài.
   Please order a few dishes.

3. 他刚到这儿，他只认识几个人。

   Tā gāng dào zhèr, tā zhǐ rènshi jǐ ge rén.
   He just got here; he only knows a few people.

4. 这几天很热。

   Zhè jǐ tiān hěn rè.
   It has been hot these few days.

4. 您跟我们一块儿去吧! Nín gēn wǒmen yíkuàir qù ba! "Why don't you go with us?"

和 hé and 跟 gēn, which both mean "and" and which were introduced in Units 3.1 (Sentence Pattern 6) and 4.2 (Sentence Pattern 5), can be used interchangeably when they link parallel nouns. However, 跟 and 和 can also be used as a preposition meaning "with," to link parties who engage in an activity together. In this usage, the adverb, 一块儿 yíkuàir or 一起 yìqǐ (both mean "together") can be added before the main verb to reinforce the jointness of the action. For example: 我跟/和他一块儿学中文 Wǒ gēn/hé tā yíkuàir xué Zhōngwén "He and I study Chinese together." Without 一块儿, the sentence 我跟他学中文 Wǒ gēn tā xué Zhōngwén would mean "I learn Chinese from him."

Note that the negative marker 不 bù or 没有 méiyǒu, as well as any auxiliary verb (such as 会 huì or 能 néng), should be placed before 跟, not before the main verb. 他没有跟你们一块儿去吗 Tā méiyǒu gēn nǐmen yíkuàir qù ma means "Didn't he go with you (guys)?"

Person₁ + 跟 + Person₂ + (一块儿/一起) + V		
	Substitution	
我会跟他一块儿/一起去图书馆。	去出差	qù chū chāi
Wǒ huì gēn tā yíkuàir/yìqǐ qù túshūguǎn.	做生意	zuò shēngyì
I will go to the library with him.	吃晚饭	chī wǎnfàn
	去买东西	qù mǎi dōngxi

5. 我一直想去看看。 **Wǒ yìzhí xiǎng qù kànkan. "I have always wanted to go see."**

When 一直 yìzhí is followed by 想 xiǎng and a main verb phrase, it indicates that the subject has been wanting to do something for a long period of time, but he/she has not yet done it.

S + 一直想 + V		
	Substitution	
我一直想去中国。	学普通话	xué pǔtōnghuà
	参观新工厂	cānguān xīn gōngchǎng
Wǒ yìzhí xiǎng qù Zhōngguó.	给她打个电话	gěi tā dǎ ge diànhuà
I have always wanted to go to China.	尝尝北京烤鸭	chángchang Běijīng kǎoyā
	约王老板见面	yuē Wáng lǎobǎn jiàn miàn

6. 我们<u>就</u>是打算到那儿去的。 **Wǒmen <u>jiù</u> shì dǎsuàn dào nàr qù de.** "That is exactly where we are planning to go."

就 jiù, meaning "exactly; precisely," is used to indicate further confirmation or affirmation of a statement. 就 emphasizes the verb that follows. For example: 他就是我们公司的 人事部经理 Tā jiù shì wǒmen gōngsī de rénshìbù jīnglǐ "He is our company's HR Manager."

就

1. 这就是我的办公室。

   Zhè jiù shì wǒ de bàngōngshì.
   This *is* my office.

2. 他们的公司就在北京。

   Tāmen de gōngsī jiù zài Běijīng.
   Their company *is* in Beijing.

3. A: 请问，张经理在不在？
   A: 我就是。

   A: Qǐngwèn, Zhāng Jīnglǐ zài bú zài?
   B: Wǒ jiù shì.

   A: Excuse me, is Manager Zhang in?
   B: This *is* he.

---

7. 我们到<u>了</u>那儿<u>再</u>决定吧! **Wǒmen dào <u>le</u> nàr <u>zài</u> juédìng ba!** "Let's make a decision after we get there!"

Using 了 le in the first verb phrase and 再 zài in the second verb phrase indicates that the action in the second verb phrase will take place after the first has been completed. In these cases, 再 is an adverb that means "then." For example: 今天晚上吃了饭, 我再去看你 Jīntiān wǎnshang chī le fàn, wǒ zài qù kàn nǐ "I will come see you after I have dinner tonight."

V₁ + 了 + (O) 再 V₂

1. 大家吃了饭再走吧!

   Dàjiā chī le fàn zài zǒu ba!
   Everybody, let's leave after we have dinner.

2. 你交了文件再下班。

   Nǐ jiāo le wénjiàn zài xià bān.
   After you submit the document, then you can leave work.

3. 我们听了报告再做决定，好吗?

   Wǒmen tīng le bàogào zài zuò juédìng, hǎo ma?
   We will make our decision after listening to the presentation. OK?

4. 我们看了计划再说吧!

   Wǒmen kàn le jìhuà zài shuō ba!
   Let's talk about it after reviewing the plan!

8. 那我们一下班就走。 **Nà wǒmen yí xià bān jiù zǒu. "We will leave as soon as we get off work."**

The pattern 一 + V₁, 就 + V₂ is used to indicate that two actions or two events occur one after another in rapid succession. The subject of the two actions can be either one person (as in this example sentence) or different people. Please note that in the second clause, 就 is an adverb, and should be placed immediately before the verb; that is, if the second clause has a subject, 就 must be placed after the subject, and not at the beginning of the second clause. It is incorrect to say *他一来, 就我们走 *Tā yì lái, jiù wǒmen zǒu.

S + 一 + V₁, 就 + V₂

Substitution	
V₁	**V₂**
学 xué	会 huì
回家 huí jia	看电视 kàn diànshì
进来 jìnlai	看见他 kànjiàn tā
下飞机 xià fēijī	去公司 qù gōngsī

我一<u>下班</u>就<u>回家</u>。

Wǒ yí xià bān, jiù huí jiā.
I go home as soon as I get off work.

S₁ + 一 + V₁, S₂ + 就 + V₂

1. 他一教，我就会。

   Tā yì jiāo, wǒ jiù huì.
   I will be able to do it as soon as he teaches me.

2. 他一来，我们就走。

   Tā yì lái, wǒmen jiù zǒu.
   We'll go as soon as he comes.

3. 经理一到，我们就开始开会。

   Jīnglǐ yí dào, wǒmen jiù kāishǐ kāi huì.
   We'll start the meeting as soon as the manager arrives.

Cultural Points

1. Socializing with Coworkers

Chinese society is not as individualistic as that of the United States. In China, focusing on oneself is frowned upon, and groups are of greater importance. This mentality begins with the immediate family and works outward to extended family, friends, and so on.

This line of thought extends into the workplace. In Western countries, the workplace is an environment in which one spends eight hours a day working; but in Asian countries such as China, it is also a focus of social life. Chinese employees are expected to socialize with their coworkers, go out with each other after work, or participate in company outings and retreats. This is also common in Japan, and has been observed in Japanese business practices since the 1980s.

2. Bar Alleys

The 后海 Hòuhǎi and 三里屯 Sānlǐtún areas are important areas for many businesspeople working in Beijing. They are known as the "Bar Alleys." In Shanghai many prefer 茂名路 Màomínglù, 新天地 Xīntiāndì or 外滩 Wàitān (the Bund) for bar-hopping. These areas can also offer enticements into illicit activities.

In the PRC, the use of recreational drugs other than alcohol or tobacco is both a crime and a social gaffe that can adversely affect an entire professional career and lead to harsh criminal penalties. To the Chinese, illegal drugs evoke unhappy memories of oppression extending from the nineteenth century Opium Wars to twentieth century atrocities. According to visa stipulations, Americans found to be involved with illicit drugs forfeit consular assistance.

Many of the Chinese women that one will meet in the bars of these areas are in reality employed by the bar. These bars hire attractive young women to talk to foreign men and persuade them to purchase drinks. At the end of the evening, the man is expected to not only pay for the drinks consumed by himself and his female companion, but also pay a large sum for the woman's "time." This is usually an exorbitant fee, and refusal to pay can generally lead to very unpleasant circumstances.

Additional Vocabulary

	Chinese	Pinyin	Part of Speech	English Equivalent
1.	重要	zhòngyào	Adj	important
2.	出来	chūlai	VC	to come out
3.	谈	tán	V	to talk; to discuss
4.	客户	kèhù	N	client; customer
5.	讨论	tǎolùn	V	to discuss
6.	高尔夫球	gāo'ěrfūqiú	N	golf
7.	书店	shūdiàn	N	bookstore
8.	交	jiāo	V	to befriend; to submit
9.	一起	yìqǐ	Adv	together
10.	老板	lǎobǎn	N	boss
11.	文件	wénjiàn	N	document
12.	计划	jìhuà	N	plan
13.	看见	kànjiàn	VC	to see
14.	下飞机	xià fēijī	VO	to get off the plane
15.	下	xià	V	to disembark from a vehicle
16.	飞机	fēijī	O	airplane
17.	三里屯	Sānlǐtún	PN	name of a place in Beijing
18.	茂名路	Màomínglù	PN	name of a road in Shanghai
19.	新天地	Xīntiāndì	PN	name of a place in Shanghai
20.	外滩	Wàitān	PN	The Bund (a popular tourist spot along the levy against the Huangpu river in Shanghai)

Unit **9.2**

Cultural Events

In this lesson we will learn:

- How to ask and respond to options for cultural events and activities.

- How to indicate your preference, and give reasons explaining your preference, for one activity over another.

- How to express conditionality when accepting others' suggestions.

高明： 您来中国以后一直很忙，明天晚上出去轻松一下，怎么样？

白有天： 好主意！您有什么建议呢？

高明： 您喜欢喝茶还是看表演？

白有天： 我比较喜欢看表演。有什么表演呢？

高明： 有京剧，还有杂技表演。

白有天： 京剧虽然有意思，可是我怕看不懂。

高明： 那么，如果买得到杂技的票，我们就去国家剧院看杂技，杂技也很好看。

白有天： 如果买不到票，我们就去茶馆喝茶吧！

Pinyin Dialogue

Gāo Míng:	Nín lái Zhōngguó yǐhòu yìzhí hěn máng, míngtiān wǎnshang chūqu qīngsōng yíxià, zěnmeyàng?
Bái Yǒutiān:	Hǎo zhǔyi! Nín yǒu shénme jiànyì ne?
Gāo Míng:	Nín xǐhuan hē chá háishi kàn biǎoyǎn?
Bái Yǒutiān:	Wǒ bǐjiào xǐhuan kàn biǎoyǎn. Yǒu shénme biǎoyǎn ne?
Gāo Míng:	Yǒu Jīngjù, hái yǒu zájì biǎoyǎn.
Bái Yǒutiān:	Jīngjù suīrán yǒu yìsi, kěshì wǒ pà kàn bu dǒng.
Gāo Míng:	Nàme, rúguǒ mǎi de dào zájì de piào, wǒmen jiù qù Guójiā Jùyuàn kàn zájì, zájì yě hěn hǎokàn.
Bái Yǒutiān:	Rúguǒ mǎi bu dào piào, wǒmen jiù qù cháguǎn hē chá ba!

Vocabulary

Chinese	Pinyin	Part of Speech	English Equivalent
1. 以后	yǐhòu	TW	after; afterwards; later; hereafter
2. 出去	chūqu	V	to go out; to get out; to exit
3. 轻松	qīngsōng	V Adj	to relax relaxed
4. 怎么样	zěnmeyàng	IP	how about; what about
5. 主意	zhǔyi	N	idea
6. 建议	jiànyì	N V	suggestion to suggest
7. 表演	biǎoyǎn	N V	performance; act; play to perform
8. 比较	bǐjiào	Adv	comparatively
9. 京剧	Jīngjù	PN	Beijing Opera
10. 杂技	zájì	N	acrobatics
11. 虽然	suīrán	Conj	although
12. 如果	rúguǒ	Conj	if
13. 票	piào	N	ticket
14. 国家剧院	Guójiā Jùyuàn	PN	National Theater
15. 剧院	jùyuàn	N	theater
16. 好看	hǎokàn	Adj	to be good to watch/read/see; interesting; pretty
17. 茶馆	cháguǎn	N	teahouse

Sentence Patterns

1. 您来中国以后，......， **Nín lái Zhōngguó yǐhòu,...** "After you came to China,..."

以后 yǐhòu, meaning "after..."can be used after a verb or a time expression (either a "time word" or a "time duration") indicating that an action will take place after a special event or a certain period of time.

V/TW/TD + 以后

1. 下班以后，我去找你。

   Xià bān yǐhòu, wǒ qù zhǎo nǐ.
   I'll look for you after we get off work.

2. 晚上十点以后，不要打电话给他。

   Wǎnshang shí diǎn yǐhòu, búyào dǎ diànhuà gěi tā.
   Don't call him after 10:00 p.m.

3. 老板一个星期以后才会回来。

   Lǎobǎn yí ge xīngqī yǐhòu cái huì huílai.
   The boss won't come back for one week.

以后 can also be used as a time word meaning "in the future, afterwards." In this structure, 以后 can stand alone without any time reference.

以后

1. 你以后想做什么？

   Nǐ yǐhòu xiǎng zuò shénme?
   What would you like to do in the future?

2. 我以后会常常跟你联系。

   Wǒ yǐhòu huì chángcháng gēn nǐ liánxì.
   I will often stay in touch with you in the future.

3. 合资的事，我们以后再谈。

   Hézī de shì, wǒmen yǐhòu zài tán.
   We will talk about the joint venture issue later.

2. 一直很忙。 <u>Yìzhí hěn máng. "(You've) been constantly busy."</u>

直 zhí literally translated means "straight." 一直 yìzhí can be used to modify a continuous status, meaning someone or something has been or was in that particular situation for a long period of time.

一直 + Adj

1. 这件事，我一直很担心。

   Zhè jiàn shì, wǒ yìzhí hěn dān xīn.
   I have been constantly worried about this matter.

2. 产品有问题，他一直很不高兴。

   Chǎnpǐn yǒu wèntí, tā yìzhí hěn bù gāoxìng.
   The product has had problems; he has been very unhappy this whole time.

3. 五月以后，天气一直很闷热。

Wǔyuè yǐhòu, tiānqì yìzhí hěn mēnrè.
The weather has been hot and humid ever since May.

4. 我们对你们的新产品一直很感兴趣。

Wǒmen duì nǐmen de xīn chǎnpǐn yìzhí hěn gǎn xìngqù.
We've always been interested in your new products.

3. 怎么样? Zěnmeyàng? "How about it?"

怎么样 zěnmeyàng is an interrogative pronoun that is used at the end of a statement to find out if the proposed statement or suggestion is agreeable or acceptable to the other party. It expresses the notion of "how about...?"

Sentence + 怎么样

1. A: 我们现在马上开会讨论一下，怎么样?
    B: 没问题，我现在有时间。

    A: Wǒmen xiànzài mǎshàng kāi huì tǎolùn yíxià, zěnmeyàng?
    B: Méi wèntí, wǒ xiànzài yǒu shíjiān.

    A: How about we call a meeting to discuss (it) immediately?
    B: No problem; I have time now.

2. A: 你跟我们一块儿去看电影，怎么样?
    B: 好啊，看什么电影?

    A: Nǐ gēn wǒmen yíkuàir qù kàn diànyǐng, zěnmeyàng?
    B: Hǎo a, kàn shénme diànyǐng?

    A: How about if you go to see a movie with us?
    B: OK. What movie?

3. A: 我们今天下班以后一起去后海吃饭，怎么样？

    B: 今天不行，因为我晚上要加班。

    A: Wǒmen jīntiān xià bān yǐhòu yìqǐ qù Hòuhǎi chī fàn, zěnmeyàng?
    B: Jīntiān bù xíng, yīnwèi wǒ wǎnshang yào jiā bān.

    A: How about if we go to Houhai for dinner after we get off work tonight?
    B: I can't today, because I'm working overtime tonight.

4. 我比较喜欢看表演。 Wǒ bǐjiào xǐhuan kàn biǎoyǎn. "I prefer to see a performance."

比较 bǐjiào can be combined with 喜欢 xǐhuan to express preference for someone/something or doing something over other alternatives. Roughly translated, it means "to prefer…" 喜欢 in turn is followed by either a noun or a verb phrase.

S + 比较喜欢 + V/N		
		Substitution
1. 他比较喜欢吃中国菜。 Tā bǐjiào xǐhuan chī Zhōngguócài. He likes Chinese food better.	喝绿茶 看京剧 看杂技 看法国电影 打高尔夫球	hē lǜchá kàn Jīngjù kàn zájì kàn Fǎguó diànyǐng dǎ gāo'ěrfūqiú
2. 我比较喜欢红酒。 Wǒ bǐjiào xǐhuan hóngjiǔ. I prefer red wine.	上海菜 京剧 足球 棒球	Shànghǎicài Jīngjù zúqiú bàngqiú

比较, meaning "comparatively; relatively; fairly," can also be used as an adverb to qualify an adjective. Please note that unlike 比, which was introduced in Unit 4.2 (Sentence Pattern 4) and which is used to compare two entities, sentences with 比较 only have one subject, and are used to indicate the relative degree of the adjective. In some cases, 比较 sentences imply comparison with something, but that something is unstated.

S + 比较 + Adj

1. 我们去宾馆接他比较好。

   Wǒmen qù bīnguǎn jiē tā bǐjiào hǎo.
   It's better if we go to the hotel to pick him up.

2. 给他发电子邮件比较快。

   Gěi tā fā diànzi yóujiàn bǐjiào kuài.
   It's faster sending him an e-mail.

3. 这个问题比较简单。

   Zhè ge wèntí bǐjiào jiǎndān.
   This problem is simpler.

4. 坐地铁比较方便。

   Zuò dìtiě bǐjiào fāngbiàn.
   Taking the subway is more convenient.

5. 京剧虽然有意思，可是我怕看不懂。 **Jīngjù suīrán yǒu yìsi, kěshì wǒ pà kàn bu dǒng. "Although Beijing Opera is interesting, I'm afraid I will not be able to understand it."**

The conjunction 虽然……可是…… is used to link two clauses, suggesting that there is a transitional relationship between them. It is used to express the notion of concession, meaning "although; though."

虽然 ……, 可是/不过……

1. 日本的产品虽然很好，可是很贵。

   Rìběn de chǎnpǐn suīrán hěn hǎo, kěshì hěn guì.
   Although Japanese products are good, they are expensive.

2. 中文虽然很难，可是会说中文很有用。

   Zhōngwén suīrán hěn nán, kěshì huì shuō Zhōngwén hěn yǒu yòng.
   Although Chinese is difficult, it is very useful if you can speak Chinese.

3. 我虽然看不懂京剧，不过我对京剧还是很感兴趣。

   Wǒ suīrán kàn bu dǒng Jīngjù, búguò wǒ duì Jīngjù háishi hěn gǎn xìngqù.
   Although I do not understand Beijing Opera, I am still interested in it.

6. 如果买得到杂技的票，我们就去国家剧院看杂技。**Rúguǒ mǎi de dào zájì de piào, wǒmen jiù qù Guójiā Jùyuàn kàn zájì. "If we are able to get tickets for acrobatics, then we'll go to the National Theater to see the acrobatics."**

The conjunction 如果 rúguǒ, which means "if" and which presents a conditional or suppositional clause, may appear before or after the subject of the first clause (dependent clause). However, the adverb 就 jiù, "then," in the second clause (main clause) must be placed immediately before the verb (i.e., after the subject if there is a subject). 就 may be omitted, especially if the second clause is in interrogative form.

如果 ... ...,（就）... ...

1. 如果你有兴趣，我给你介绍一下新产品。

   Rúguǒ nǐ yǒu xìngqù, wǒ gěi nǐ jièshào yíxià xīn chǎnpǐn.
   If you are interested, I will introduce the new products to you.

2. 你如果不想慢跑，我们就打篮球。

   Nǐ rúguǒ bù xiǎng mànpǎo, wǒmen jiù dǎ lánqiú.
   If you don't like to go jogging, then we'll play basketball.

3. 如果有钱，你想买什么？

   Rúguǒ yǒu qián, nǐ xiǎng mǎi shénme?
   If you had money, what would you buy?

7. 买得到杂技的票... **Mǎi de dào** zájì de piào... "to be able to buy tickets for acrobatics"

In Unit 2.2 (Sentence Pattern 7), we introduced the concept of "complement of degree," in which some Chinese verbs use an adjective to describe the degree to which the action is conducted. In this lesson, we will introduce the concept of "complement of result," in which a verb is followed by another verb or an adjective indicating the result of the action indicated by the first verb. This type of verb complement is called a "resultative verb."

There are two forms of resultative verbs: one is called "potential" and the other is called "actual." Both forms may be either positive or negative. The positive potential form consists of V_1 + 得 + V_2 and the negative potential form consists of V_1 + 不 + V_2. For example: 我看得懂中文 Wǒ kàn de dǒng Zhōngwén "I'm able to understand Chinese (by reading) or 我看不懂中文 Wǒ kàn bu dǒng Zhōngwén "I'm unable to understand Chinese (by reading)." It is important to note that, as illustrated by these examples, the word "potential" does not mean "latent" here, but rather indicates "capability." The actual form will be introduced in Unit 10.2 (Sentence Pattern 3).

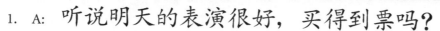

1. A: 听说明天的表演很好，买得到票吗？
   B: 试试看，大概买得到。

   A: Tīngshuō míngtiān de biǎoyǎn hěn hǎo, mǎi de dào piào ma?
   B: Shìshi kàn, dàgài mǎi de dào.

   A: I heard tomorrow's show is very good; will we be able to get tickets?
   B: Let's try; we probably will.

2. A: 你找得到他吗？
   B: 找得到，他就在会议室。

   A: Nǐ zhǎo de dào tā ma?
   B: Zhǎo de dào, tā jiù zài huìyìshì.

   A: Can you find him?
   B: Yes, I can; he is in the conference room.

3. A: 下个星期你回得来吗？
   B: 我怕回不来。

   A: Xià ge xīngqī nǐ huí de lái ma?
   B: Wǒ pà huí bu lái.

   A: Are you able to come back next week?
   B: I'm afraid I won't be able to come back.

4. A: 坐在后面的人能听得见吗？
   B: 听得见，可是听不清楚。

   A: Zuò zài hòumian de rén néng tīng de jiàn ma?
   B: Tīng de jiàn, kěshì tīng bu qīngchu.

   A: Can people sitting in the back hear?
   B: We can hear, but not very clearly.

Cultural Points

1. Chinese Local Opera

While there are references to theatrical entertainments in China as early as 1500 BC, Chinese theater developed during the Yuan Dynasty (1279 to 1368) and was based on story cycles popularized by traveling storytellers. Yuan dynasty theatre spread across China and took on various local forms; thus, Chinese opera is rich in local cultural characteristics, with each region boasting its own signature form of drama. Today, Beijing Opera is the most well-known form. Actions were taken to eradicate Chinese historical opera during the Cultural Revolution (1966 -1976); however, the robustness of the cultural history, literature, and art found in the opera withstood this test of time.

2. Popular Entertainment

Going to see Chinese opera or a Chinese acrobatic troupe is not just entertainment—these activities are uniquely classical Chinese art forms and they are favorably regarded as forms of intellectual and artistic cultivation. As there are relatively few venues for these popular activities, it would be best to ask your Chinese colleagues to assist you in the process of identifying an interesting show and purchasing tickets in advance.

Additional Vocabulary

	Chinese	Pinyin	Part of Speech	English Equivalent
1.	件	jiàn	M	(a measure word for , luggage, or clothing)
2.	担心	dān xīn	VO	to worry
3.	闷热	mēnrè	Adj	hot and humid
4.	加班	jiā bān	VO	to work overtime
5.	足球	zúqiú	N	soccer

6.	棒球	bàngqiú	N	baseball
7.	简单	jiǎndān	Adj	simple
8.	地铁	dìtiě	N	subway
9.	难	nán	Adj	difficult
10.	有用	yǒu yòng	Adj	useful
11.	慢跑	mànpǎo	N V	jogging to jog
12.	篮球	lánqiú	N	basketball
13.	会议室	huìyìshì	N	meeting room
14.	后面	hòumian	N	at the back; in the rear; behind (in space or position)
15.	面	miàn	Suf	used with terms of direction or localization such as 前面 qiánmian "front," 外面 wàimian "outside," 里面 lǐmian "inside"

UNIT
10

出门
Chū mén
Going Out

Unit **10.1**

Asking Directions from Taxi Drivers

In this lesson we will learn:

- About taking a taxi in China.

- About the layout of Beijing, in order to more successfully navigate your way around the city.

- How to convey your destination to taxi drivers.

⊙ Chinese Dialogue

出租车司机： 请问，先生，您上哪儿?

白有天： 师傅，我去天安门广场。

出租车司机： 走二环还是三环?

白有天： 要是二环不堵的话，就走二环吧。

出租车司机： 二环这个时候经常堵车，走三环可能会更快。

白有天： 长安街怎么样?

出租车司机： 长安街现在应该不会太堵。

白有天： 那我们先上三环，再走长安街吧!

Pinyin Dialogue

Chūzūchē sījī:	Qǐng wèn, xiānsheng, nín shàng nǎr?
Bái Yǒutiān:	Shīfu, wǒ qù Tiān'ānmén Guǎngchǎng.
Chūzūchē sījī:	Zǒu Èrhuán háishi Sānhuán?
Bái Yǒutiān:	Yàoshi Èrhuán bù dǔ dehuà, jiù zǒu Èrhuán ba.
Chūzūchē sījī	Èrhuán zhè ge shíhou jīngcháng dǔ chē, zǒu Sānhuán kěnéng huì gèng kuài.
Bái Yǒutiān:	Cháng'ānjiē zěnmeyàng?
Chūzūchē sījī:	Cháng'ānjiē xiànzài yīnggāi bú huì tài dǔ.
Bái Yǒutiān:	Nà wǒmen xiān shàng Sānhuán, zài zǒu Cháng'ānjiē ba!

Vocabulary

Chinese	Pinyin	Part of Speech	English Equivalent
1. 出门	chū mén	VO	to go out
2. 门	mén	N	door; gate
3. 出租车	chūzūchē	N	taxi
4. 司机	sījī	N	driver (of a car)
5. 师傅	shīfu	N	driver; master in a given field
6. 天安门	Tiān'ānmén	PN	Tiananmen
7. 广场	guǎngchǎng	N	square
8. 二环	Èrhuán	PN	Second Ring (Road)
9. 三环	Sānhuán	PN	Third Ring (Road)
10. 要是	yàoshi	Conj	if
11. 堵	dǔ	V	to have a traffic jam; to block up
12. ……的话	…dehuà	Conj	if
13. 堵车	dǔ chē	VO N	to have a traffic jam traffic congestion
14. 可能	kěnéng	Adv	possibly; likely; perhaps
15. 更	gèng	Adv	even more
16. 长安街	Cháng'ānjiē	PN	Chang'an Street
17. 怎么样	zěnmeyàng	IP	how is…
18. 应该	yīnggāi	AV	should; ought to
19. 先	xiān	Adv	first

Sentence Patterns

1. 您上哪儿？ Nín shàng nǎr? "Where are you going?"

In Units 3.1 (Sentence Pattern 9) and 5.1 (Sentence Pattern 2), we learned that 去 qù means "to go" to a place that is away from the speaker. Here we learn that 您上哪儿 Nín shàng nǎr "Where are you going?" can also be used interchangeably with 您去哪儿 Nín qù nǎr. 上 is a colloquial way to say "to go (to a place)" in northern China, but it is used only if the destination is not far, therefore, *他想上美国 Tā xiǎng shàng Měiguó is incorrect.

S + 上 + place word	
	Substitution
我要上街。 Wǒ yào shàng jiē. I want to go (stroll on) the street.	洗手间　xǐshǒujiān 邮局　　yóujú 银行　　yínháng 商店　　shāngdiàn 医院　　yīyuàn

2. 要是二环不堵的话，就走二环吧。 Yàoshi Èrhuán bù dǔ dehuà, jiù zǒu Èrhuán ba. "If the Second Ring (Road) is not congested, then take the Second Ring (Road)."

We learned the conjunction 如果 rúguǒ… …, 就 jiù… … is used to express the notion of "If… then…" in Unit 9.2 (Sentence Pattern 6). 要是 yàoshi is an alternative form of 如果 and is used more often in spoken Chinese. In addition, 的话 dehuà can be added at the end of the "if" clause to reinforce the cause/effect nature of the sentence, and either 要是/如果 or 的话 can be omitted without changing the overall meaning. For example, 要是/如果买得到票 yàoshi/rúguǒ mǎi de dào piào has the same meaning as 买得到票的话 mǎi de dào piào dehuà.

要是/如果 ... ... (的话)，就 ... ...

1. 要是您有时间的话，我给您介绍一下市场部的经理。

   Yàoshi nín yǒu shíjiān dehuà, wǒ gěi nín jièshào yíxià shìchǎngbù de jīnglǐ.
   If you have time, I will introduce the manager of the marketing department to you.

2. 要是我们下周去北京，我们就能在那儿见到张总经理。

   Yàoshi wǒmen xià zhōu qù Běijīng, wǒmen jiù néng zài nàr jiàndào Zhāng Zǒngjīnglǐ.
   If we go to Beijing next week, we could meet with the General Manager Zhang there.

3. (要是) 王经理不在的话，就帮我找他的秘书吧。

   (Yàoshi) Wáng Jīnglǐ bú zài dehuà, jiù bāng wǒ zhǎo tā de mìshū ba.
   If Manager Wang is not here, then look for his secretary for me.

3. 走三环可能会更快。 **Zǒu Sānhuán kěnéng huì gèng kuài.**
"Taking the Third Ring (Road) will probably be much faster."

可能 kěnéng is an adverb used to make an estimation or supposition of a certain fact. The negative form of 可能 can take two formats. The first is 可能不 kěnéng bù, and is equivalent to the English phrase "unlikely." The second negative form is 不可能 bù kěnéng, and is the equivalent of "impossible."

可能

1. 我们没有见过她，她可能是新来的会计师。

Wǒmen méiyǒu jiàn guò tā, tā kěnéng shì xīn lái de kuàijìshī.
We have never met her before; she is probably the recently hired accountant.

2. 这道菜太辣，你可能不爱吃。

Zhè dào cài tài là, nǐ kěnéng bú ài chī.
This dish is too spicy; you probably won't like it.

3. 王经理出差去了，不可能来开会。

Wáng Jīnglǐ chū chāi qù le, bù kěnéng lái kāi huì.
The manager is on a business trip; it's impossible for him to come for the meeting.

4. 走三环可能会更快。 **Zǒu Sānhuán kěnéng huì gèng kuài.**
"Taking the Third Ring (Road) will probably be much faster."

更 gèng, meaning "even more," is an adverb used to modify an adjective. It implies that the degree of the adjective is much stronger, when compared with something else.

更 + Adj

1. 听了李总的介绍，我们对这个项目更有信心了。

   Tīng le Lǐ Zǒng de jièshào, wǒmen duì zhè ge xiàngmù gèng yǒu xìnxīn le.
   After hearing President Li's introduction, we're even more confident about this project.

2. 我们安排在这周见面吧，您下周可能会更忙。

   Wǒmen ānpái zài zhè zhōu jiàn miàn ba, nín xià zhōu kěnéng huì gèng máng.
   Let's plan on meeting this week; you probably will be even busier next week.

3. A: 二环比三环堵吗？

   B: 三环很堵，不过二环更堵。

   A: Èrhuán bǐ Sānhuán dǔ ma?
   B: Sānhuán hěn dǔ, búguò Èrhuán gèng dǔ.

   A: Is Second Ring Road more congested than Third Ring Road?
   B: Third Ring Road is quite congested, but Second Ring is even more so.

5. 长安街<u>怎么样</u>？ **Cháng'ānjiē <u>zěnmeyàng</u>? "What about Chang'an Street?"**

In Unit 9.2 (Sentence Pattern 3), we learned that 怎么样 zěnmeyàng is used to find out if a proposal or suggestion is acceptable. In this lesson, 怎么样 is still used as an interrogative pronoun, but it is used to inquire about the nature, condition, or state of something, and means "how is…?" For example: 你怎么样 Nǐ zěnmeyàng "How are things with you?" or "What's up with you?"

Compare the following two sentences:

长安街怎么样？ Cháng'ānjiē zěnmeyàng? "What is the condition of Chang'an Street?"

走长安街，怎么样？ Zǒu Cháng'ānjiē, zěnmeyàng? "How about if we take Chang'an Street?"

1. A: 你父亲身体怎么样?
   B: 他每天锻炼，身体挺好。

   A: Nǐ fùqin shēntǐ zěnmeyàng?
   B: Tā měitiān duànliàn, shēntǐ tǐng hǎo.

   A: How is your father's health?
   B: He exercises every day; he is in good health (he is quite healthy).

2. A: 今年的生意怎么样?
   B: 今年比去年更好。

   A: Jīnnián de shēngyì zěnmeyàng?
   B: Jīnnián bǐ qùnián gèng hǎo.

   A: How is business this year?
   B: This year is even better than last year.

3. A: 他的报告写得怎么样?
   B: 写得非常好。

   A: Tā de bàogào xiě de zěnmeyàng?
   B: Xiě de fēicháng hǎo.

   A: How is his (written) report?
   B: (It is) very well-written.

6. 长安街现在<u>应该</u>不会太堵。 **Cháng'ānjiē xiànzài <u>yīnggāi</u> bú huì tài dǔ. "Chang'an Street shouldn't have too much traffic right now."**

应该 yīnggāi, meaning "should," is an auxiliary verb used before a verb. As is the case with the English word "should," 应该 may be used to convey an assessment or logical conclusion about a situation. 吧 is sometimes added to the end of the sentence to solicit concurrence from the listener.

1. 我明天没有会议，我们应该有时间讨论这个问题。

   Wǒ míngtiān méiyǒu huìyì, wǒmen yīnggāi yǒu shíjiān tǎolùn zhè ge wèntí.
   I do not have meetings tomorrow; we should have time to discuss this issue.

2. 现在八点了，他们应该已经吃过晚饭了吧？

   Xiànzài bā diǎn le, tāmen yīnggāi yǐjīng chī guò wǎnfàn le ba?
   It's already 8:00; they should have had dinner by now, right?

3. 要是不堵车，我们应该不会迟到。

   Yàoshi bù dǔ chē, wǒmen yīnggāi bú huì chídào.
   If there is no traffic jam, we should be able to make it in time.

7. 那我们先上三环，再走长安街吧！ **Nà wǒmen xiān shàng Sānhuán, zài zǒu Cháng'ānjiē ba! "Then we'll get on Third Ring (Road) first, and then go by Chang'an Street!"**

"先 + V, 再 + V" is the pattern used to express the idea of "doing something first, and then something else next," meaning "first V₁, then V₂." The subjects of these two clauses can be the same or different. If the subjects are the same, the subject in the second clause can be omitted. Otherwise, it should be included. For example: 你先来，我们再一块儿去 Nǐ xiān lái, wǒmen zài yíkuàir qù "You come first, then we will go together later."

S_1 + 先 + V_1, (S_2) + 再 + V_2				
我们先接您，再去分公司。 Wǒmen xiān jiē nín, zài qù fēngōngsī. We'll pick you up first, then go to the branch office.	**Substitution**			
	V_1		V_2	
	想想看	xiǎngxiang kàn	决定	juédìng
	参观	cānguān	听报告	tīng bàogào
	打电话约他	dǎ diànhuà yuē tā	跟他见面	gēn tā jiàn miàn
	吃饭	chī fàn	去看电影	qù kàn diànyǐng

Cultural Points

1. Taxi Drivers

In China, when a taxi driver picks up a foreigner, the foreigner may be asked many questions if language is shared. These questions may range from the amount of money you earn (not considered impolite to ask in China) to contemporary Sino-U.S. relations. Cab drivers are talkative and inquisitive, and usually very friendly and open. Reticence on your part to make conversation could be construed as aloofness or even rudeness.

Here are some more tips about taking cabs in China. Most Chinese people do not wear seatbelts, so as soon as you buckle your seatbelt, the driver may think that you lack confidence in his/her driving. Of course, it is still best that you put on your seatbelt anyway because many cab drivers do not follow the rules of traffic and may take you on nerve-rattling adventure rides. Also be aware that some cab drivers may take you on long "scenic tours." Most cabs have meters that indicate the fee, so usually you don't need to bargain for the fare, nor is it necessary to include a tip.

2. The Layout of Beijing's Streets

The city of Beijing is laid out in concentric circles. The Second Ring Road is nearest the center. Each successive "ring road" has a radius a few miles longer than that of the previous road. Development has proceeded to include the Fifth and Sixth Ring Roads.

There is no First Ring Road per se. At the center of the city are the Forbidden City (also called the Palace Museum) and Tiananmen Square. In antiquity, the Forbidden City was encircled by a stone wall topped by a wide walkway ample enough to have been considered the first ring road, and it was used by palace guards walking their guard circuit. Chang'an Street runs east-west (continuing as Jian Guo Men Road in the east and Fu Xing Men Road in the west), cutting through Tiananmen Square just south of the Forbidden City, and bisecting the city, north and south.

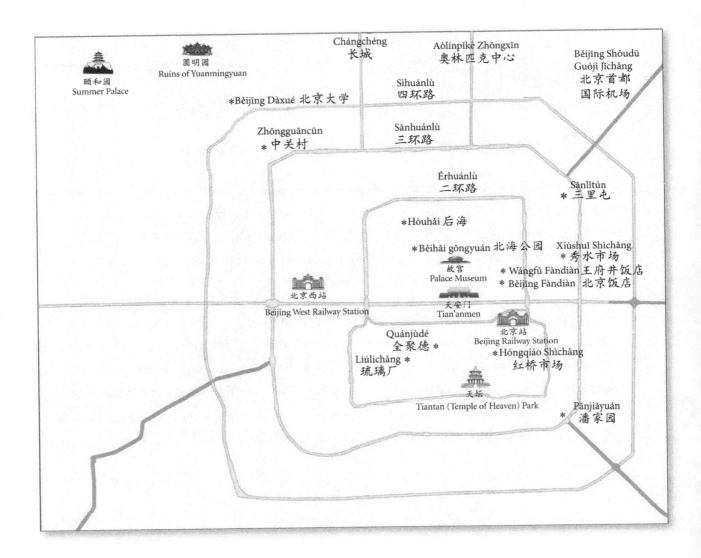

Additional Vocabulary

	Chinese	Pinyin	Part of Speech	English Equivalent
1.	上街	shàng jiē	VO	to go on the street; to stroll on the street (usually when shopping)
2.	洗手间	xǐshǒujiān	N	restroom
3.	邮局	yóujú	N	post office
4.	商店	shāngdiàn	N	shop
5.	医院	yīyuàn	N	hospital
6.	爱	ài	V	to love; to like
7.	项目	xiàngmù	N	project
8.	信心	xìnxīn	N	confidence
9.	锻炼	duànliàn	V	to exercise; to work out
10.	会议	huìyì	N	meeting
11.	迟到	chídào	V	to arrive late

Unit **10.2**

Asking Directions from Pedestrians

In this lesson you will learn:

- How to navigate while on foot.
- How to ask for directions.
- How to express distances and directions.

Chinese Dialogue

白有天： 请问，去东方广场怎么走？

过路人： 从这里一直向北走，第二个红绿灯右转，就到了。

白有天： 对不起，我没听清楚，请您再说一遍。

过路人： 从这里一直往前走，第二个路口右拐。

白有天： 右拐以后，还要走多远？

过路人： 不远，一拐弯就能看到。

白有天： 在路的哪边？

过路人： 在左边。

白有天： 谢谢！

过路人： 不客气！

Pinyin Dialogue

Bái Yǒutiān: Qǐngwèn, qù Dōngfāng Guǎngchǎng zěnme zǒu?

Guòlùrén: Cóng zhèli yìzhí xiàng běi zǒu, dì èr ge hónglǜdēng yòu zhuǎn, jiù dào le.

Bái Yǒutiān: Duìbuqǐ, wǒ méi tīng qīngchu, qǐng nín zài shuō yí biàn.

Guòlùrén: Cóng zhèli yìzhí wǎng qián zǒu, dì èr ge lùkǒu yòu guǎi.

Bái Yǒutiān: Yòu guǎi yǐhòu, hái yào zǒu duō yuǎn?

Guòlùrén: Bù yuǎn, yì guǎi wān jiù néng kàn dào.

Bái Yǒutiān: Zài lù de nǎ biān?

Guòlùrén: Zài zuǒ biān.

Bái Yǒutiān: Xièxie!

Guòlùrén: Bú kèqi!

Vocabulary

	Chinese	Pinyin	Part of Speech	English Equivalent
1.	东方	dōngfāng	N/PN	east; the East; the Orient
2.	东	dōng	N	east
3.	怎么	zěnme	IP	how to…
4.	向	xiàng	Prep	towards
5.	红绿灯	hónglǜdēng	N	traffic light
6.	灯	dēng	N	light
7.	右转	yòu zhuǎn	V	to turn right
8.	转	zhuǎn	V	to make a turn
9.	遍	biàn	M	(a measure word for actions)
10.	往	wǎng	Prep	towards; in the direction of
11.	前	qián	N	ahead; front (opposite of 后 hòu)
12.	路口	lùkǒu	N	intersection
13.	拐	guǎi	V	to make a turn
14.	拐弯	guǎi wān	VO	to turn at a corner
15.	路	lù	N	road
16.	边/边儿	biān/biānr	Suf	side (used with terms of direction)
17.	不客气	bú kèqi	UE	You are welcome; don't be so polite

Sentence Patterns

1. 去东方广场**怎么走**？ **Qù Dōngfāng Guǎngchǎng zěnme zǒu?**
"**How do I get to the Oriental Plaza?**"

怎么 zěnme is an interrogative pronoun meaning "how to do (something)," and it precedes a verb to inquire in what way or manner and by what means an action is to be carried out.

怎么 + V

1. 你知道怎么做中国菜吗？

   Nǐ zhīdào zěnme zuò Zhōngguócài ma?
   Do you know how to make Chinese food?

2. "Human Resources" 用中文怎么说？

   "Human Resources" yòng Zhōngwén zěnme shuō?
   How do you say "Human Resources" in Chinese?

3. 你的中文讲得很好，是怎么学的？

   Nǐ de Zhōngwén jiǎng de hěn hǎo, shì zěnme xué de?
   You speak Chinese very well; how did you learn it?

4. A: 我怎么去你们公司呢？
   B: 你可以坐地铁，也可以坐出租车，都很方便。

   A: Wǒ zěnme qù nǐmen gōngsī ne?
   B: Nǐ kěyǐ zuò dìtiě, yě kěyǐ zuò chūzūchē, dōu hěn fāngbiàn.

   A: How do I get to your company?
   B: You may take a subway or a taxi; both are very convenient.

2. 从这里<u>一直</u>向北走。 **Cóng zhèli <u>yìzhí</u> xiàng běi zǒu. "From here go straight north."**

In Unit 9.2 (Sentence Pattern 2) we learned that 直 zhí literally means "straight" and 一直 conveys the idea that a certain condition has been sustained or continues without change for a period of time. In this lesson, 一直 is used to indicate straight linear movement (in going to a place). Thus, 一直走 means "to go straight (in a certain direction)."

一直

1. 向前一直走，就到了。

   Xiàng qián yìzhí zǒu, jiù dào le.
   Go straight ahead, and you will be there.

2. 你从这里一直走，不要拐弯。

   Nǐ cóng zhèli yìzhí zǒu, búyào guǎi wān.
   You go straight ahead from here. Do not make any turns.

3. 你先向右拐，再一直走。

   Nǐ xiān xiàng yòu guǎi, zài yìzhí zǒu.
   First, you turn right, and then go straight ahead.

4. 一直向西走差不多一公里，就到地铁站了。

   Yìzhí xiàng xī zǒu chàbuduō yì gōnglǐ, jiù dào dìtiězhàn le.
   Go toward the west for about one kilometer, and then you will arrive at the subway station.

一直 can also modify a verb to indicate that an action has extended from one point of time to another without interruption.

一直 + V

1. 她一直不说话，不知道她有什么意见。

   Tā yìzhí bù shuō huà, bù zhīdào tā yǒu shénme yìjiàn.
   She has not yet said a word, and we don't know what opinions she has.

2. 他一直做进出口生意。

   Tā yìzhí zuò jìnchūkǒu shēngyì.
   He has always been doing import and export business.

3. 虽然住在同一个城市，可是我们一直没有见过面。

   Suīrán zhù zài tóng yí ge chéngshì, kěshì wǒmen yìzhí méiyǒu jiàn guò miàn.
   Although we live in the same city, we have never met.

3. 我没听<u>清楚</u>。 **Wǒ méi <u>tīng qīngchu</u>. "I didn't hear clearly."**

In Unit 9.2 (Sentence Pattern 7), we introduced the "potential" resultative verb form. Now we will introduce the "actual" resultative verb form. The "potential" form indicates what can or cannot be accomplished, whereas the "actual" form indicates what has or hasn't actually transpired, or what will or will not actually transpire. The positive form of the "actual" resultative verb construction is: $V_1 + V_2 + 了$.

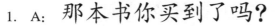

1. A: 那本书你买到了吗?

    B: 我已经买到了。

   A: Nà běn shū nǐ mǎi dào le ma?
   B: Wǒ yǐjīng mǎi dào le.

   A: Have you already bought that book?
   B: I've already bought (it).

2. A: 你找到工作了吗?

    B: 找到了。

   A: Nǐ zhǎo dào gōngzuò le ma?
   B: Zhǎo dào le.

   A: Have you found a job yet?
   B: Yes, I have found one.

3. A: 你听懂他的报告了吗?

    B: 我都听懂了。

   A: Nǐ tīng dǒng tā de bàogào le ma?
   B: Wǒ dōu tīng dǒng le.

   A: Did you understand his (spoken) presentation?
   B: I understood it all.

4. A: 这本书你看懂了吗?

    B: 这本书不难, 我看懂了。

   A: Zhè běn shū nǐ kàn dǒng le ma?
   B: Zhè běn shū bù nán, wǒ kàn dǒng le.

   A: Did you understand (by reading) this book?
   B: This book is not difficult; I understood it.

5. A: 那就是中国银行, 你看见了吗?

    B: 我看见了。

   A: Nà jiù shì Zhōngguó Yínháng, nǐ kàn jiàn le ma?
   B: Wǒ kàn jiàn le.

   A: That *is* the Bank of China; did you see it?
   B: I saw it.

The negative structure of the "actual form" is: 没 (有) + V₁ + V₂.

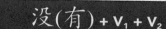

没(有) + V₁ + V₂

1. 我今天一直没有看到他，他可能出去了。

   Wǒ jīntiān yìzhí méiyǒu kàn dào tā, tā kěnéng chūqu le.
   I didn't see him all day today; he probably went out.

2. 我们去得太晚，没买到票。

   Wǒmen qù de tài wǎn, méi mǎi dào piào.
   We went too late, and didn't succeed in buying the tickets.

3. 人太多，我没找到他。

   Rén tài duō, wǒ méi zhǎo dào tā.
   There were too many people; I didn't find him.

4. 这个报告我看了三遍，还是没有看懂。

   Zhè ge bàogào wǒ kàn le sān biàn, háishi méiyǒu kàn dǒng.
   I've read this report three times, and still didn't understand it.

4. 请您<u>再</u>说一<u>遍</u>。 **Qǐng nín <u>zài</u> shuō yí <u>biàn</u>. "Please say it again."**

In Units 9.1 (Sentence Pattern 7) and 10.1 (Sentence Pattern 7), we learned to use 再 in the sense of "then." Now we will introduce another meaning, the meaning of "again," for this word. In both usages, 再 is an adverb and therefore must immediately precede the verb it modified, as in 再见 "see you again." It indicates that an action will be repeated in the future.

再 + V

1. 我没听懂，可不可以再讲一遍？

   Wǒ méi tīng dǒng, kě bù kěyǐ zài jiǎng yí biàn?
   I didn't understand (you); could you repeat that?

2. 要是大家还不清楚，我们请他再解释一遍。

   Yàoshi dàjiā hái bù qīngchu, wǒmen qǐng tā zài jiěshì yí biàn.
   If everyone is still unclear, we can ask him to explain it once more.

3. 这个报告请你帮我再看一下，好吗？

   Zhè ge bàogào qǐng nǐ bāng wǒ zài kàn yíxià, hǎo ma?
   Please help me to review this report once more, OK?

In Unit 7.1 (Sentence Pattern 5) we learned that 次 cì is a measure word indicating the frequency of an action (how many times it occurs). 遍 biàn is another frequently used measure word for counting the number of occurrences of an action. The difference between 次 and 遍 is a subtle one: 次 simply indicates the specific number of times that an action has occurred, whereas 遍 implies the reoccurrence of an entire process, from the beginning to the end. Compare the following examples:

请你再解释一遍 Qǐng nǐ zài jiěshì yí biàn "Please go over it again (from beginning to end)."

请你再解释一次 Qǐng nǐ zài jiěshì yí cì "Please explain it one more time."

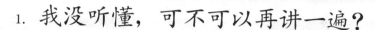

遍/次

1. 我没听懂，可不可以再讲一遍？

   Wǒ méi tīng dǒng, kě bù kěyǐ zài jiǎng yí biàn?
   I didn't understand (it); could you repeat it again?

2. 这个报告我看了两遍了。

   Zhè ge bàogào wǒ kàn le liǎng biàn le.
   I've already read the report twice from beginning to end.

3. 请他再表演一次。

   Qǐng tā zài biǎoyǎn yí cì.
   Ask him to perform one more time.

Cultural Points

1. Directions

In general, Chinese people want to be helpful, especially to foreign visitors. This desire to be helpful may sometimes act to your detriment. For instance, when asking a person in the street for directions, their desire to provide you with an answer may compel them to give you directions even when they do not really know the way. Chinese people are not in the habit of reading maps and may not know locations you are seeking to find. Some people may simply give you their best estimate, rather than admitting that they do not know. It is always a good idea to confirm the directions by asking a second person along the way.

Additional Vocabulary

	Chinese	Pinyin	Part of Speech	English Equivalent
1.	用	yòng	V	to use
2.	西	xī	N	west
3.	地铁站	dìtiězhàn	N	subway station
4.	意见	yìjiàn	N	opinion
5.	最近	zuìjìn	TW	lately; recently
6.	同	tóng	Adj	same
7.	解释	jiěshì	V	to explain

UNIT
11

购物
Gòuwù
Shopping

Unit **11.1**

Places for Purchasing Gifts

In this lesson we will learn:

• About popular outdoor markets in Beijing and Shanghai.

• How to ask about shopping areas.

• How to make sure it is not a burden on your Chinese colleagues to arrange such outings.

Chinese Dialogue

白有天： 我太太要我买一些珠宝回去。

高明： 买珠宝应该去红桥市场。您以前去过红桥市场吗?

白有天： 没去过，因为每次来时间都太紧了。

高明： 明天我有空，我可以陪您去。

白有天： 好极了，但是会不会太麻烦您了?

高明： 不会。我也刚好想去那儿买点儿东西。

白有天： 从这里到红桥市场有多远?

高明： 红桥市场在天坛路，大约十公里吧。

白有天： 我们怎么去呢?

高明： 叫一辆出租车吧!

白有天： 行，我听您安排。

Pinyin Dialogue

Bái Yǒutiān： Wǒ tàitai yào wǒ mǎi yìxiē zhūbǎo huíqu.

Gāo Míng： Mǎi zhūbǎo yīnggāi qù Hóngqiáo Shìchǎng. Nín yǐqián qù guò Hóngqiáo Shìchǎng ma?

Bái Yǒutiān： Méi qù guò, yīnwèi měi cì lái shíjiān dōu tài jǐn le.

Gāo Míng： Míngtiān wǒ yǒu kòng, wǒ kěyǐ péi nín qù.

Bái Yǒutiān： Hǎo jí le, dànshì huì bú huì tài máfan nín le?

Gāo Míng： Bú huì. Wǒ yě gānghǎo xiǎng qù nàr mǎi diǎnr dōngxi.

Bái Yǒutiān： Cóng zhèli dào Hóngqiáo Shìchǎng yǒu duō yuǎn?

Gāo Míng： Hóngqiáo Shìchǎng zài Tiāntánlù, dàyuē shí gōnglǐ ba.

Bái Yǒutiān： Wǒmen zěnme qù ne?

Gāo Míng： Jiào yí liàng chūzūchē ba!

Bái Yǒutiān： Xíng, wǒ tīng nín ānpái.

Vocabulary

Chinese	Pinyin	Part of Speech	English Equivalent
1. 些	xiē	M	(a measure word for multiple things or people)
2. 珠宝	zhūbǎo	N	jewelry; precious gems
3. 红桥市场	Hóngqiáo Shìchǎng	PN	Hongqiao Market
4. 以前	yǐqián	TW	before; ago; previously
5. 因为	yīnwèi	Conj	because
6. 紧	jǐn	Adj	tight; urgent; pressing; tense
7. 陪	péi	V	to accompany
8. ......极了	...jí le	Adv	extremely
9. 但是	dànshì	Conj	but
10. 麻烦	máfan	V N Adj	to bother; to trouble trouble troublesome
11. 刚好	gānghǎo	Adv	by coincidence; by chance
12. 天坛路	Tiāntánlù	PN	Tiantan Road
13. 天坛	Tiāntán	PN	Temple of Heaven
14. 大约	dàyuē	Adv	approximately; about
15. 叫	jiào	V	to call (a taxi); to order
16. 辆	liàng	M	(a measure word for vehicles)

Sentence Patterns

1. 我太太要我买一些珠宝回去。 **Wǒ tàitai yào wǒ mǎi yìxiē zhūbǎo huíqu. "My wife wants me to buy some jewelry to bring back."**

些 xiē is a measure word used to signify an indefinite, but fairly small, quantity. 一 yī is the only numeral that can be used with 些, and it can be omitted when it is understood in usage. For example: 他给我 (一) 些书 Tā gěi wǒ (yì) xiē shū "He gave me some books." When 一 is omitted, 些 can be used with pronouns such as 这 zhè, 那 nà, 哪 nǎ to signify "these," "those," and "which," respectively.

一些

1. 今天下班以后，我没有时间跟你去，因为我得上街买一些家具。

   Jīntiān xià bān yǐhòu, wǒ méiyǒu shíjiān gēn nǐ qù, yīnwèi wǒ děi shàng jiē mǎi yìxiē jiājù.
   After we get off work today, I won't have time to go with you because I must go buy some furniture.

2. 这些杂志，你还要吗？

   Zhèxiē zázhì, nǐ hái yào ma?
   Do you still want these magazines?

3. 他们那些产品是在哪儿生产的？

   Tāmen nàxiē chǎnpǐn shì zài nǎr shēngchǎn de?
   Where were their products manufactured?

4. 哪些新产品比较有市场？

   Nǎxiē xīn chǎnpǐn bǐjiào yǒu shìchǎng?
   Which new products are more marketable?

---

2. 买珠宝应该去红桥市场。 **Mǎi zhūbǎo yīnggāi qù Hóngqiáo shìchǎng.** "To buy jewelry, you should go to Hongqiao Market."

In Unit 10.1 (Sentence Pattern 6), we learned that 应该 yīnggāi is used as an auxiliary verb to express a probability or logical conclusion. In this lesson, 应该 is also used as an auxiliary verb preceding a verb, to indicate the notion of necessity or obligation. In English, this is roughly equivalent to "should" or "ought to."

应该 + V

1. 这几天太忙了，我们应该出去轻松一下。

    Zhè jǐ tiān tài máng le, wǒmen yīnggāi chūqu qīngsōng yíxià.
    We've been too busy these few days; we should go out and relax a bit.

2. 他身体不好，不应该喝太多咖啡。

    Tā shēntǐ bù hǎo, bù yīnggāi hē tài duō kāfēi.
    His health is not too good; he shouldn't drink too much coffee.

3. 你不应该在这儿吸烟。

    Nǐ bù yīnggāi zài zhèr xī yān.
    You shouldn't smoke here.

4. 这个问题非常重要，我们应该去问谁？

    Zhè ge wèntí fēicháng zhòngyào, wǒmen yīnggāi qù wèn shéi?
    This issue is very important; to whom should we go to ask (about it)?

3. 您以前去过红桥市场吗？ **Nín yǐqián qù guò Hóngqiáo Shìchǎng ma?** "Have you ever been to Hongqiao Market before?"

以前 yǐqián means "before; previously; ago," and its sentence structure is the same as 以后, explained in Unit 9.2 (Sentence Pattern 1).

以前

1. 我们的财务经理以前在联想工作过。

   Wǒmen de cáiwù jīnglǐ yǐqián zài Liánxiǎng gōngzuò guò.
   Our financial manager worked at Lenovo before.

2. 他以前经常来我们的商店买东西。

   Tā yǐqián jīngcháng lái wǒmen de shāngdiàn mǎi dōngxi.
   He used to come to our store quite often to shop.

3. A: 你以前看过京剧吗？
   B: 我以前没看过。

   A: Nǐ yǐqián kàn guò Jīngjù ma?
   B: Wǒ yǐqián méi kàn guò.

   A: Have you ever seen Beijing Opera before?
   B: I've never seen it before.

V/TW/TD + 以前

1. 我来中国以前，听不懂中文。

   Wǒ lái Zhōngguó yǐqián, tīng bu dǒng Zhōngwén.
   Before I came to China, I did not understand (through listening) Chinese.

2. 睡觉以前，我喜欢看一会儿书。

   Shuì jiào yǐqián, wǒ xǐhuan kàn yìhuǐr shū.
   Before I go to bed, I like to read for awhile.

3. 这个报告明天早上十点以前可以交给经理吗？

   Zhè ge bàogào míngtiān zǎoshang shí diǎn yǐqián kěyǐ jiāo gěi jīnglǐ ma?
   Are you able to submit this report to the manager by 10:00 a.m. tomorrow?

4. 我们是三年以前认识的。

   Wǒmen shì sān nián yǐqián rènshi de.
   It was three years ago that we met each other.

4. <u>因为</u>每次来时间都太紧了。 **<u>Yīnwèi</u> měi cì lái shíjiān dōu tài jǐn le. "Because every time my schedule was too tight."**

The conjunction 因为……，所以…… yīnwèi…, suǒyǐ…, meaning "because…, therefore…" is used to indicate a cause-and-effect relationship. The 因为 clause usually precedes the 所以 clause, although this ordering may be switched. Either 因为 or 所以 may be omitted, though not both in a single sentence.

因为 …… ，所以 ……

1. 因为明天要见客户，我不能来开会。

   Yīnwèi míngtiān yào jiàn kèhù, wǒ bù néng lái kāi huì.
   Because I have to meet with a client tomorrow, I won't be able to come to the meeting.

2. 坐地铁会更快，因为长安街经常堵车。

   Zuò dìtiě huì gèng kuài, yīnwèi Cháng'ānjiē jīngcháng dǔ chē.
   Because Chang'an Street is often congested, it will be faster if we take the subway.

3. 因为怕麻烦您，所以我没有和您谈这件事。

   Yīnwèi pà máfan nín, suǒyǐ wǒ méiyǒu hé nín tán zhè jiàn shì.
   Because I was afraid to bother you, I did not talk to you about this matter.

4. 我们今天不能去看球赛，因为没买到票。

   Wǒmen jīntiān bù néng qù kàn qiúsài, yīnwèi méi mǎi dào piào.
   We can not go to watch the ballgame today, because we could not get tickets.

---

5. 好极了。 **Hǎo _jí le_. "Excellent."**

极了 _jí le_ is added after an adjective or a verb that expresses emotion or opinion (such as 喜欢 _xǐhuan_) to express the highest possibly degree or extent, and is equivalent to "extremely..." in English.

Adj + 极了

1. 因为开了一天的会，我累极了。

   Yīnwèi kāi le yì tiān de huì, wǒ lèi jí le.
   Because I had meetings all day long, I'm absolutely exhausted.

2. 我们的项目做得很好，客户高兴极了。

   Wǒmen de xiàngmù zuò de hěn hǎo, kèhù gāoxìng jí le.
   We did well on this project; our clients are extremely happy.

3. 那个商店的东西贵极了。

   Nà ge shāngdiàn de dōngxi guì jí le.
   The stuff at that store is extremely expensive.

6. 我也刚好想去那儿买点儿东西。 **Wǒ yě gānghǎo xiǎng qù nàr mǎi diǎnr dōngxi. "It just so happens that I have been thinking about going there to buy some things."**

刚好 gānghǎo is an adverb used in a verb phrase to convey the idea of a fortuitous coincidence, so it can be translated roughly as "coincidently." This type of sentence often occurs as the first clause in a two-clause sentence, with the second clause being a follow-up of the first clause that stated the fortuitous coincidence.

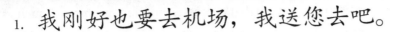
1. 我刚好也要去机场，我送您去吧。

   Wǒ gānghǎo yě yào qù jīchǎng, wǒ sòng nín qù ba.
   I happen to be going to the airport; I'll take you there.

2. 马经理刚好下周出差回来，可以安排你们在下周四见面。

   Mǎ Jīnglǐ gānghǎo xià zhōu chū chāi huílai, kěyǐ ānpái nǐmen zài xià zhōusì jiàn miàn.
   It just so happens that Manager Ma is returning next week from a business trip. I can arrange for you two to meet next Thursday.

3. 对不起，我没有出来见你，因为我刚好有事。

   Duìbuqǐ, wǒ méiyǒu chūlai jiàn nǐ, yīnwèi wǒ gānghǎo yǒu shì.
   I'm sorry I didn't come out to see you, I was tied up with something at that time.

4. 今天刚好有空，我陪你上街买东西吧。

   Jīntiān gānghǎo yǒu kòng, wǒ péi nǐ shàng jiē mǎi dōngxi ba.
   I just happen to have some free time today; I'll accompany you to go shopping.

7. 从这里到红桥市场有多远？ **Cóng zhèli dào Hóngqiáo Shìchǎng yǒu duō yuǎn? "How far is it from here to the Hongqiao Market?"**

"从 cóng X 到 dào Y," meaning "from X to Y," can be used to state a range between two points in location, price, time, etc. In this lesson, "从 X 到 Y" is used to specify the path or distance between two places. The pattern can also be used to indicate a period of time from one point in time to another.

从 X 到 Y

1. 从北京到旧金山，要坐十几个小时的飞机。

    Cóng Běijīng dào Jiùjīnshān, yào zuò shí jǐ ge xiǎoshí de fēijī.
    It takes more than ten hours to get to San Francisco from Beijing by plane.

2. 从我家到公司的路上，一直堵车。

    Cóng wǒ jiā dào gōngsī de lùshang, yìzhí dǔ chē.
    The traffic was terrible all the way from my home to the company.

3. 明天我会很忙，因为从上午九点到下午三点都有会议。

    Míngtiān wǒ huì hěn máng, yīnwèi cóng shàngwǔ jiǔ diǎn dào xiàwǔ sān diǎn dōu yǒu huìyì.
    I'll be busy tomorrow, because I have meetings all day from 9:00 a.m. to 3:00 p.m.

4. 她从早到晚都忙公司的事。

    Tā cóng zǎo dào wǎn dōu máng gōngsī de shì.
    She is busy with the company business from morning to night.

8. 大约十公里吧。 **Dàyuē shí gōnglǐ ba. "It's about ten miles, I suppose."**

An important function of 吧 ba is to indicate uncertainty or supposition, as was introduced in Unit 2.2 (Sentence Pattern 6). Another function, learned in Units 6.1 (Sentence Pattern 6) and 8.1 (Sentence Pattern 3), is to signal a suggestion or a piece of advice. In addition to these two functions, 吧 also can be added to a statement to soften the tone, implying the preceding phrase is only an estimate, not a hard fact. In this third usage of 吧, adverbs indicating approximation, such as 大约 dàyuē or 差不多 chàbuduō, are often used together with this particle. Note that the intonation of 吧 varies depending on which of the three usages is intended.

1. 地铁站离这儿很近，走路大概五分钟吧。

   Dìtiězhàn lí zhèr hěn jìn, zǒu lù dàgài wǔ fēn zhōng ba.
   The subway station is very near here, it takes about five minutes to walk there,
   I would guess.

2. 这个花瓶很便宜，差不多一百块钱吧。

   Zhè ge huāpíng hěn piányi, chàbuduō yìbǎi kuài qián ba.
   This vase is very inexpensive; it's about 100 dollars, I think.

3. A: 他们公司有多少员工？
   B: 一共六百人吧。

   A: Tāmen gōngsī yǒu duōshǎo yuángōng?
   B: Yígòng liùbǎi rén ba.

   A: How many employees are there in their company?
   B: Altogether there are about 600, I guess.

4. A: 现在几点了？
   B: 大约九点差一刻吧。

   A: Xiànzài jǐ diǎn le?
   B: Dàyuē jiǔ diǎn chà yí kè ba.

   A: What time is it now?
   B: It's about a quarter to nine (8:45).

9. 叫一辆出租车吧! Jiào yí liàng chūzūchē ba! "Let's call a taxi!"

In Unit 1.1 (Sentence Pattern 3), we learned that 叫 jiào can mean "to call; to be called" when referring to names. In this lesson, the meaning of 叫 is "to call on a person to do a task." We learned that 请 qǐng is a polite form of "asking someone to do something." In this sense, the meaning of 叫 and 请 are the same, though the usages are different: 叫 has a more commanding tone, while 请 is a polite request.

叫

1. 经理叫我准备一份文件，明天开会要用。

    Jīnglǐ jiào wǒ zhǔnbèi yí fèn wénjiàn, míngtiān kāi huì yào yòng.
    The manager asked me to prepare a document to be used for tomorrow's meeting.

2. 请你叫司机等我一会儿。

    Qǐng nǐ jiào sījī děng wǒ yìhuǐr.
    Please ask the driver to wait for me for a while.

请

1. 现在我们请总经理说几句话。

    Xiànzài wǒmen qǐng zǒngjīnglǐ shuō jǐ jù huà.
    Now, we'll ask the general manager to say a few words.

2. 如果有问题的话，可以请他帮忙。

    Rúguǒ yǒu wèntí dehuà, kěyǐ qǐng tā bāng máng.
    If there are problems, you can ask him for help.

Cultural Points

1. Shopping

Travelers in China, whether there for business or for pleasure, will find many shopping destinations for a wide variety of goods. In Beijing, Hongqiao Market is famous for pearls, jewelry, handicrafts, and "knock-off" Western brand name products such as shoes, handbags, backpacks, and luggage items. There is another popular shopping destination in Beijing known as Xiushui Market, 秀水市场 Xiùshuǐ Shìchǎng. This used to be known to foreign travelers as "Silk Alley" and up until recently was a quasi-black market for foreigners wishing to buy bargain fashionable products and Western brand name knock-offs. Backpacks, silks, neckties, t-shirts, blue jeans and other fashion items are plentiful there. An interesting feature of the Xiushui Market is its proximity to one of Beijing's largest Embassy areas. Now, Xiushui Market is a legitimate market that is regulated by the Beijing municipal government.

For travelers to Shanghai, there was a market similar to Beijing's Xiushui Market known as Xiangyang Market, 襄阳市场 Xiāngyáng Shìchǎng. One could expect to find the same motley variety of clothing, jewelry, watches, and cheap knock-offs there as in Beijing. However, on June 30, 2006, this market was shut down by the Chinese government in an effort to control intellectual property rights violations.

Like markets in many developing nations, in most Chinese open air or warehouse-style markets such as Hongqiao it is expected that shoppers will "haggle," or bargain with vendors over the price of their wares. It is advisable for foreign business travelers to learn this skill, as it is very similar to the business negotiations that occur in real business situations in China. Bear in mind, you should always present a lower counter offer to what is first stated by the vendor. However, there is a tendency for some foreign travelers to take advantage of the opportunity of haggling and put too much pressure on vendors to lower the price. Not only can this cause the vendors to lose face, it also puts unnecessary financial strain on merchants who may already be collecting very thin margins on their products. A friendly, polite negotiation style will guarantee a win-win shopping experience.

Additional Vocabulary

	Chinese	Pinyin	Part of Speech	English Equivalent
1.	家具	jiājù	N	furniture
2.	财务	cáiwù	N	finance
3.	联想	Liánxiǎng	PN	Lenovo
4.	一会儿	yíhuìr	TD	a little while
5.	球赛	qiúsài	N	ballgame
6.	送	sòng	V	to send; to take someone somewhere; to see someone off; to give as a gift
7.	旧金山	Jiùjīnshān	PN	San Francisco
8.	路上	lùshang	N	on the road
9.	走路	zǒu lù	VO	to walk; to go on foot
10.	花瓶	huāpíng	N	vase
11.	便宜	piányi	Adj	inexpensive; cheap
12.	块	kuài	M	(a measure word for the basic unit of Chinese currency; the spoken form of "yuán")
13.	元	yuán	M	(a measure word for the basic unit of Chinese currency)
14.	准备	zhǔnbèi	V	to prepare
15.	秀水市场	Xiùshuǐ Shìchǎng	PN	Xiushui Market (in Beijing)
16.	襄阳市场	Xiāngyáng Shìchǎng	PN	Xiangyang Market (in Shanghai)

Unit **11.2**

Gifts for Others

In this lesson we will learn:

- About buying gifts in China.
- How to express decisions on what gifts to buy.
- How to discuss the best location to purchase a particular item.

Chinese Dialogue

高明： 您快回国了，还有什么事需要帮忙吗？

白有天： 我得带一些礼物回美国，上哪儿买比较好呢？

高明： 您需要买什么东西呢？

白有天： 我想买一些中国的工艺品。

高明： 您可以去琉璃厂或者潘家园，那里的商店什么都有。

白有天： 能买到中国字画吗？

高明： 当然，那儿的商店除了字画以外，还有古董。

白有天： 太好了。我明天开完会就去。

Pinyin Dialogue

Gāo Míng: Nín kuài huí guó le, hái yǒu shénme shì xūyào bāng máng ma?

Bái Yǒutiān: Wǒ děi dài yìxiē lǐwù huí Měiguó, shàng nǎr mǎi bǐjiào hǎo ne?

Gāo Míng: Nín xūyào mǎi shénme dōngxi ne?

Bái Yǒutiān: Wǒ xiǎng mǎi yìxiē Zhōngguó de gōngyìpǐn.

Gāo Míng: Nín kěyǐ qù Liúlichǎng huòzhě Pānjiāyuán, nàli de shāngdiàn shénme dōu yǒu.

Bái Yǒutiān: Néng mǎi dào Zhōngguó zìhuà ma?

Gāo Míng: Dāngrán, nàr de shāngdiàn chúle zìhuà yǐwài, hái yǒu gǔdǒng.

Bái Yǒutiān: Tài hǎo le. Wǒ míngtiān kāi wán huì jiù qù.

 # Vocabulary

Chinese	Pinyin	Part of Speech	English Equivalent
1. 得	děi	AV	must; have to
2. 带	dài	V	to take; to bring; to carry
3. 礼物	lǐwù	N	present; gift
4. 工艺品	gōngyìpǐn	N	handicraft article
5. 琉璃厂	Liúlichǎng	PN	name of a place known as the Scholars Market (see Cultural Points in this lesson)
6. 或者	huòzhě	Conj	or (used in statement)
7. 潘家园	Pānjiāyuán	PN	name of a place known as the Dirt Market (see Cultural Points in this lesson)
8. 字画	zìhuà	N	calligraphy and painting
9. 除了......以外	chúle...yǐwài	Conj	besides; in addition to
10. 古董	gǔdǒng	N	antique
11. 完	wán	V	to be finished; to be done

Sentence Patterns

1. 您<u>快</u>回国<u>了</u>。 **Nín <u>kuài</u> huí guó <u>le</u>. "You are going back to your country soon."**

When 快 kuài, literally meaning "fast; quick; soon," is used with 了 le, it implies that an action or event is imminent and will happen soon. For example: 他快来了 Tā kuài lái le "He is coming soon."

快 + V + 了

1. 现在已经五点半了，快下班了。

   Xiànzài yǐjīng wǔ diǎn bàn le, kuài xià bān le.
   It is 5:30 already; we'll be getting off work soon.

2. 快开会了，王经理为什么还没到呢？

   Kuài kāi huì le, Wáng Jīnglǐ wèishénme hái méi dào ne?
   We're going to have a meeting soon. Why hasn't Manager Wang arrived yet?

3. 春节快到了，你有什么计划呢？

   Chūnjié kuài dào le, nǐ yǒu shénme jìhuà ne?
   Spring Festival is coming soon; what plans do you have?

4. 他的太太快生小孩了。

   Tā de tàitai kuài shēng xiǎohái le.
   His wife is going to give birth soon.

2. 还有什么事<u>需要</u>帮忙吗？ **Hái yǒu shénme shì <u>xūyào</u> bāng máng ma? "Is there anything else you need help with?"**

需要 xūyào can be translated into English as "to need to (followed by a verb); to require (followed by a noun)." In certain cases, 需 may be omitted and 要 alone carries the meaning. This usage of 要 is the same as the one described in Unit 6.1 (Sentence Pattern 4).

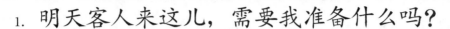

需要

1. 明天客人来这儿，需要我准备什么吗？

   Míngtiān kèrén lái zhèr, xūyào wǒ zhǔnbèi shénme ma?
   Tomorrow the guests are coming here; do you need me to prepare anything?

2. 下周三是小王的生日，我们需要买些礼物吗？

   Xià zhōusān shì Xiǎo Wáng de shēngrì, wǒmen xūyào mǎi xiē lǐwù ma?
   Next Wednesday is Xiao Wang's birthday; do we need to buy some gifts?

3. 这个报告我已经写完了，可是还需要请经理再看一遍。

   Zhè ge bàogào wǒ yǐjīng xiě wán le, kěshì hái xūyào qǐng jīnglǐ zài kàn yí biàn.
   I've already finished writing the report, but I need to ask the manager to review it again.

4. 你需要多长时间做完这个方案？

   Nǐ xūyào duō cháng shíjiān zuò wán zhè ge fāng'àn?
   How long do you need to finish this proposal?

3. 我<u>得</u>带一些礼物回美国。 **Wǒ <u>děi</u> dài yìxiē lǐwù huí Měiguó.**
"I must take some gifts back to the United States."

得 děi is an auxiliary verb used mostly in spoken Chinese in mainland China, and it signifies the notion of "must; need." 得 is mostly interchangeable with 需要 xūyào, as described in the previous sentence pattern. However, 需要 conveys a sense of urgency and necessity that 得 lacks. 需要 can also take a noun as its object, whereas 得 is used only with a verb phrase. The negative form of 得 is 不必 búbì or 不用 búyòng, but never *不得.

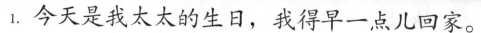
得

1. 今天是我太太的生日，我得早一点儿回家。

   Jīntiān shì wǒ tàitai de shēngrì, wǒ děi zǎo yìdiǎnr huí jiā.
   Today is my wife's birthday; I must go home a little earlier.

2. 这几天太累了，你得多休息。

   Zhè jǐ tiān tài lèi le, nǐ děi duō xiūxi.
   You've been too tired these last few days; you must rest more.

3. 这个问题比较难，我得和大家商量一下。

   Zhè ge wèntí bǐjiào nán, wǒ děi hé dàjiā shāngliang yíxià.
   This issue is rather difficult; I must consult with everybody.

4. 请你先走，我还得问他几个问题。

   Qǐng nǐ xiān zǒu, wǒ hái děi wèn tā jǐ ge wèntí.
   Please, you go first; I still need to ask him a few questions.

4. 上哪儿买<u>比较好呢</u>? **Shàng nǎr mǎi <u>bǐjiào hǎo ne</u>? "Where would be the best place to go?"**

比较好呢 bǐjiào hǎo ne is used at the end of an interrogative sentence to solicit opinions or seek the best option on a proposed course of action. This phrase is used only in questions using interrogative pronouns such as 什么 shénme, 哪 nǎ, 怎么 zěnme and 谁 shéi. While speaking, 比较 can be omitted, as it is understood.

... ... (比较) 好呢

1. 他们快结婚了，我们买什么礼物给他们(比较)好呢？

   Tāmen kuài jié hūn le, wǒmen mǎi shénme lǐwù gěi tāmen (bǐjiào) hǎo ne?
   They are getting married soon; what would be the best gift to buy for them?

2. 明天有两个会要开，时间怎么安排比较好呢？

   Míngtiān yǒu liǎng ge huì yào kāi, shíjiān zěnme ānpái bǐjiào hǎo ne?
   There are two meetings that I need to go to tomorrow; what's the best way to arrange the time?

3. 这个方案怎么写比较好呢？

   Zhè ge fāng'àn zěnme xiě bǐjiào hǎo ne?
   What's the best way to write up this business plan?

5. 您可以去琉璃厂或者潘家园。**Nín kěyǐ qù Liúlichǎng huòzhě Pānjiāyuán. "You can either go to Liúlichǎng or Pānjiāyuán."**

The English word "or" is tricky to translate into Chinese. The Chinese equivalent to "or" can be 还是 háishi or 或者 huòzhě, depending on its meaning in context. In 3.1 (Sentence Pattern 5) we learned that 还是 is used to form a choice-type question asking "X or Y?" In this lesson, 或者" is used in a statement sentence meaning "either X or Y." Note that 或者 cannot be used to form questions; it can only be used in a statement.

1. 您可以坐地铁或者出租车，都差不多一样快。

Nín kěyǐ zuò dìtiě huòzhě chūzūchē, dōu chàbuduō yíyàng kuài.
You may either take the subway or a taxi; they're about the same speed.

2. 明天你来我们公司或者我去宾馆接你，都行。

Míngtiān nǐ lái wǒmen gōngsī huòzhě wǒ qù bīnguǎn jiē nǐ, dōu xíng.
Tomorrow, you could either come to our company or I could pick you up at the hotel; either way is fine.

3. 他对中国工艺品有兴趣的话，您可以买古董或者字画给他。

Tā duì Zhōngguó gōngyìpǐn yǒu xìngqù dehuà, nín kěyǐ mǎi gǔdǒng huòzhě zìhuà gěi tā.
If he is interested in Chinese art, you can buy him either some antiques, or some calligraphy and paintings.

6. 那儿的商店除了字画以外，还有古董。 **Nàr de shāngdiàn chúle zìhuà yǐwài, hái yǒu gǔdǒng. "In addition to Chinese calligraphy and paintings, the shops there also carry antiques."**

除了 chúle means "besides." This 除了 phrase appears before the main clause in a sentence, and is coupled with the adverb 还 hái or 也 yě in the main clause. Together, they convey the idea that, in addition to what has been mentioned, there is still more. Please note, either 除了 or 以外 in this phrase can be omitted. For example:

那儿的商店除了有字画，还有古董。(以外 yǐwài is omitted)

Nàr de shāngdiàn chúle yǒu zìhuà, hái yǒu gǔdǒng.
In addition to calligraphy and paintings, the shops there also have antiques.

那儿的商店卖字画以外，还卖古董。(除了 chúle is omitted)

Nàr de shāngdiàn mài zìhuà yǐwài, hái mài gǔdǒng.
In addition to calligraphy and paintings, the shops there also sell antiques.

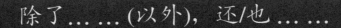

1. 这件事除了总经理，还有谁知道？

    Zhè jiàn shì chúle zǒngjīnglǐ, hái yǒu shéi zhīdào?
    Besides the general manager, who else knows about this matter?

2. 这个问题除了工程师，还要和律师一起讨论。

    Zhè ge wèntí chúle gōngchéngshī, hái yào hé lǜshī yìqǐ tǎolùn.
    In addition to the engineer, the lawyer also needs to be included in discussions concerning this problem.

3. 除了杭州的工厂以外，我们在东莞也有一个分工厂。

    Chúle Hángzhōu de gōngchǎng yǐwài, wǒmen zài Dōngguǎn yě yǒu yí ge fēngōngchǎng.
    In addition to the factory in Hangzhou, we also have a factory in Dongguan.

4. 除了京剧，我也喜欢看话剧。

    Chúle Jīngjù, wǒ yě xǐhuan kàn huàjù.
    Besides Bejing Opera, I also like to see stage plays.

除了......以外 can also be used to express the concept of exclusion, meaning "except." For example: 除了他以外，没有人去过那家饭店 Chúle tā yǐwài, méiyǒu rén qù guò nà jiā fàndiàn "Nobody has been to that restaurant except him" or 除了看电视，他什么事都不做 Chúle kàn diànshì, tā shénme shì dōu bú zuò "He does not do anything except watch TV."

7. 我明天开完会就去。 **Wǒ míngtiān kāi wán huì jiù qù. "I will go tomorrow right after the meeting is over."**

完 wán is a verb meaning "to finish; to be over," e.g., 这个项目快完了 Zhè ge xiàngmù kuài wán le means "This project will soon be over."

完 can also be used as a complement to another verb to indicate a resultative ending. In this instance, it indicates the completion of an action and can be used with many different verbs, such as 吃 chī, 喝 hē, 做 zuò, etc. The object of the verb is usually placed after 完, as in 吃完晚饭 chī wán wǎnfàn; it can also be placed before the verb if the object is to be emphasized. For example: 晚饭吃完了 Wǎnfàn chī wán le.

V + 完

1. 我们上完课就去看电影。

   Wǒmen shàng wán kè jiù qù kàn diànyǐng.
   We'll go to see a movie after we finish classes.

2. 这份报告我一写完就交给你。

   Zhè fèn bàogào wǒ yì xiě wán jiù jiāo gěi nǐ.
   I'll submit the report to you as soon as I finish writing it.

3. 下班以前，如果这个项目做不完，怎么办呢？

   Xià bān yǐqián, rúguǒ zhè ge xiàngmù zuò bu wán, zěnme bàn ne?
   If I cannot finish doing this project before we get off work, what should I do?

4. A: 这个会下午两点以前能开得完吗？
   B: 这个问题很麻烦，大概开不完。

   A: Zhè ge huì xiàwǔ liǎng diǎn yǐqián néng kāi de wán ma?
   B: Zhè ge wèntí hěn máfan, dàgài kāi bu wán.

   A: Are we able to finish this meeting before two o'clock?
   B: The issue is very troublesome; we probably will not be able to finish the meeting (by two o'clock).

5. A: 那本小说你快看完了吗？
   B: 最近比较忙，还没看完。

   A: Nà běn xiǎoshuō nǐ kuài kàn wán le ma?
   B: Zuìjìn bǐjiào máng, hái méi kàn wán.

   A: Will you be able to finish reading the book soon?
   B: I've been rather busy recently; I still haven't finished reading it.

Cultural Points

1. Buying Gifts

Gift buying, whether it is for family members, friends, or colleagues, is another aspect of business trips. Various shopping areas often specialize in different types of goods, so one should be aware of which districts are best suited to one's particular shopping needs. For example, 潘家园 Pānjiāyuán (Dirt Market/Ghost Market) and 琉璃厂 Liúlichǎng (Scholars Market) in Beijing are famous for Chinese fine art and other handicrafts. These are popular destinations for foreign travelers who want to bring gifts back to their home countries. 潘家园 is located in the southeast of Beijing and primarily sells replicas of Chinese antiques. 琉璃厂 is located south of Hepingmen ("Peace Gate") within walking distance of 全聚德 Quánjùdé (Quanjude Peking Duck Restaurant).

Additional Vocabulary

	Chinese	Pinyin	Part of Speech	English Equivalent
1.	春节	Chūnjié	PN	Spring Festival; Chinese New Year
2.	生	shēng	V	to give birth
3.	小孩	xiǎohái	N	child
4.	客人	kèrén	N	guest
5.	生日	shēngrì	N	birthday
6.	方案	fāng'àn	N	proposal; plan
7.	商量	shāngliang	V	to consult with someone; to discuss
8.	工程师	gōngchéngshī	N	engineer
9.	东莞	Dōngguǎn	PN	name of a place in Guangdong
10.	话剧	huàjù	N	stage play
11.	办	bàn	V	to do; to handle; to tackle

UNIT

12

话别
Huàbié
Farewells

Unit **12.1**

Showing Gratitude

In this lesson we will learn:

- About different ways of showing gratitude in Chinese.
- How to say good-bye and show your appreciation to business colleagues at the end of a trip.
- How to express your willingness to come back in the future.

◉ Chinese Dialogue

马经理：	高明告诉我，您后天就要回美国了，是吗？
白有天：	是的，我后天中午就走了。
马经理：	真高兴我们这次合作得这么愉快。
白有天：	我也很高兴，非常感谢您对我的支持。
马经理：	您下次什么时候再来？
白有天：	不一定，得看情况。大概八月吧。
马经理：	希望下次您能带太太和孩子一起来。
白有天：	我也非常希望他们能来中国，我想让孩子有机会多学学中国的文化。
马经理：	那如果八月份能来，我们那个时候北京见！
白有天：	一言为定！

Pinyin Dialogue

Mǎ Jīnglǐ:	Gāo Míng gàosu wǒ, nín hòutiān jiù yào huí Měiguó le, shì ma?
Bái Yǒutiān:	Shì de, wǒ hòutiān zhōngwǔ jiù zǒu le.
Mǎ Jīnglǐ:	Zhēn gāoxìng wǒmen zhè cì hézuò de zhème yúkuài.
Bái Yǒutiān:	Wǒ yě hěn gāoxìng, fēicháng gǎnxiè nín duì wǒ de zhīchí.
Mǎ Jīnglǐ:	Nín xià cì shénme shíhòu zài lái?
Bái Yǒutiān:	Bùyídìng, děi kàn qíngkuàng. Dàgài bāyuè ba.
Mǎ Jīnglǐ:	Xīwàng xià cì nín néng dài tàitai hé háizi yìqǐ lái.
Bái Yǒutiān:	Wǒ yě fēicháng xīwàng tāmen néng lái Zhōngguó, wǒ xiǎng ràng háizi yǒu jīhuì duō xuéxue Zhōngguó de wénhuà.
Mǎ Jīnglǐ:	Nà rúguǒ bāyuèfèn néng lái, wǒmen nà ge shíhou Běijīng jiàn!
Bái Yǒutiān:	Yìyán wéidìng!

Vocabulary

Chinese	Pinyin	Part of Speech	English Equivalent
1. 话别	huà bié	VO N	to say good-bye good-byes
2 告诉	gàosu	V	to tell
3. 后天	hòutiān	TW	the day after tomorrow
4. 中午	zhōngwǔ	TW	noon; midday
5. 真	zhēn	Adv	truly; really
6. 合作	hézuò	V N	to cooperate cooperation; collaboration
7. 这么	zhème	Adv	so; such; like this
8. 愉快	yúkuài	Adj	happy; joyful; cheerful
9. 感谢	gǎnxiè	V N	to thank; to be grateful thanks
10. 支持	zhīchí	N V	support to support
11. 下次	xià cì	TW	next time
12. 不一定	bùyídìng	UE	not for sure
13. 情况	qíngkuàng	N	situation; condition
14. 希望	xīwàng	V	to hope; to wish; to expect
15. 让	ràng	V	to let; to allow; to make
16. 文化	wénhuà	N	culture
17. 月份	yuèfèn	N	month
18. 份	fèn	N	portion (of a larger whole)
19. 一言为定	yìyán wéidìng	UE	it's a deal; that's settled then

Sentence Patterns

1. 您<u>后天</u><u>就要</u>回美国<u>了</u>。Nín <u>hòutiān</u> <u>jiù yào</u> huí Měiguó <u>le</u>.
"You are going back to the United States the day after tomorrow."

The pattern 要 yào + V + 了 is basically the same as 快 kuài + V + 了, which was introduced in 11.2 (Sentence Pattern 1). Both are used to signal imminent action. The main difference between these two patterns is that 要 + V + 了 is typically used in conjunction with a specific time expression, while 快 + V + 了 is not. 就 can be added before the 要 + V + 了 construction to show an even greater sense of imminence.

(就)要 + V + 了

1. 我们要下班了，我明天上午再帮您联系。

   Wǒmen yào xià bān le, wǒ míngtiān shàngwǔ zài bāng nín liánxì.
   We'll soon be off work; I'll help you get in touch tomorrow morning.

2. 你快准备一下，客户马上就要来参观我们的公司了。

   Nǐ kuài zhǔnbèi yíxià, kèhù mǎshàng jiù yào lái cānguān wǒmen de gōngsī le.
   Hurry up and get ready; the clients will be coming to visit our company soon.

3. 我们谈得很顺利，下周就要签合同了。

   Wǒmen tán de hěn shùnlì, xià zhōu jiù yào qiān hétong le.
   Our talks are going very smoothly; we are about to sign the contract next week.

4. 今天下午就要开会讨论了，可是我的报告还没有写完，怎么办呢?

   Jīntiān xiàwǔ jiù yào kāi huì tǎolùn le, kěshì wǒ de bàogào hái méiyǒu xiě wán, zěnme bàn ne?
   We're just about to have the meeting this afternoon, but I haven't finished writing my report. What should I do?

---

2. 非常感谢您对我的支持。 **Fēicháng gǎnxiè nín <u>duì</u> wǒ de zhīchí.**
"**I very much appreciate your support.**"

对 duì was previously introduced in Unit 7.2 (Sentence Pattern 1) as a preposition to show one's attitude towards something. For example: 经理对这个项目非常关心 Jīnglǐ duì zhè ge xiàngmù fēicháng guān xīn "The manager is very concerned about this project." In this lesson, 对 is also used as a preposition to show the direction of an action towards another person. In this sense, 对 is like the word "to," "towards," or "for." See the following examples:

对

1. 他对同事一直都很客气。

   Tā duì tóngshì yìzhí dōu hěn kèqi.
   He is always polite to his colleagues.

2. 他对我们的帮助很大，我们应该感谢他。

   Tā duì wǒmen de bāngzhù hěn dà, wǒmen yīnggāi gǎnxiè tā.
   He is very helpful to us; we should be grateful to him.

3. 我对我们的合作很有信心。

   Wǒ duì wǒmen de hézuò hěn yǒu xìnxīn.
   I am very confident about our collaboration.

3. 得<u>看</u>情况。 **Děi <u>kàn</u> qíngkuàng. "It depends on the situation."**

In Unit 6.2 (Sentence Pattern 5) we learned that 看 kàn is added to a reduplicated verb to convey the idea of "doing something and seeing what happens." In this lesson, 看 is also used to express the idea of "to see." 得看情况 literally means "(I) have to see the situation."

看 can also be used to express one's opinion. The subject of the sentence is usually either 我 or 我们, and the sentence generally conveys one's opinion or judgment, which is based on observation. In an interrogative sentence involving this usage of 看, the subject is usually 你. For example: 你看他的表现怎么样 Nǐ kàn tā de biǎoxiàn zěnmeyàng "What do you think of his performance?" 看 can have many different usages depending on the context. Below are examples of the various usages of the word 看.

看 *"Opinion"*

1. 我看明天会很热。

   Wǒ kàn míngtiān huì hěn rè.
   It seems to me that tomorrow will be hot.

2. 我看他的表现很不错。

   Wǒ kàn tā de biǎoxiàn hěn búcuò.
   I think/In my opinion his performance is pretty good.

3. 我看他很能干，你看呢?

   Wǒ kàn tā hěn nénggàn, nǐ kàn ne?
   (To me) he appears to be very capable; what do you think?

4. 我们合作得这么顺利，我看这个项目下个月
   就可以做完。

   Wǒmen hézuò de zhème shùnlì, wǒ kàn zhè ge xiàngmù xià ge yuè jiù kěyǐ zuò wán.
   Our collaboration has been going so well, I believe this project can be completed
   next month.

看 *"to See; to Read; to Watch"*

1. 他正在看电视。

   Tā zhèngzài kàn diànshì.
   He is in the middle of watching TV.

2. 她一直很喜欢看小说。

   Tā yìzhí hěn xǐhuan kàn xiǎoshuō.
   She has always liked to read novels.

3. 我一有时间就来看您。

Wǒ yì yǒu shíjiān jiù lái kàn nín.
I'll come to see you as soon as I have time.

4. 因为我们工作太忙，我们请了一个阿姨帮我们看小孩。

Yīnwèi wǒmen gōngzuò tài máng, wǒmen qǐng le yí ge āyí bāng wǒmen kān xiǎohái.

(Please note that 看 is pronounced in the first tone here.)
Because we're so busy with work, we hire a nanny to watch the kids for us.

5. 如果第一次做得不好，我们可以再试试看。

Rúguǒ dì yí cì zuò de bù hǎo, wǒmen kěyǐ zài shìshi kàn.
If we don't do well the first time, we can try again and see.

4. 希望下次您能<u>带</u>太太和孩子一起来。 **Xīwàng xià cì nín néng <u>dài</u> tàitai hé háizi yìqǐ lái. "I hope that next time you can bring your wife and children with you."**

带 dài means to carry something or someone with oneself. 带 can further be used with the directional complement 来 to signify "to bring" or 去 "to take," as in 是谁带你们来这儿的 Shì shéi dài nǐmen lái zhèr de "Who brought you here?"

带

1. 我刚好也要去天坛，我带你们一起去吧。

Wǒ gānghǎo yě yào qù Tiāntán, wǒ dài nǐmen yìqǐ qù ba.
I also happen to want to go to the Temple of Heaven; how about I take you along?

2. 我需要去超市买些东西，你能带我去吗?

Wǒ xūyào qù chāoshì mǎi xiē dōngxi, nǐ néng dài wǒ qù ma?
I need to go to the supermarket to buy some things; could you take me there?

3. 今天要是没有别的安排，我带你们出去轻松一下。

   Jīntiān yàoshi méiyǒu biéde ānpái, wǒ dài nǐmen chūqu qīngsōng yíxià.
   If you do not have any other arrangements today, I'll take you out to relax a little.

4. 坐飞机可以带几件行李？

   Zuò fēijī kěyǐ dài jǐ jiàn xíngli?
   How many pieces of luggage can one take when flying?

5. 我想让孩子有机会多学学中国的文化。 **Wǒ xiǎng ràng háizi yǒu jīhuì duō xuéxue Zhōngguó de wénhuà. "I want to let my children have opportunities to learn more about Chinese culture."**

让 ràng has many different uses. Below are examples of several usages of 让.

The basic meaning of 让 is "to let," which is used in imperative sentences to express a suggestion or request. For example: 让他走 Ràng tā zǒu "Let him go."

让 "to Let"

1. 他最近太累了，让他休息几天吧。

   Tā zuìjìn tài lèi le, ràng tā xiūxi jǐ tiān ba.
   He has been too tired lately; let him rest for a few days.

2. 看他有什么意见，让他说说看。

   Kàn tā yǒu shénme yìjiàn, ràng tā shuōshuo kàn.
   Let's see what his opinions are; let him speak up.

3. 让我先想想，我们再讨论。

   Ràng wǒ xiān xiǎngxiang, wǒmen zài tǎolùn.
   Let me think about it first; then we'll discuss it.

4. 对不起，让你久等了。

   Duìbuqǐ, ràng nǐ jiǔ děng le.
   Sorry to make (let) you wait for so long.

让 can also be used in the sense of "to ask someone to perform a task." The meaning is the same as 请 qǐng and 叫 jiào, as explained in Unit 11.1 (Sentence Pattern 9). However, as explained in that lesson, 请 is used to make a request of someone who is your superior and it conveys respect, whereas 让 and 叫 are used in a more imperative tone with subordinates.

让 "to Ask"

1. 总经理让我们介绍一下分公司的情况。

   Zǒngjīnglǐ ràng wǒmen jièshào yíxià fēngōngsī de qíngkuàng.
   The general manager asked us to brief you on the branch's situation.

2. 我们自己去机场吧，你不要让他送我们。

   Wǒmen zìjǐ qù jīchǎng ba, nǐ búyào ràng tā sòng wǒmen.
   We'll go to the airport ourselves; don't ask him to take us there.

3. 这件礼物是张总让我带给您的。

   Zhè jiàn lǐwù shì Zhāng Zǒng ràng wǒ dài gěi nín de.
   President Zhang asked me to bring this gift to you.

让 can also mean "to allow" or "to permit." It is often used in its negative form to indicate prohibition.

让 "to Permit"

1. 这个路口不让左拐，我们下个路口再拐。

   Zhè ge lùkǒu bú ràng zuǒ guǎi, wǒmen xià ge lùkǒu zài guǎi.
   This intersection doesn't permit left turns; we'll turn at the next intersection.

2. 公司不让迟到早退。

   Gōngsī bú ràng chídào zǎotuì.
   The company doesn't allow us to come in late and leave early.

3. 会议室让抽烟吗？

   Huìyìshì ràng chōu yān ma?
   Are we permitted to smoke in the meeting room?

Cultural Points

1. Returning to China

The opportunities for Western managers (i.e., expatriates) of foreign corporations to live and work full-time in China are many. This remains true even as cities such as Shanghai and Beijing are attracting less expatriates than before, because of the increasing competency of local talent and the high expense of foreign expatriates. Higher-level managers and engineers are the dominant professionals working as expatriates in China. It should be noted that it is now more common for a Chinese national to be a branch manager in charge of an office of a foreign enterprise in China. These local managers may be responsible to yet higher levels of management in the company. The foreign upper management often supervises and inspects the activities of many single offices on a rotating basis. This makes it necessary for foreign managers to travel frequently to multiple offices in China to briefly oversee operations (the normal duration may now just be a matter of days or weeks), thus they must constantly be preparing for their next trip to China.

2. Referring to Someone as 阿姨 āyí "Aunt"

阿姨 literally means "mother's sister" and thus "aunt," but is also commonly used to refer to nannies, housekeepers, and female family friends (usually in the same age group as parents). It is a common practice for many expatriates and native Chinese alike to hire housekeepers, nannies, and drivers to help them with household duties. Usually these services require only modest compensation. So, using 阿姨 to refer to female helpers is an affectionate way of expressing the feeling that they are almost like part of the family.

Additional Vocabulary

Chinese	Pinyin	Part of Speech	English Equivalent
1. 顺利	shùnlì	Adj	smooth
2. 签	qiān	V	to sign
3. 合同	hétong	N	contract
4. 关心	guān xīn	VO	to care for or about, to be concerned with
		N	concern
5. 帮助	bāngzhù	N	help
		V	to help
6. 表现	biǎoxiàn	N	performance
		V	to manifest
7. 不错	búcuò	Adj	not bad; pretty good
8. 能干	nénggàn	Adj	capable
9. 阿姨	āyí	N	nanny; housekeeper; aunt; female family friends close to one's parents' age
10. 超市	chāoshì	N	supermarket
11. 别的	biéde	Adj	other
12. 行李	xíngli	N	luggage
13. 自己	zìjǐ	Pr	oneself
14. 早退	zǎotuì	V	to leave early
15. 抽烟	chōu yān	VO	to smoke

Unit **12.2**

Good-byes and Future Plans

In this lesson we will learn:

- About proper etiquette when saying good-bye.

- How to entrust business colleagues with responsibilities in order to show confidence in their abilities.

- How to reassure business contacts that you'll keep in touch after leaving.

Chinese Dialogue

高明：　明天早上我开车送您去机场。

白有天：太感谢您了。

高明：　您的行李都收拾好了吗？

白有天：还没呢，今天晚上吃完饭再收拾，还来得及。

白有天：您回去以后，我一定会经常和您联系的。

白有天：谢谢。我不在的时候，公司的业务就请您多费心了。

高明：　您放心吧，我一定会努力的。

Pinyin Dialogue

Gāomíng: Míngtiān zǎoshang wǒ kāi chē sòng nín qù jīchǎng.

Bái Yǒutiān: Tài gǎnxiè nín le.

Gāomíng: Nín de xíngli dōu shōushi hǎo le ma?

Bái Yǒutiān: Hái méi ne, jīntiān wǎnshang chī wán fàn zài shōushi, hái lái de jí.

Gāomíng: Nín huíqu yǐhòu, wǒ yídìng huì jīngcháng hé nín liánxì de.

Bái Yǒutiān: Xièxie. Wǒ bú zài de shíhou, gōngsī de yèwù jiù qǐng nín duō fèi xīn le.

Gāomíng: Nín fàng xīn ba, wǒ yídìng huì nǔlì de.

Vocabulary

Chinese	Pinyin	Part of Speech	English Equivalent
1. 收拾	shōushi	V	to pack
2. 来得及	lái de jí	V	to be able to do something in time
3. ……的时候	…de shíhou	Conj.	when…; while…; at the time of…
4. 业务	yèwù	N	business; professional work
5. 费心	fèi xīn	VO	to exert one's heart/mind (polite expression used when asking for help)
6. 放心	fàng xīn	VO	to be at ease; to set one's mind at rest

Sentence Patterns

1. 明天早上我开车<u>送</u>您去机场。**Míngtiān zǎoshang wǒ kāi chē <u>sòng</u> nín qù jīchǎng. "I will drive you to the airport tomorrow morning."**

The verb 送 sòng has various meanings depending on the context. In the following examples, it means "to take or to escort someone someplace; to see someone off." It is the antonym of 接 jiē, which was introduced in Unit 8.1. Another meaning of 送 is "to give something to someone as a gift." Below are examples of each usage.

送 "to Escort"

1. 太晚了，我让司机送您回去吧。

   Tài wǎn le, wǒ ràng sījī sòng nín huíqu ba.
   It's too late; I'll have the driver take you back.

2. 你要是能送我去车站的话，我就不必打的了。

   Nǐ yàoshi néng sòng wǒ qù chēzhàn dehuà, wǒ jiù búbì dǎ dī le.
   If you can take me to the station, then I won't have to take a cab.

3. 白先生明天就要回美国了，谁去机场送他呢？

   Bái Xiānsheng míngtiān jiù yào huí Měiguó le, shéi qù jīchǎng sòng tā ne?
   Mr. Bai is returning to the United States tomorrow. Who is going to the airport to see him off?

送 "to Give as a Gift"

1. 中国人结婚，朋友们是送钱还是送礼物呢？

   Zhōngguórén jié hūn, péngyoumen shì sòng qián háishi sòng lǐwù ne?
   When Chinese people get married, do their friends give them money or do they give gifts?

2. 他的太太快生小孩了，我们送什么礼物比较好呢？

   Tā de tàitai kuài shēng xiǎohái le, wǒmen sòng shénme lǐwù bǐjiào hǎo ne?
   His wife is having a baby soon; what gift should we give?

3. 新年的时候，我们公司会送红包给员工。

   Xīnnián de shíhou, wǒmen gōngsī huì sòng hóngbāo gěi yuángōng.
   During the Chinese New Year, our company will give the employees "red envelopes."

2. 您的行李都收拾<u>好了</u>吗? **Nín de xíngli dōu shōushi <u>hǎo le</u> ma?**
"Have you finished all your packing?"

The 好 hǎo in a V + 好了 hǎo le construction indicates the satisfactory completion of an action. The usage and sentence structure is similar to V + 完 wán, which was explained in Unit 11.2 (Sentence Pattern 7). However, the difference between V + 好了 and V + 完了 is that the pattern V + 好了 also implies that there is continuity in the completion of the action, signifying readiness for another action. The typical example is: 晚饭做好了, 我们吃吧 Wǎnfàn zuò hǎo le, wǒmen chī ba. "Dinner is ready—let's eat." The negative form of V + 好了 is 还没 hái méi V + 好. Please note that if 了 is used in the question, then it must be dropped in a negative response.

V + 好了

1. 财务报告我已经写好了, 你现在看吗?

   Cáiwù bàogào wǒ yǐjīng xiě hǎo le, nǐ xiànzài kàn ma?
   I have finished writing the financial report; do you want to read it now?

2. 计划都安排好了, 我们上午听报告, 下午开会讨论。

   Jìhuà dōu ānpái hǎo le, wǒmen shàngwǔ tīng bàogào, xiàwǔ kāi huì tǎolùn.
   The plans are all set; we'll listen to the report in the morning, and we'll meet to discuss it in the afternoon.

3. A: 文件都准备好了吗?
   B: 还没准备好, 正在准备。

   A: Wénjiàn dōu zhǔnbèi hǎo le ma?
   B: Hái méi zhǔnbèi hǎo, zhèngzài zhǔnbèi.

   A: Have you finished preparing the documents?
   B: They are not ready yet; I'm getting them ready right now.

---

3. 还来得及。 **Hái lái de jí. "There is still enough time."**

来得及 lái de jí is a resultative verb, meaning "there is still enough time to do something." For example: 你现在马上走, 还来得及 Nǐ xiànzài mǎshàng zǒu, hái lái de jí "If you leave right away, you can still make it." The negative form is 来不及, and it means "there is not enough time to do something; will not make it in time."

来得及/来不及

1. 我下午三点送你去机场，来得及吗？

   Wǒ xiàwǔ sān diǎn sòng nǐ qù jīchǎng, lái de jí ma?
   I'll take you to the airport at 3:00 p.m. Is that enough time?

2. 能快点吗？我上班来不及了。

   Néng kuài diǎn ma? Wǒ shàngbān lái bu jí le.
   Can you go a little faster? I'm late for work.

3. 我来不及自己去买礼物，你能不能帮我去琉璃厂
   买一幅中国画？

   Wǒ lái bu jí zìjǐ qù mǎi lǐwù, nǐ néng bù néng bāng wǒ qù Liúlichǎng
   mǎi yì fú Zhōngguó huà?
   I don't have the time to go buy a gift myself; can you help me by going to Liulichang
   to buy a Chinese painting?

4. 我不在的时候, … **Wǒ bú zài de shíhou, … "While I'm not here…"**

Like 以前 yǐqián "before" and 以后 yǐhòu "after," 的时候 de shíhou is used at the end of a phrase or clause to provide a time reference for an action, meaning "while; during." 正在 zhèngzài, which indicates an ongoing action and which we learned in Unit 9.1 (Sentence Pattern 2), will frequently be used in conjunction with a 的时候 clause.

1. 你进来的时候，我正在打电话。

   Nǐ jìnlai de shíhou, wǒ zhèngzài dǎ diànhuà.
   I was on the phone when you came in.

2. 生病的时候，要多喝水，多注意休息。

   Shēng bìng de shíhou, yào duō hē shuǐ, duō zhùyì xiūxi.
   When you're sick, you should drink more water and get more rest.

3. 我跟我太太是在上大学的时候认识的。

   Wǒ gēn wǒ tàitai shì zài shàng dàxué de shíhou rènshi de.
   It was when we studied in the University that my wife and I got to know each other.

4. 你打电话来的时候，我正在看你的报告。

   Nǐ dǎ diànhuà lái de shíhou, wǒ zhèngzài kàn nǐ de bàogào.
   When your call came in, I was in the middle of reading your report.

5. 我一定会经常和您联系<u>的</u>。 **Wǒ yídìng huì jīngcháng hé nín liánxì <u>de</u>. "I will certainly be in touch with you often."**

We learned in Unit 2.1 (Sentence Patterns 2 & 4) that 的, a particle, can function as a possessive or descriptive marker when placed between a modifier and a noun. In this lesson we are going to learn that when 的 is placed at the end of a statement, it expresses certainty. When spoken by a subordinate, this function becomes one of signifying reassurance.

1. 这种手机谁都会喜欢的。

   Zhè zhǒng shǒujī shéi dōu huì xǐhuan de.
   I'm sure everybody will like this kind of cell phone.

2. 你帮她这么多忙，她一定会感谢你的。

   Nǐ bāng tā zhème duō máng, tā yídìng huì gǎnxiè nǐ de.
   You've helped her so much; I know she will definitely appreciate it.

3. 这件事这么重要，你应该先问他的。

   Zhè jiàn shì zhème zhòngyào, nǐ yīnggāi xiān wèn tā de.
   This matter is so important, you should ask him first.

4. 我们保持联系，以后还有机会见面的。

   Wǒmen bǎochí liánxì, yǐhòu hái yǒu jīhuì jiàn miàn de.
   We'll stay in touch; I'm sure we'll have opportunities to meet again.

Cultural Points

1. Etiquette when Preparing for Departure

When preparing to leave and return to your home country, talking about the next possible trip is important to facilitate the building of long-term relationships. As the departure time nears, it is necessary to talk about keeping in touch after leaving and offering the promise of return trips in the future. Chinese contacts and colleagues should be reassured that they will be entrusted with the company's responsibilities after you leave. This is a way of demonstrating respect for and confidence in their abilities.

2. 公司的业务就请您多费心了。 **Gōngsī de yèwù jiù qǐng nín duō fèi xīn le.**

The expression of 请您多费心了 Qǐng nín duō fèi xīn le or 让您多费心了 Ràng nín duō fèi xīn le could be directly translated as "Please take the trouble to (help me do something)" or "Sorry to make you go to the trouble (of helping me do something)." However, the best, most culturally appropriate translations of these expressions may be "I would really appreciate it if you could (help me do something)" or "I really appreciate your (helping me do something)." The difficulty in finding equivalent translations stems from the differences in cultural values. Traditionally, Chinese culture has the characteristic of "interdependency" in which people within the same circle tend to rely upon one another. Western culture, on the other hand, tends to place more value on independence, self-reliance, and individual responsibility. It should be noted that as the Chinese economy is becoming more developed, people are becoming more individualistic, although this expression is still commonly used.

3. 红包 **Hóngbāo "Red Envelopes"**

For Chinese people and other Asians, the 红包 hóngbāo or "Red Envelope" is a common way to give monetary gifts on special occasions and, increasingly, in business settings. The Red Envelope (or Red Packet) is a very old gift-giving tradition in China and in many parts of Asia that have been influenced by Chinese culture. The overseas Chinese diaspora continues the tradition of giving gifts through the use of the Red Envelope. The red color of the envelope symbolizes good fortune. In Cantonese, the Red Envelope is known as 利是 "Lai Si."

The Red Envelope was originally used to give gifts of money during Chinese New Year. This tradition is also known as 压岁钱 yāsuìqián. This practice involves parents, grandparents, and other senior relatives (usually married) giving money to children and other younger, single relatives. Upon receiving the Red Envelope, the recipient normally utters an auspicious saying or a saying of gratitude.

Red Envelopes are also presented at weddings, on birthdays, to newborn babies, on other holidays (for some, this might include Christmas) and on other special occasions. Businesspeople now often use Red Envelopes to give gifts to clients, partners, and the like. Red Envelopes are also the most common method by which political bribes are transmitted.

Additional Vocabulary

	Chinese	Pinyin	Part of Speech	English Equivalent
1.	打的	dǎ dī	VO	to take a cab
2.	新年	xīnnián	N	New Year
3.	红包	hóngbāo	N	red envelope
4.	幅	fú	M	(a measure word for paintings)
5.	生病	shēng bìng	VO	to get sick
6.	注意	zhùyì	V	to pay attention to
7.	保持	bǎochí	V	to keep
8.	压岁钱	yāsuìqián	N	money given as a gift to children during the Chinese New Year

English Translations of the Dialogues

Unit 1 Greetings

1.1 Exchanging Names

Gao Ming:	How do you do!
Bai Youtian:	How do you do!
Gao Ming:	What's your surname?
Bai Youtian:	My surname is Bai.
Gao Ming:	What's your (full) name?
Bai Youtian:	My name is Bai Youtian. And you?
Gao Ming:	My surname is Gao. My (full) name is Gao Ming.
Bai Youtian:	Mr. Gao, I am very happy to meet you.
Gao Ming:	I am very happy to meet you too, Mr. Bai.

1.2 Exchanging Greetings

Bai Youtian:	Good morning!
Gao Ming:	Good morning!
Bai Youtian:	Mr. Gao, are you busy today?
Gao Ming:	I am busy today.
Bai Youtian:	How about tomorrow? Are you busy tomorrow?
Gao Ming:	Tomorrow I won't be busy. How about you?
Bai Youtian:	Tomorrow I won't be busy, either.
Gao Ming:	Then we will meet tomorrow!
Bai Youtian:	Fine, goodbye!

Unit 2 Introductions

2.1 Meeting the Company Manager

Gao Ming:	This is Manager Ma.
Bai Youtian:	How do you do, Manager Ma. I'm glad to see you.
Gao Ming:	This is Mr. Bai from our American company.
Ma Jingli:	Welcome to China, Mr. Bai.
Bai Youtian:	Mr. Ma, are you from Beijing?
Ma Jingli:	No, I am from Shanghai.
Bai Youtian:	My wife is also Shanghainese. Shanghai is a very nice place.
Ma Jingli:	Mr. Bai, your Chinese is very good.
Bai Youtian:	You're too kind.

2.2 Getting to Know the Company Staff

Bai Youtian:	Excuse me, who is Linda?
Gao Ming:	She is the manager of Human Resources.
Bai Youtian:	What country is she from?
Gao Ming:	She is American.
Bai Youtian:	Can she speak Chinese?
Gao Ming:	She can speak a little.
Bai Youtian:	Who is that lady?
Gao Ming:	She is the company's secretary, Ms. Wang Ying.
Bai Youtian:	She can speak English, right?
Gao Ming:	Yes, she speaks English very well.

Unit 3 Family

3.1 Marital Status and Family

Gao Ming:	Mr. Bai, are you married?
Bai Youtian:	Yes, I am married.
Gao Ming:	Do you have any children?
Bai Youtian:	Yes.
Gao Ming:	How many?
Bai Youtian:	Two.
Gao Ming:	Boys or girls?
Bai Youtian:	One boy and one girl.
Gao Ming:	How old are they now?
Bai Youtian:	My son is twelve and is a middle school student. My daughter is eight and is in primary school.
Gao Ming:	Will they come to China?
Bai Youtian:	Yes, they will come to China next year.

3.2 Family Members and Relatives

Bai Youtian:	Are your mother and father in good health?
Gao Ming:	They are both fine. They are both retired.
Bai Youtian:	How old are your parents?
Gao Ming:	My father is sixty-three and my mother is fifty-nine.
Bai Youtian:	Do you have siblings?
Gao Ming:	Yes I do. I have an older brother and a younger sister.
Bai Youtian:	What do they do?
Gao Ming:	My older brother is doing business and my younger sister is still a student.
Bai Youtian:	What kind of business does your brother do?
Gao Ming:	He does import and export business.

Unit 4 The Company

4.1 Company Type

Lin Xiǎojie:	I heard your company is a computer company.
Bai Youtian:	Yes, it's a computer company.

Lin Xiǎojie:	Is it a wholly owned enterprise?
Bai Youtian:	No, it's a Sino-US joint venture.
Lin Xiǎojie:	Where is the company's headquarters located?
Bai Youtian:	In Beijing.
Lin Xiǎojie:	How many branch offices do you have in China?
Bai Youtian:	There are three. One is in Shanghai, one is in Guangzhou and another is in Shenzhen.

Unit 4.2 Company Size

Lin Xiǎojie:	How many people are there in your company?
Bai Youtian:	There are approximately one hundred and fifty people.
Lin Xiǎojie:	Are they all Chinese?
Bai Youtian:	No, some are Chinese, and some are foreigners.
Lin Xiǎojie:	Are there more Chinese or more foreigners?
Bai Youtian:	There are more Chinese than foreigners.
Lin Xiǎojie:	Is your company as big as Fangzheng Company?
Bai Youtian:	No, Fangzheng Company is much bigger than we are.

Unit 5 Inquiries

5.1 Inquiring about Someone's Whereabouts

Bai Youtian:	Is Manager Ma in?
Wang Ying:	He's not in. He went to the Computer City.
Bai Youtian:	Will Manager Ma come back to the office this afternoon?
Wang Ying:	Sorry, I'm not sure.
Bai Youtian:	May I go there to find him?
Wang Ying:	Of course you may.
Bai Youtian:	Where is the Computer City?
Wang Ying:	It's located in Zhongguancun.
Bai Youtian:	Is Zhongguancun far from here?
Wang Ying:	Not too far, It's very close. It's only three kilometers (from here).

5.2 Inquiring after Someone's Profession

Bai Youtian:	Miss Lin, where do you work?
Lin Xiǎojie:	I work at the Bank of China.
Bai Youtian:	What time do you go to work?
Lin Xiǎojie:	We go to work at 9:00 a.m., and leave work at 5:30 p.m.
Bai Youtian:	What time is it now?
Lin Xiǎojie:	It's now a quarter after nine.
Bai Youtian:	Then why haven't you gone to work yet?
Lin Xiǎojie:	Today is Saturday. We have weekends off.

Unit 6 Making Appointments

6.1 Setting up an Appointment

Bai Youtian:	Xiao Wang, could you help me contact Fangzheng Company?
Wang Ying:	Do you mean Fangzheng Computer Company?
Bai Youtian:	Yes.
Wang Ying:	Who are you looking for?
Bai Youtian:	I want to meet with Manager Zhang from the marketing department.
Wang Ying:	When?
Bai Youtian:	Next Monday.
Wang Ying:	Next Monday is June 3. You have meetings all day.
Bai Youtian:	Then make it Tuesday.
Wang Ying:	Okay, I will contact him immediately.

6.2 Rescheduling an Appointment

Bai Youtian:	Xiao Wang, did you give Fangzheng Company a call?
Wang Ying:	I called, but Manager Zhang left for a business trip.
Bai Youtian:	Do you know when he will be back?
Wang Ying:	He won't be back until next Wednesday.
Bai Youtian:	Then can we arrange to meet next Thursday?
Wang Ying:	I will see what I can do. What time next Thursday is convenient for you?
Bai Youtian:	Two-thirty in the afternoon.
Wang Ying:	Okay, I will give his secretary a call right now.

Unit 7 Visiting

7.1 Visiting a Company for the First Time

Bai Youtian:	Hello, I am Bai Youtian, the manager of Blue Star Computer Company.
Zhang Guoqiang:	Hello, Manager Bai. My name is Zhang Guoqiang. Welcome to Fangzheng Company.
Bai Youtian:	Thank you. Manager Zhang, this is my business card.
Zhang Guoqiang:	This is my business card. Please instruct me in many areas.* Please have a seat.
Bai Youtian:	Manager Zhang, I hear that you just came back from a business trip.
Zhang Guoqiang:	Yes, I just came back from Sichuan the day before yesterday. I'm sorry I couldn't meet with you last week.
Bai Youtian:	Not a problem. I know you are busy.
Zhang Guoqiang:	Is this your first trip to China?
Bai Youtian:	No, I come (here) often. I come two or three times a year.
Zhang Guoqiang:	How long will you stay this time?
Bai Youtian:	About a month.

*See Lesson 7.1 Cultural Point 2.

7.2 Introducing Products and Plants

Bai Youtian:	I am here to introduce our new product.
Zhang Guoqiang:	Great. We are very interested in your product.
Bai Youtian:	This type of product was produced at our factory in Jiangsu.

Zhang Guoqiang:	Really? Which city in Jiangsu?
Bai Youtian:	In Suzhou. We built a branch factory there.
Zhang Guoqiang:	When was it built?
Bai Youtian:	It was built last year.
Zhang Guoqiang:	How many employees are there?
Bai Youtian:	Altogether there are 1,300 people.
Zhang Guoqiang:	That's quite a lot!
Bai Youtian:	It's a fair amount. If you have time, you are welcome to tour our factory.
Zhang Guoqiang:	Thank you. If I have the chance, I certainly will come.

Unit 8 Dining

8.1 Dining Invitations

Zhang Guoqiang:	Mr. Bai, I would like to invite you for dinner tonight.
Bai Youtian:	Thank you. You are too kind!
Zhang Guoqiang:	Have you ever had Peking duck?
Bai Youtian:	I have never had it. But I heard Peking duck is Beijing's signature dish.
Zhang Guoqiang:	That's right. Then let's go to Quanjude for Peking duck. Which hotel are you staying at?
Bai Youtian:	I'm staying at Wangfu Hotel.
Zhang Guoqiang:	I'll go to the hotel to pick you up tonight at 6:00. Is that all right?
Bai Youtian:	All right, I will be waiting for you in the hotel lobby.

8.2 Dining Etiquette

Zhang Guoqiang:	Mr. Bai, what would you like to drink?
Bai Youtian:	I'm flexible. Anything is fine.
Zhang Guoqiang:	Would you like to try Chinese Maotai?
Bai Youtian:	Chinese liquor is very strong. I'm afraid that I will get drunk!
Zhang Guoqiang:	In that case, we will drink beer, OK?
Bai Youtian:	OK.
Zhang Guoqiang:	Do you like Tsingtao or Yanjing beer?
Bai Youtian:	Tsingtao beer. What is this dish?
Zhang Guoqiang:	This is Kung Pao Chicken. Is it too spicy?
Bai Youtian:	No, no, I can take spicy food.
Zhang Guoqiang:	In that case, have some more. Don't be shy.

Unit 9 Social Events

9.1 Nightlife

Gao Ming:	Sorry to disturb you. Are you busy now?
Bai Youtian:	Please come in. I'm reading a report.
Gao Ming:	Do you already have plans for tonight?
Bai Youtian:	Not yet. Do you have something in mind?
Gao Ming:	I made plans with a few friends to go out to a bar. Why don't you come with us?
Bai Youtian:	Great! I hear that Houhai has a few new bars. I've always wanted to go to see them.
Gao Ming:	That's exactly where we are planning to go.
Bai Youtian:	Great! Which one?

| Gao Ming: | Let's make a decision after we get there. |
| Bai Youtian: | Good. We will leave as soon as we get off work. |

9.2 Cultural Events

Gao Ming:	You've been constantly busy since coming to China. How about we go out tomorrow night to relax a little?
Bai Youtian:	Great idea! Do you have any suggestions?
Gao Ming:	Would you prefer drinking tea or seeing a performance?
Bai Youtian:	I would prefer to see a performance. What shows are there?
Gao Ming:	There is Beijing Opera as well as acrobatics.
Bai Youtian:	Although Beijing Opera is interesting, I'm afraid I will not be able to understand it.
Gao Ming:	In that case, if we are able to buy tickets for acrobatics, then we'll go to the National Theater to see acrobatics. Acrobatics is also very entertaining.
Bai Youtian:	If we are unable to get the tickets, then we will go to a teahouse to drink tea.

Unit 10 Going Out

10.1 Asking Directions from Taxi Drivers

Driver:	Excuse me, sir, where are you going?
Bai Youtian:	Sir, I'm going to Tiananmen Square.
Driver:	Do you want to take the Second or Third Ring (Road)?
Bai Youtian:	If the Second Ring is not congested, then take the Second Ring.
Driver:	Second Ring is often congested at this time. Taking the Third Ring will probably be much faster.
Bai Youtian:	What about Chang'an Street?
Driver:	Chang'an Street shouldn't have too much traffic right now.
Bai Youtian:	Then we'll get on Third Ring first, and then go by Chang'an Street!

10.2 Asking Directions from Pedestrians

Bai Youtian:	Excuse me, how do I get to the Oriental Plaza?
Passerby:	From here go straight north. At the second traffic light, turn right and you'll be there.
Bai Youtian:	I'm sorry, I didn't hear you clearly. Please say it again.
Passerby:	From here, go straight ahead. Turn right at the second intersection.
Bai Youtian:	After the right turn, how much further must I walk?
Passerby:	Not far. You can see it as soon as you make the turn.
Bai Youtian:	Which side of the road is it on?
Passerby:	It's on the left.
Bai Youtian:	Thank you!
Passerby:	You're welcome!

Unit 11 Shopping

11.1 Gifts for Family

| Bai Youtian: | My wife wants me to buy some jewelry to bring back. |
| Gao Ming: | To buy jewelry, you should go to Hongqiao Market. Have you ever been to Hongqiao Market before? |

Bai Youtian:	I have never been because every time I come to China my schedule is too tight.
Gao Ming:	I have some free time tomorrow. I can accompany you.
Bai Youtian:	Excellent! But wouldn't it be too much trouble for you?
Gao Ming:	Not at all. It just so happens that I have been thinking about going there to buy some things.
Bai Youtian:	How far is it from here to Hongqiao Market?
Gao Ming:	Hongqiao Market is on Tian Tan Road. It's about 10 kilometers, I think.
Bai Youtian:	How do we get there?
Gao Ming:	Let's call a taxi!
Bai Youtian:	Okay, whatever you say!

11.2 Gifts for Others

Gao Ming:	You are going back to your country soon. Is there anything else you need help with?
Bai Youtian:	I must bring some gifts back to the United States. What are the better places to go buy gifts?
Gao Ming:	What do you need to buy?
Bai Youtian:	I want to buy some Chinese handicrafts.
Gao Ming:	You can either go to Liulichang or Panjiayuan; the shops there have everything.
Bai Youtian:	Can you get Chinese calligraphy and paintings there?
Gao Ming:	Of course. In addition to calligraphy and paintings, the shops there also have antiques.
Bai Youtian:	That's great. I'll go tomorrow right after the meeting is over.

Unit 12 Farewells

12.1 Showing Gratitude

Ma Jingli:	Gao Ming told me that you are going back to the United States the day after tomorrow. Is that true?
Bai Youtian:	That's correct. I will be leaving the day after tomorrow at noon.
Ma Jingli:	I'm very glad that we were able to work together so well this time.
Bai Youtian:	I'm also very happy. I very much appreciate your support.
Ma Jingli:	When will you be coming back next time?
Bai Youtian:	I'm not sure. It depends on the situation, but probably in August.
Ma Jingli:	I hope that next time you can bring your wife and children with you.
Bai Youtian:	I also hope they can come to China. I want to let my children have opportunities to learn more about Chinese culture.
Ma Jingli:	Then if you can make it in August, we will meet again in Beijing!
Bai Youtian:	It's a deal!

12.2 Good-byes and Future Plans

Gao Ming:	I will drive you to the airport tomorrow morning.
Bai Youtian:	I appreciate it very much.
Gao Ming:	Have you finished all your packing?
Bai Youtian:	Not yet. I will do it tonight after dinner. There is still enough time.
Gao Ming:	After you go back, I will definitely be in touch with you often.
Bai Youtian:	Thank you. While I'm not here, I'd really appreciate it if you could look after the company's affairs for me.*
Gao Ming:	You can rest assured I will work hard.

*See Lesson 12.2 Cultural Point 2.

Key World Capitals

Country	Capital	Country: Chinese Name	Country: Pinyin	Capital: Chinese Name	Capital: Pinyin
Brazil	Brasilia	巴西	Bāxī	巴西利亚	Bāxīlìyà
Canada	Ottawa	加拿大	Jiānádà	渥太华	Wòtàihuá
France	Paris	法国	Fǎguó	巴黎	Bālí
Germany	Berlin	德国	Déguó	柏林	Bólín
India	New Delhi	印度	Yìndù	新德里	Xīndélǐ
Italy	Rome	意大利	Yìdàlì	罗马	Luómǎ
Japan	Tokyo	日本	Rìběn	东京	Dōngjīng
Mexico	Mexico City	墨西哥	Mòxīgē	墨西哥城	Mòxīgē Chéng
Russia	Moscow	俄国	Éguó	莫斯科	Mòsīkē
Singapore	Singapore	新加坡	Xīnjiāpō	新加坡	Xīnjiāpō
South Korea	Seoul	南韩	Nánhán	首尔	Shǒuěr
Spain	Madrid	西班牙	Xībānyá	马德里	Mǎdélǐ
United Kingdom	London	英国	Yīngguó	伦敦	Lúndūn
United States	Washington, D.C.	美国	Měiguó	华盛顿特区	Huáshèngdùn tèqū

Major Business Provinces in China

Major Business Cities in China

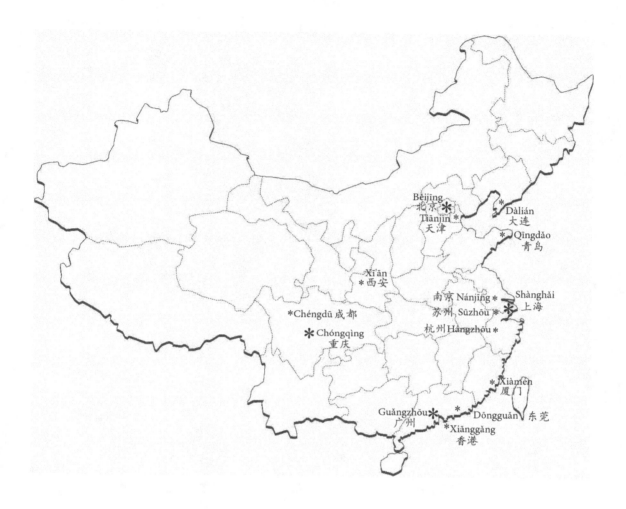

Chinese-English Wordlist

Note: An "a" after a lesson number refers to the "Additional Vocabulary" lists in the textbook.

Pinyin	Chinese	Part of Speech	English	Unit
A				
a	啊	P	(a particle used after 好/是 to indicate agreement)	8.1a
āyí	阿姨	N	nanny; housekeeper; aunt; female family friend close to one's parents' age	12.1a
ǎi	矮	Adj	short; low	5.1a
ài	爱	V	to love; to like	10.1a
ānpái	安排	V/N	to arrange; arrangement; plans	6.2
B				
ba	吧	P	(a particle that implies a supposition)	2.2
ba	吧	P	(a particle that implies suggestion or advice)	6.1
bā	八	Nu	eight	Intro
bàba	爸爸	N	dad	2.1a
bái	白	PN/Adj	a surname; white	1.1
báijiǔ	白酒	N	white wine; a strong Chinese liquor	6.1a
Bái Yǒutiān	白有天	PN	the full name of a fictional person in this text	1.1
bǎi	百	Nu	hundred	Intro
bàn	半	Nu	half (an hour)	5.2
bàn	办	V	to do; to handle; to tackle	11.2a
bànfǎ	办法	N	way to handle things; solution	6.1a
bàngōngshì	办公室	N	office	3.1a
bāng	帮	V	to help	6.1
bāng máng	帮忙	VO	to help	6.1a
bāngzhù	帮助	N/V	help; to help	12.1a
bàngqiú	棒球	N	baseball	9.2a
bǎochí	保持	V	to keep	12.2a
bàogào	报告	N	report; presentation	6.2a
bàozhǐ	报纸	N	newspaper	2.1a
bēi	杯	M	(a measure word for cups or glasses)	3.1a
běi	北	N	north	2.1
Běijīng	北京	PN	Beijing	2.1
běn	本	M	(a measure word for nouns that are "bound together")	3.1a
bǐ	笔	N	pen	2.1a
bǐjìběn	笔记本	N	note book	6.2a
bǐjìběn diànnǎo	笔记本电脑	N	lap top	6.2a
bǐ	比	Prep	a comparison marker; than	4.2
bǐjiào	比较	Adv	comparatively; relatively; rather	9.2
biān/biānr	边/边儿	Suf	side; used with terms of direction	10.2
biàn	遍	M	(a measure word for actions)	10.2
biǎoxiàn	表现	N/V	performance; to manifest	12.1a
biǎoyǎn	表演	N/V	performance; act; play; to perform	9.2

bié	别	Adv	don't	8.2
biéde	别的	Adj	other	12.1a
bīnguǎn	宾馆	N	hotel	7.1a
bīng	冰	N	ice	6.1a
bīngshuǐ	冰水	N	ice water	6.1a
bù	不	Adv	no; not	1.2
búbì	不必	AV	need not; not necessary	6.1a
búcuò	不错	Adj	not bad; pretty good	12.1a
búguò	不过	Conj	but	8.1
bú kèqi	不客气	UE	You are welcome; don't be so polite	10.2
bùyídìng	不一定	UE	not for sure	12.1
búyòng	不用	AV	need not; not necessary	6.1a
bù	部	N	department	2.2

C

cái	才	Adv	not until; as late as	6.2
cáiwù	财务	N	finance	11.1a
cài	菜	N	dish (of food); vegetables	2.2a
cài	菜	N	cuisine of a place (e.g., 中国菜 Zhōngguócài=Chinese cuisine/food)	6.1a
cānguān	参观	V	to visit; to observe; to tour (a company/factory, etc.)	7.2
cāntīng	餐厅	N	cafeteria; restaurant	4.1a
chá	茶	N	tea	3.1a
cháguǎn	茶馆	N	teahouse	9.2
chà	差	V/Adj	to be short by; to lack; inferior	5.2a
chàbuduō	差不多	Adv	about; almost	4.2
chǎnpǐn	产品	N	product	7.2
cháng	常	Adv	often	7.1
chángcháng	常常	Adv	often; frequently	7.1a
cháng	长	Adj	long	7.1a
Cháng'ānjiē	长安街	PN	Chang'an Street	10.1
Chángchéng	长城	N	The Great Wall	8.1a
cháng	尝	V	to taste; to try the flavor of	8.2
chàng	唱	V	to sing	8.1a
chāo	超	Adv	very; super (Taiwanese usage among youth)	3.2a
chāoshì	超市	N	supermarket	12.1a
chē	车	N	vehicle	2.2a
chēzhàn	车站	N	station (usually for a bus or train)	5.1a
chēzi	车子	N	car	2.1a
chéng	城	N	city; town	5.1
chéngshì	城市	N	city	7.2
chī	吃	V	to eat	2.2a
chī fàn	吃饭	VO	to eat a meal	5.2a
chídào	迟到	V	to arrive late	10.1a
chōu yān	抽烟	VO	to smoke	12.1a
chū	出	V	to be out; opposite of 进	3.2
chū chāi	出差	VO	to be on a business trip	6.1a
chūkǒu	出口	V/N	to export; export; exit	3.2
chūlai	出来	VC	to come out	9.1a
chū mén	出门	VO	to go out	10.1
chūqu	出去	V	to go out; to get out	9.2

chūzūchē	出租车	N	taxi	10.1
chúle…yǐwài	除了……以外	Conj	besides; in addition to	11.2
chuánzhēn	传真	N	fax	6.2a
Chūnjié	春节	PN	Spring Festival; Chinese New Year	11.2a
cì	次	M	(a measure word for frequency)	7.1
cóng	从	Prep	from	7.1

D

dǎ	打	V	to hit	2.2a
dǎ dī	打的	VO	to take a cab	12.1a
dǎ diànhuà	打电话	VO	to call; to make a phone call	6.2
dǎ qiú	打球	VO	to hit a ball; to play a ball game	2.2a
dǎrǎo	打扰	V	to disturb	9.1
dǎrǎo yíxià	打扰一下	UE	May I disturb/interrupt you a bit	9.1
dǎsuàn	打算	V	to plan (to do something)	9.1
dǎ zì	打字	VO	to type (characters)	2.2a
dà	大	Adj	big; huge; old in age	2.1a
dàgài	大概	Adv	probably; most likely	7.1
dàjiā	大家	Pr	everybody	8.1a
dàtáng	大堂	N	lobby	8.1
dàxué	大学	N	university; college	7.1a
dàyuē	大约	Adv	approximately; about	11.1
dāi	待	V	to stay	7.1
dài	带	V	to take; to bring; to carry	11.2
dàifu	大夫	N	doctor	2.1a
dān xīn	担心	VO	to worry	9.2a
dànshì	但是	Conj	but	11.1
dāngrán	当然	Adv	of course	5.1
dào	道	M	(a measure word for courses of meals)	8.2
dào	到	V	to arrive	3.1a
dào…lái	到……来	V	to come to (a place)	3.1
de	的	P	(a particle that indicates a possessive or descriptive form)	2.1
dehuà	……的话	Conj	if	10.1
de shíhou	……的时候	Conj	when…; while…; at the time of…	12.2
de	得	P	(a particle that indicates degree complement)	2.2
děi	得	AV	must; have to	11.2
dēng	灯	N	light	10.2
děng	等	V	to wait	6.2a
dì	第	Pre	prefix for ordinal numbers; -th/-nd/-rd	7.1
dìdi	弟弟	N	younger brother	2.1a
dìfang	地方	N	place	2.1
dìtiě	地铁	N	subway	9.2a
dìtiězhàn	地铁站	N	subway station	10.2a
dìtú	地图	N	map	2.1a
dìzhǐ	地址	N	address	2.1a
diǎn	点	M	(a measure word for telling time; "o'clock")	3.1a
diǎn	点	V	to order (food)	8.2a
diàn	电	N/Adj	electricity; electric; electrical	2.1a
diànhuà	电话	N	telephone	2.1a
diànnǎo	电脑	N	computer	2.1a

Diànnǎochéng	电脑城	PN	Computer City	5.1
diànshì	电视	N	television	7.1a
diànyǐng	电影	N	movie	4.2a
diànzǐ yóujiàn	电子邮件	N	e-mail	6.2a
dōng	东	N	east	10.2
dōngfāng	东方	N/PN	east; the East; the Orient	10.2
Dōngguǎn	东莞	PN	name of a place in Guangzhou	11.2a
dōngxi	东西	N	stuff; things	6.1a
dǒng	懂	V	to understand	5.1a
dōu	都	Adv	both; all	3.2
dúzī	独资	N	wholly owned foreign enterprise (WOFE)	4.1
dǔ	堵	V	to have a traffic jam; to block up	10.1
dǔ chē	堵车	VO/N	to have a traffic jam; traffic congestion	10.1
duànliàn	锻炼	V	to exercise; to work out	10.1a
duì	对	Prep	in; signifies the object of an interest or action	7.2
duì	对	Adj	right; correct	8.1
duìbuqǐ	对不起	UE	sorry; excuse me (an apology)	5.1
duō	多	Adj	many; much; a lot	2.2a
duō	多	IP	used to inquire about amount	3.2
duōshao	多少	IP	how many; how much	4.2

E

è	饿	Adj	hungry	1.2a
érzi	儿子	N	son	3.1
èr	二	Nu	two	Intro
Èrhuán	二环	PN	Second Ring (Road)	10.1

F

fā	发	V	to send; to dispatch; to distribute	6.2a
fàn	饭	N	(cooked) rice; meal	6.1a
fàndiàn	饭店	N	restaurant; hotel	7.1a
fāng'àn	方案	N	proposal; plan	11.2a
fāngbiàn	方便	Adj	available; convenient	6.2
Fāngzhèng Gōngsī	方正公司	PN	name of a fictional company in this text	4.2
fángzi	房子	N	house	5.2a
fǎngwèn	访问	V	to visit	7.1
fàng	放	V	to put	8.1a
fàng xīn	放心	VO	to be at ease; to set one's mind at rest	12.2
fēi	飞	V	to fly	5.1a
fēijī	飞机	N	airplane	9.1a
fēicháng	非常	Adv	very; extremely; highly	7.2
fèi xīn	费心	VO	to exert one's heart/ mind (polite expression used when asking for help)	12.2
fēn	分	M	(a measure word for minutes when stating a specific time)	5.2a
fēnchǎng	分厂	N	branch factory	7.2
fēngōngsī	分公司	N	branch office	4.1
fēnzhōng	分钟	TD	duration or period of minutes	7.1a
fèn	份	M	(a measure word for things which come in a set or pile, such as reports, newspapers, etc.)	9.1
fèn	份	N	portion (of a larger whole)	12.1
fú	幅	M	(a measure word for paintings)	12.2a

fùmǔ	父母	N	parents	3.2
fùqin	父亲	N	father	3.2

G

gān bēi	干杯	UE/VO	Cheers!; to make a toast	8.2a
gǎn	感	V	to feel; to sense	7.2
gǎnxiè	感谢	V/N	to thank; to be grateful; thanks	12.1
gāng	刚	Adv	just now; a short while ago	7.1
gānghǎo	刚好	Adv	by coincidence; by chance	11.1
gāo	高	N/Adj	a surname; tall; high	1.1
gāo'ěrfūqiú	高尔夫球	N	golf	9.1a
Gāo Míng	高明	PN	the full name of a fictional person in this text	1.1
gāoxìng	高兴	Adj	glad; pleased; happy	1.1
gàosu	告诉	V	to tell	12.1
gēge	哥哥	N	older brother	2.1a
gè	个	M	(a measure word for objects in general)	2.1
gěi	给	Prep/V	to; for; to give	6.2
gēn	跟	Conj/Prep	and; with	4.2
gèng	更	Adv	even more	10.1
gōngbǎo jīdīng	宫保鸡丁	N	Kung Pao Chicken	8.2
gōngchǎng	工厂	N	factory	7.2
gōngchéngshī	工程师	N	engineer	11.2a
gōngrén	工人	N	worker	4.1a
gōnglǐ	公里	M	(a measure word for distance in kilometers)	5.1
gōngsī	公司	N	company	2.1
gōngyìpǐn	工艺品	N	handicraft article	11.2
gōngyù	公寓	N	apartment	5.1a
gōngyuán	公园	N	park	3.1a
gōngzuò	工作	V/N	to work; job	3.2
gǔdǒng	古董	N	antique	11.2
guǎi	拐	V	to make a turn	10.2
guǎi wān	拐弯	VO	to turn at a corner	10.2
guān xīn	关心	VO/N	to care for or about, to be concerned with; concern	12.1a
guǎnlǐ	管理	N	management	7.2a
guàn	罐	M	(a measure word for cans or jars)	6.2a
guǎngchǎng	广场	N	square	10.1
Guǎngzhōu	广州	PN	Guangzhou	4.1
guì	贵	Adj	the honorific form of "your"; expensive	1.1
guì xìng	贵姓	UE	an honorific form of asking a person's surname	1.1
guó	国	N	country	2.1
guójiā	国家	N	country; nation	2.1a
Guójiā Jùyuàn	国家剧院	PN	National Theater	9.2
guóyǔ	国语	N	Mandarin Chinese (term used in Taiwan); official national language of a country	2.2a
guǒzhī	果汁	N	fruit juice	6.1a
guò	过	P	(a particle that indicates a past action or state)	8.1

H

hái	还	Adv	still; yet; in addition; as well as; also	3.2, 4.1
hái kěyǐ	还可以	UE	it's OK; not bad (a humble expression)	7.2
hái méi(yǒu)	还没(有)	Adv	not yet	5.2

háishi	还是	Conj	or	3.1
háir	孩儿	N	child	3.1
háizi	孩子	N	child; children; kids	3.1
hǎi	海	N	sea	2.1
Hàn	汉	PN	a reference to China; the original tribe from which 97 percent of ethnic Chinese trace their origins	2.2a
Hànyǔ	汉语	PN	Chinese language	2.2a
Hànzì	汉字	PN	Chinese characters	2.2a
hǎo	好	Adj	fine; good	1.1
hǎokàn	好看	Adj	to be good to watch/read/see; interesting; pretty	9.2
hào	号	N	day of the month; number	6.1
hàomǎ	号码	N	number	6.2a
hē	喝	V	to drink	6.1a
hēzuì	喝醉	VC	to drink to excess	8.2
hé	和	Conj/Prep	and; with	3.1
hétong	合同	N	contract	12.1a
hézī	合资	N	joint venture	4.1
hézuò	合作	V/N	to cooperate; cooperation; collaboration	12.1
hěn	很	Adv	very	1.1
hóng	红	Adj	red	6.1a
hóngbāo	红包	N	red envelope	12.2a
hóngchá	红茶	N	black tea	6.1a
hóngjiǔ	红酒	N	red wine	6.1a
hónglùdēng	红绿灯	N	traffic light	10.2
Hóngqiáo Shìchǎng	红桥市场	PN	Hongqiao Market	11.1
Hòuhǎi	后海	PN	name of a park-like area in Beijing	9.1
hòumian	后面	N	at the back; in the rear; behind (in space or position)	9.2a
hòutiān	后天	TW	the day after tomorrow	12.1
huāpíng	花瓶	N	vase	11.1a
huā qián	花钱	VO	to spend money	8.2a
huà	画	N	painting	3.1a
huàbào	画报	N	illustrated magazine or newspaper	3.1a
huà	话	N	spoken language; words; speech	2.2
huà bié	话别	VO/N	to say good-bye; good-byes	12.1
huàjù	话剧	N	stage play	11.2a
huānyíng	欢迎	V/UE	to welcome; to greet; Welcome!	2.1
huángdì	皇帝	N	emperor	3.1a
huí	回	V	to return	5.1
huí...lái	回......来	V	to return to (a place)	5.1
huí guó	回国	VO	to return to one's own country	5.1a
huí jiā	回家	VO	to return home	5.1a
huílai	回来	VC	to come back	5.1a
huíqu	回去	VC	to go back	5.1a
huì	会	AV/V	can; to know how to	2.2
huì	会	AV	will	3.1
huìyì	会议	N	meeting	10.1a
huìyìshì	会议室	N	meeting room	9.2a
huǒchē	火车	N	train	7.2a
huòzhě	或者	Conj	or (used in statements)	11.2

jīchǎng	机场	N	airport	7.1a
jīhuì	机会	N	opportunity; chance	7.2
…jí le	… …极了	Adv	extremely	11.1
jǐ	几	IP	how many	3.1
jǐ	几	Nu	several; a few	9.1
jìhuà	计划	N	plan	9.1a
jìsuànjī	计算机	N	computer (used in mainland China); calculator (used in Taiwan)	6.2a
jiā	家	M/N	(a measure word for business establishments such as companies, stores, or restaurants); family; home	4.1
jiājù	家具	N	furniture	11.1.a
jiārén	家人	N	family member(s)	6.1a
jiātíng	家庭	N	family	3.1
jiābān	加班	V	to work overtime	9.2a
jiǎndān	简单	Adj	simple	9.2a
jiàn	见	V	to see	1.2
jiàndào	见到	VC	to see; to meet	2.1
jiàn miàn	见面	VO	to meet; to see	6.2
jiàn	件	M	(a measure word for 事, luggage or clothing)	9.2a
jiàn	建	V	to build	7.2
jiànyì	建议	N/V	suggestion; to suggest	9.2
Jiāngsū	江苏	N	Jiangsu province	7.2
jiǎng	讲	V	to speak; to say	2.2a
jiāo	交	V	to befriend; to submit	9.1a
jiāo	教	V	to teach	2.2a
jiāo shū	教书	VO	to teach (academic courses)	2.2a
jiào	叫	V	to be called (first name/full name); to call	1.1
jiào	叫	V	to call (a taxi); to order	11.1
jiē	接	V	to pick up (people); to answer (the telephone)	8.1
jié hūn	结婚	VO	to get married	3.1
jiějie	姐姐	N	older sister	2.1a
jiěshì	解释	V	to explain	10.2a
jièshào	介绍	V/N	to introduce; introduction	2.1
jīnnián	今年	TW	this year	3.1
jīntiān	今天	TW	today	1.2
jǐn	紧	Adj	tight; urgent; pressing; tense	11.1
jǐnzhāng	紧张	Adj	nervous	7.2a
jìn	进	V	to enter	3.2
jìnchūkǒu	进出口	N/V	import and export; to import and export	3.2
jìnkǒu	进口	V/N	to import; import; entrance	3.2
jìnlai	进来	VC	to come in	2.2a
jìnqu	进去	VC	to go in	5.1a
jìn	近	Adj	close; near	5.1
jīng	京	N	indicates a capital city	2.1
Jīngjù	京剧	PN	Beijing Opera	9.2
jīngcháng	经常	Adv	often; frequently; constantly	7.1a
jīnglǐ	经理	N	manager	2.1
jiǔ	九	Nu	nine	Intro
jiǔ	久	Adj/TD	long; for a long time	7.1
jiǔ	酒	N	alcohol; wine	6.1a

jiǔbā	酒吧	N	pub; bar	9.1
jiù	就	Adv	right away; as early as	6.2
jiù	就	Adv	exactly; precisely; just	9.1
jiù	旧	Adj	old (opposite of 新 xīn)	7.2a
Jiùjīnshān	旧金山	PN	San Francisco	11.1a
jù	句	M	(a measure word for sentences)	8.1a
jùyuàn	剧院	N	theater	9.2
juédìng	决定	V/N	to decide; decision; resolution	9.1

K

kāfēi	咖啡	N	coffee	3.1a
Kǎlā OK	卡拉 OK	N	Karaoke	7.1a
kāi	开	V	to drive; to operate; to open	2.2a
kāi	开	V	to hold (a meeting/party, etc.)	6.1
kāi chē	开车	VO	to drive a car	2.2a
kāi huì	开会	VO	to attend (have) a meeting	6.1
kāishǐ	开始	V	to begin; to start	8.1a
kāixīn	开心	Adj	to be happy	7.2a
kàn	看	V	to read; to watch; to take a look	2.2a
kànjiàn	看见	VC	to see	9.1a
kàn shū	看书	VO	to read books	2.2a
kǎoyā	烤鸭	N	roast duck	8.1
kělè	可乐	N	cola	3.1a
kěnéng	可能	Adv	possibly; likely; perhaps	10.1
kěshì	可是	Conj	but	6.2
kěyǐ	可以	AV	to allow; may; to be able to; can	5.1
kè	刻	M	(a measure word meaning a quarter of an hour; 15 minutes)	5.2
kèhù	客户	N	client; customer	9.1a
kèqi	客气	Adj	polite; courteous	8.1
kèrén	客人	N	guest	11.2a
kòng	空	N	free time; spare time	3.1a
kǒu	口	N	mouth; an aperture of a place	3.2
kuàijì	会计	N	accounting	7.1a
kuàijìshī	会计师	N	accountant	2.1a
kuài	块	M	(a measure word for basic unit of Chinese currency; spoken form equivalent to 元 yuán)	11.1a
kuài	快	Adj	fast	2.2a

L

là	辣	Adj	spicy; hot; peppery	8.2
lái	来	V	to come	2.1
lái de jí	来得及	V	to be able to do something in time	12.2
lán	蓝	Adj	blue	7.1
Lánxīng	蓝星	PN	the name of a fictional company in this text	7.1
lánqiú	篮球	N	basketball	9.2a
lǎobǎn	老板	N	boss	9.1a
lǎoshī	老师	N	teacher	1.1a
le	了	P	(a particle that indicates completion of an action)	3.1
lèi	累	Adj	tired	1.2a
lěng	冷	Adj	cold	1.2a

lí	离	Prep	away from (indicates distance between two places)	5.1
lǐbài	礼拜	N	week (= 星期, but more colloquial)	5.2a
líkāi	离开	VC	to leave	5.1a
lǐwù	礼物	N	present; gift	11.2
Lǐ Zǒng	李总	PN	President Li (of a company)	4.1a
lìhai	厉害	Adj	strong; severe	8.2
liánxì	联系	V	to contact	6.1
Liánxiǎng	联想	PN	Lenovo	11.1a
liáng	凉	Adj	cool	1.2a
liǎng	两	Nu	two	Intro
liàng	辆	M	(a measure word for vehicles)	11.1
lín	林	PN/N	a surname; forest	4.1
líng	零	Nu	zero	Intro
Liúlichǎng	琉璃厂	PN	name of a place known as the Scholars Market	11.2
liù	六	Nu	six	Intro
liùshísān	六十三	Nu	sixty three	3.2
lù	路	N	road	10.2
lùkǒu	路口	N	intersection	10.2
lùshang	路上	N	on the road	11.1a
lǜshī	律师	N	lawyer	2.1a
lǜ	绿	Adj	green	6.1a
lǜchá	绿茶	N	green tea	6.1a

M

māma	妈妈	N	mom	2.1a
máfan	麻烦	V/N/Adj	to bother; to trouble; trouble; troublesome	11.1
mǎ	马	PN/N	a surname; horse	2.1
mǎshàng	马上	Adv	immediately; right away	6.1
ma	吗	IP	a particle used to form a question	1.2
mǎi	买	V	to buy	5.2a
mǎi cài	买菜	VO	to buy groceries	7.1a
mài	卖	V	to sell	5.2a
màn	慢	Adj	slow	2.2a
mànpǎo	慢跑	N/V	jogging; to jog	9.2a
máng	忙	Adj	busy	1.2
máobǐ	毛笔	N	calligraphy brush	3.1a
Máotáijiǔ	茅台酒	PN	Maotai (a Chinese liquor)	8.2
Màomínglù	茂名路	PN	name of a place in Shanghai	9.1a
màoyì	贸易	N	trade	3.2
méi guānxi	没关系	UE	It doesn't matter; never mind	7.1
méiyǒu	没有	V/Adv	do not have; there is/are not; (negative marker)	3.1
měi	每	Pr	every; each	7.1a
měitiān	每天	TW	everyday	7.1a
měi	美	Adj	beautiful	2.1
Měiguó	美国	PN	America	2.1
mèimei	妹妹	N	younger sister	2.1a
mēn	闷	Adj	humid; stifling	5.1a
mēnrè	闷热	Adj	hot and humid	9.2a
mén	门	N	door; gate	10.1
men	们	Suf	pluralizes pronouns and human nouns	1.2

mǐ	米	M	(a measure word for length in meters)	7.1a
mǐ	米	N	(uncooked) rice	6.1a
mǐfàn	米饭	N	rice	6.1a
mìshū	秘书	N	secretary	2.2
miàn	面	Suf	used with terms of direction or localization such as 前面 qiánmian "front," 外面 wàimiàn "outside," 里面 lǐmian "inside"	9.2a
míng	明	PN/Adj	the given name of a fictional character in this text; bright	1.1
míngnián	明年	TW	next year	3.1
míngtiān	明天	TW	tomorrow	1.2
míngcài	名菜	N	signature dish	8.1
míngpiàn	名片	N	name card; business card	7.1
míngzi	名字	N	full name; given name	1.1
mǔqin	母亲	N	mother	3.2

N

nǎ/něi	哪	IP	which	2.2
nǎli	哪里	UE	polite rejection of a compliment	2.1
nǎli	哪里	IP	where	5.2
nǎr	哪儿	IP	where	4.1a
nà	那	Conj	in that case; then	1.2
nà/nèi	那	Spe	that	2.1a
nàli	那里	Pr	there	5.2a
nàme	那么	Conj	then; in that case	6.1
nàr	那儿	Pr	there	5.1
nán	男	N	male	3.1
nánhái'ér	男孩儿	N	boy	3.1
nán	难	Adj	difficult	9.2a
nǎo	脑	N	brain; mind	2.1a
ne	呢	P	(a particle used to form an elliptical question)	1.1
néng	能	AV	to be able to; can	5.1
nénggàn	能干	Adj	capable	12.1a
nǐ	你	Pr	you	1.1a
nián	年	N	year	3.1
niánjì	年纪	N	age	3.2
niàn shū	念书	VO	to read books; to study	5.2a
nín	您	Pr	you (the honorific form of "you")	1.1
nǔlì	努力	Adj/V	diligent; to work hard	4.2a
nǚ	女	N	female	3.1
nǚ'ér	女儿	N	daughter	3.1
nǚhái'ér	女孩儿	N	girl	3.1
nǚshì	女士	N	lady	1.2a

P

pà	怕	V	to be afraid; to fear	8.2
Pānjiāyuán	潘家园	PN	name of a place known as the Dirt Market	11.2
péi	陪	V	to accompany	11.1
péngyou	朋友	N	friend	2.1a
píjiǔ	啤酒	N	beer	6.1a
piányi	便宜	Adj	inexpensive; cheap	11.1a
piào	票	N	ticket	9.2

píng	瓶	M	(a measure word for bottles)	6.2a
pǔtōng	普通	Adj	common; ordinary	2.2
pǔtōnghuà	普通话	N	common speech; a reference to Mandarin Chinese	2.2

Q

qī	七	Nu	seven	Intro
qǐlái	起来	VC	to get up	6.2a
qìchē	汽车	N	automobile	2.1a
qiān	千	Nu	thousand	Intro
qiān	签	V	to sign	12.1a
qián	前	N	ahead; front (opposite of 后 hòu)	10.2
qiántiān	前天	TW	the day before yesterday	7.1
qián	钱	N	money	3.1a
Qīngdǎo Píjiǔ	青岛啤酒	PN	Tsingtao beer	8.2
qīngsōng	轻松	V/Adj	to relax; relaxed	9.2
qīngchu	清楚	Adj	clear; distinct	5.1
qíngkuàng	情况	N	situation; condition	12.1
qǐng	请	Adv/V	please; to request; to invite	2.2
qǐng wèn	请问	UE	Excuse me…; May I ask…	2.2
qiú	球	N	ball	2.2a
qiúsài	球赛	N	ballgame	11.1a
qù	去	V	to go	3.1a
qùnián	去年	TW	last year	7.2
Quánjùdé	全聚德	PN	a famous roast duck restaurant in Beijing	8.1

R

ràng	让	V	to let; to allow; to make	12.1
rè	热	Adj	hot	1.2a
rén	人	N	person; people	2.1
rénshì	人事	N	human resources; human concerns	2.2
rénshìbù	人事部	N	human resources department	2.2
rènshi	认识	V	to know (someone); to be acquainted with (a person)	1.1
rì	日	N	day; the sun	6.1a
rúguǒ	如果	Conj	if	9.2

S

sān	三	Nu	three	Intro
Sānhuán	三环	PN	Third Ring (Road)	10.1
Sānlǐtún	三里屯	PN	name of a place in Beijing	9.1a
shāngdiàn	商店	N	shop	10.1a
shāngliang	商量	V	to consult with someone; to discuss	11.2a
shàng	上	N	above; on top of	2.1
shàng	上	V	to attend a school or class; to go to	3.1
shàng	上	Adj	last; previous	6.1a
shàng bān	上班	VO	to go to work	5.2
shàng (ge) xīngqī	上(个)星期	TW	last week	6.1a
shàng ge yuè	上个月	TW	last month	6.1a

Shànghǎi	上海	PN	Shanghai	2.1
shàng jiē	上街	VO	to go on the street; to stroll on the street (usually for shopping)	10.1a
shàng kè	上课	VO	to go to class; to begin a class	5.2a
shàngwǔ	上午	TW	morning	5.2
shàngxiàwǔ	上下午	TW	morning and afternoon	6.1
shāo	稍	Adv	slightly; for a moment	6.2a
shāoděng	稍等	UE	to wait for a moment	6.2a
shǎo	少	Adj	few; little	2.2a
shéi/shuí	谁	IP	who; whom	2.2
shēntǐ	身体	N	health; body	3.2
Shēnzhèn	深圳	PN	Shenzhen	4.1
shénme	什么	Pr	what	1.1
shēng	生	V	to give birth	11.2a
shēng bìng	生病	VO	to get sick	12.2a
shēngchǎn	生产	V	to manufacture; to produce	7.2
shēngrì	生日	N	birthday	11.2a
shēngyì	生意	N	business	3.2
shīfu	师傅	N	driver; master in a given field	10.1
shí	十	Nu	ten	Intro
shí'èr	十二	Nu	twelve	3.1
shíhou	时候	N	(a point of) time	6.2
shíjiān	时间	N	time	3.1a
shítáng	食堂	N	canteen; dining hall	4.1a
shìchǎng	市场	N	market	6.1
shì	是	V	to be (am; are; is)	2.1
shì	事	N	matter; affair; thing; business	3.1a
shì	试	V	to try; to attempt	6.2
shōushi	收拾	V	to pack	12.2
shǒujī	手机	N	cellular phone	6.2a
shū	书	N	book	2.1a
shūdiàn	书店	N	book store	9.1a
shuǐ	水	N	water	3.1a
shuì	睡	V	to sleep	6.2a
shuì jiào	睡觉	VO	to sleep	8.2a
shùnlì	顺利	Adj	smooth	12.1a
shuō	说	V	to speak; to say	2.2
shuō huà	说话	VO	to talk; to speak	2.2a
shuōmíng	说明	V	to explain	8.1a
sījī	司机	N	driver (of a car)	10.1
sì	四	Nu	four	Intro
Sìchuān	四川	PN	Sìchuān province	7.1
sòng	送	V	to send; to take someone somewhere; to see someone off; to give as a gift; to deliver	7.1a, 11.1a
sòng xìn	送信	VO	to deliver mail	7.1a
Sūzhōu	苏州	PN	Suzhou	7.2
suīrán	虽然	Conj	although	9.2
suíbiàn	随便	UE	as one pleases	8.2
suì	岁	M	(a measure word for years of age)	3.1

T

tā	他	Pr	he; him	1.1a
tā	她	Pr	she; her	1.1a
tái	台	M	(a measure word for certain machinery, apparatuses, etc.)	6.2a
tài	太	Adv	too; overly	5.1
tàitai	太太	N	Mrs.; wife	1.2a
tán	谈	V	to talk; to discuss	9.1a
tǎolùn	讨论	V	to discuss	9.1a
tiān	天	PN/N	used as part of a name in this text; day; sky	1.1
Tiān'ānmén	天安门	PN	Tiananmen	10.1
Tiāntán	天坛	PN	The Temple of Heaven	11.1
Tiāntánlù	天坛路	PN	Tiantan Road	11.1
tīng	听	V	to hear; to listen	4.1
tīngshuō	听说	V	to have heard it said	4.1
tǐng	挺	Adv	very; rather; quite	3.2
tóng	同	Adj	same	10.2a
tóngshì	同事	N	colleagure; co-worker	2.1a
tóngxué	同学	N	classmate	2.1a
tóuzī	投资	N	investment	7.2a
túshūguǎn	图书馆	N	library	3.1a
tuìxiū	退休	V	to retire	3.2

W

wài	外	N	outside	3.1a
wàiguó	外国	N	foreign country	3.1a
wàiguórén	外国人	N	foreigner	3.1a
Wàitān	外滩	PN	The Bund (a popular tourist spot along the levy against the Huangpu river in Shanghai)	9.1a
wán/wánr	玩/玩儿	V	to have fun; to play	6.1a
wán	完	V	to be finished; to be done	11.2
wǎn'ān	晚安	UE	Good night!	1.2a
wǎncān	晚餐	N	dinner	8.1
wǎnfàn	晚饭	N	dinner; supper	8.1a
wǎnshang	晚上	TW	evening	1.2a
wàn	万	Nu	ten thousand	Intro
wáng	王	PN/N	a surname; king	2.2
Wáng Yīng	王英	PN	the full name of a fictional person in this text	2.2
Wángfǔ Fàndiàn	王府饭店	PN	Wangfu Hotel	8.1
wǎng	往	Prep	towards; in the direction of	10.2
wǎngqiú	网球	N	tennis	5.2a
wèi	位	M	(a measure word for addressing people politely)	2.1
wèishénme	为什么	IP	why	5.2
wén	文	N	language; written language	2.2
wénhuà	文化	N	culture	12.1
wénjiàn	文件	N	document	9.1a
wèn	问	V	to ask (a question)	2.2
wènhǎo	问好	V/N	to greet; greetings	1.1
wèntí	问题	N	problem; question	6.1a
wǒ	我	Pr	I; me	1.1

wǒmen	我们	Pr	we; us	1.2
				Intro
wǔ	五	Nu	five	3.2
wǔshíjiǔ	五十九	Nu	fifty nine	1.2a
wǔ'ān	午安	UE	Good afternoon!	5.2a
wǔfàn	午饭	N	lunch	

X

xī	西	N	west	10.2a
xī yān	吸烟	VO	to smoke	5.1a
xīwàng	希望	V	to hope; to wish; to expect	12.1
xǐshǒujiān	洗手间	N	restroom	10.1a
xǐhuan	喜欢	V	to like; to love; to be fond of	8.2
xià	下	V	to disembark from a vehicle	9.1a
xià	下	Adj	next; below	6.1
xià bān	下班	VO	to get off work	5.2
xià cì	下次	TW	next time	12.1
xià fēijī	下飞机	VO	to get off the plane	9.1a
xià ge yuè	下个月	TW	next month	6.1a
xiàwǔ	下午	TW	afternoon	1.2a
xià xīngqī	下星期	TW	next week	6.1
xiān	先	Adv	first	10.1
xiānsheng	先生	N	Mr.; husband	1.1
xiànzài	现在	TW	now; at present	5.2
Xiānggǎng	香港	PN	Hong Kong	7.1a
xiāngyān	香烟	N	cigarette	3.1a
Xiāngyáng Shìchǎng	襄阳市场	PN	Xiangyang Market (in Shanghai)	11.1a
xiǎng	想	AV/V	would like to; to think of (doing something); to think; to miss	6.1
xiǎng jiā	想家	VO/Adj	to miss home; homesick	6.1a
xiàng	向	Prep	towards	10.2
xiàngmù	项目	N	project	10.1a
xiǎo	小	Adj	small; little; young (for people only)	3.1
xiǎo	小	Adj	a title used to address one who is younger than you	6.1
xiǎohái	小孩	N	child	11.2a
xiǎo huángdì	小皇帝	N	"little emperor"	3.1a
xiǎojie	小姐	N	Miss; young lady	2.2
xiǎoshí	小时	TD	hour	7.1a
xiǎoshuō	小说	N	novel	2.1a
Xiǎo Wáng	小王	PN	Little Wang	6.1
xiǎoxīn	小心	Adj/Adv	careful; to do something carefully	6.1a
xiǎoxué	小学	N	elementary school	3.1
xiē	些	M	(a measure word for multiple things or people)	11.1
xiě	写	V	to write	2.2a
xièxie	谢谢	UE	thank you	2.1a
xīn	新	Adj	new	7.2
xīnnián	新年	N	New Year	12.2a
Xīntiāndì	新天地	PN	name of a place in Shanghai	9.1a
xìn	信	N	letter	6.1a
xìnxīn	信心	N	confidence	10.1a
xīng	星	N	star	7.1
xīngqī	星期	N	week	5.2

xīngqī'èr	星期二	TW	Tuesday	6.1
xīngqīliù	星期六	TW	Saturday	5.2
xīngqīyī	星期一	TW	Monday	6.1
xīngfèn	兴奋	Adj	excited	7.2a
xíng	行	Adj/V	all right; OK	8.2
xíngli	行李	N	luggage	12.1a
xìng	姓	V/N	to be named (surname); surname	1.1
xìngqu	兴趣	N	interest	7.2
xiōngdi jiěmèi	兄弟姐妹	N	brothers and sisters; siblings	3.2
xiūxi	休息	V	to rest; to take a break	5.2
Xiùshuǐ Shìchǎng	秀水市场	PN	Xiushui Market (in Beijing)	11.1a
xūyào	需要	V	to need	6.1a
xué	学	V	to learn; to study	1.2a
xuésheng	学生	N	student	1.2a
xuéxí	学习	V	to study (mainland China usage)	5.2a
xuéxiào	学校	N	school; campus	2.1a
Xuěbì	雪碧	PN	Sprite	6.2a
xúnwèn	询问	V	to ask about; to inquire	5.1

Y

ya	呀	P	used in place of 啊 when the preceding word ends with the sound of *a, o, e, i,* or *ü*	7.2
yāsuìqián	压岁钱	N	New Year money gift to children	12.2a
Yànjīng Píjiǔ	燕京啤酒	PN	Yanjing beer	8.2
yào	要	AV/V	must; have to; need to; to want to; to desire to have (something)	6.1
yàoshi	要是	Conj	if	10.1
yě	也	Adv	also	1.2
yèwù	业务	N	business	12.2
yī	一	Nu	one	Intro
yīshēng	医生	N	doctor	6.2a
yīyuàn	医院	N	hospital	10.1a
yídìng	一定	Adv	definitely; for sure	7.2
yígòng	一共	Adv	all together; totally	7.2
yíhuìr	一会儿	TD	a little while	11.1a
yíkuàir	一块儿	Adv	together	9.1
yíxià	一下	TD	used after a verb to indicate that an action is only for a moment; a short while	9.1
yíyàng	一样	Adj	same	4.2
yǐjīng	已经	Adv	already	3.1
yǐhòu	以后	TW	after; afterwards; later; hereafter	9.2
yǐqián	以前	TW	before; ago; previously	11.1
yìdiǎn	一点	Adj	a little	2.2
yìdiǎnr	一点儿	Adj	a little (Beijing pronunciation)	2.2
yìqǐ	一起	Adv	together	9.1a
yìyán wéidìng	一言为定	UE	it's a deal; that's settled then	12.1
yìzhí	一直	Adv	always; all along; straight through	9.1
yì	亿	Nu	hundred million	Intro
yìjiàn	意见	N	opinion	10.2a
yīnwèi	因为	Conj	because	11.1
yínháng	银行	N	bank	5.2
yǐnliào	饮料	N	drinks; beverage (usually non-alcoholic drinks)	6.1a
yīnggāi	应该	AV	should; ought to	10.1

Yīng	英	PN	the given name of a fictional character in this text	2.2
Yīngwén	英文	PN	English	2.2
yìngchou	应酬	V/N	to engage in social activities (when off duty); (work-related) social activities	9.1
yòng	用	V	to use	10.2a
yóujú	邮局	N	post office	10.1a
yǒu	有	PN/V	used as part of a name in this text; (cf Unit 3.1); to have; there is; there are	1.1, 3.1
yǒude...yǒude...	有的…… 有的……	Adj	some...some...	4.2
yǒu qián	有钱	Adj	rich; wealthy	4.2a
yǒu yìsi	有意思	Adj	interesting	4.2a
yǒu yòng	有用	Adj	useful	9.2a
yòu	右	N/Adj	right	7.1
yòu zhuǎn	右转	V	to turn right	10.2
yúkuài	愉快	Adj	happy; joyful; cheerful	12.1
yuán	元	M	(a measure word for the basic unit of Chinese currency)	11.1a
yuángōng	员工	N	employee; staff; personnel	7.2
yuǎn	远	Adj	far; remote	5.1
yuē	约	V	to invite; to make a date or appointment in advance	9.1
yuējiàn	约见	V	to make an appointment to meet	6.1
yuè	月	N	month	6.1
yuèfèn	月份	N	month	12.1
yùndòng	运动	V	to exercise; to work out	7.1a

Z

zájì	杂技	N	acrobatics	9.2
zázhì	杂志	N	magazine	2.1a
zài	在	V	to be at a place	4.1
zài	在	V	to be present	5.1
zài	在	Prep	at; in; on	5.2
zài	再	Adv	again	1.2
zài	再	Adv	then	9.1
zàijiàn	再见	UE	good-bye; see you again	1.2
zánmen	咱们	Pr	we; us	1.2a
zǎo	早	UE/Adj	Good morning!; early	1.2a
zǎo'ān	早安	UE	Good morning!	1.2a
zǎofàn	早饭	N	breakfast	7.1a
zǎoshang	早上	TW	(early) morning	1.2
zǎoshang hǎo	早上好	UE	Good morning!	1.2
zǎotuì	早退	V	to leave early	12.1a
zěnme	怎么	IP	how to…	10.2
zěnmeyàng	怎么样	IP	how about; what about	9.2
zěnmeyàng	怎么样	IP	how is…	10.1
zhàn	站	V	to stand	8.1a
zhànqǐlái	站起来	VC	to stand up	8.1a
zhāng	张	M	(a measure word for flat objects)	3.1a
Zhāng	张	PN	a surname	6.1
Zhāng Guóqiáng	张国强	PN	the full name of a fictional person in this text	7.1
zhǎo	找	V	to look for; to search	5.1
zhào	兆	Nu	trillion	Intro
zhè/zhèi	这	Spe	this	2.1
zhè cì	这次	TW	this time	7.1

zhèli	这里	Pr	here	5.2a
zhème	这么	Adv	so; such; like this	12.1
zhèr	这儿	Pr	here	5.1
zhēn	真	Adv	truly; really	12.1
zhèngzài	正在	Adv	in the midst of; in the middle of	9.1
zhī	支	M	(a measure word for stick-like objects)	3.1a
zhīchí	支持	N/V	support; to support	12.1
zhīdao	知道	V	to know; to have the knowledge of	6.2
zhǐ	只	Adv	only; just	5.1
zhǐjiào	指教	V	to give advice (polite expression used when meeting for the first time)	7.1
zhōng	钟	N	o'clock; time as measured in minutes or seconds; clock	5.2
zhōng	中	Adj	middle; medium	2.1
Zhōngguāncūn	中关村	PN	a name of a district in Beijing	5.1
Zhōngguó	中国	PN	China	2.1
Zhōng-Měi	中美	Adj	Sino-American	4.1
Zhōngwén	中文	PN	Chinese language	2.1
zhōngwǔ	中午	TW	noon; midday	12.1
zhōngxué	中学	N	middle/high school	3.1
zhōngxuéshēng	中学生	N	middle/high school student	3.1
zhǒng	种	M	(a measure word for types/kinds/sorts)	7.2
zhòngyào	重要	Adj	important	9.1a
zhōu	周	N	week (= 星期, but more formal)	6.2
zhōumò	周末	TW	weekend	5.2
zhūbǎo	珠宝	N	jewelry; precious gems	11.1
zhǔyi	主意	N	idea	9.2
zhùyì	注意	V	to pay attention to	12.2a
zhù	住	V	to reside; to stay (at a hotel)	8.1
zhuǎn	转	V	to make a turn	10.2
zhǔnbèi	准备	V	to prepare	11.1a
zǐgōngsī	子公司	N	a subsidiary company	8.1a
zìjǐ	自己	Pr	oneself	12.1a
zì	字	N	character	2.2a
zìdiǎn	字典	N	dictionary	2.1a
zìhuà	字画	N	calligraphy and painting	11.2
zǒngbù	总部	N	headquarters	4.1
zǒngjīnglǐ	总经理	N	general manager	4.1a
zǒu	走	V	to walk	2.2a
zǒu	走	V	to leave	3.1a
zǒu lù	走路	VO	to walk; to go on foot	11.1a
zúqiú	足球	N	soccer	9.2a
zuì	醉	V/Adj	to get drunk; drunk	8.2
zuìjìn	最近	TW	lately; recently	10.2a
zuótiān	昨天	TW	yesterday	1.2a
zuǒ	左	N/Adj	left	7.1
zuǒyòu	左右	Adv	about; around; approximately	7.1
zuò	作	V	to do	6.2a
zuò	坐	V	to sit	2.2a
zuò	坐	V	to travel by; to take (a means of transportation)	7.2a
zuò huǒchē	坐火车	VO	to take a train	7.2a
zuò	做	V	to make; to do	2.2a
zuò cài	做菜	VO	to cook (make dishes)	2.2a

English-Chinese Wordlist

Note: An "a" after a lesson number refers to the "Additional Vocabulary" lists in the textbooks.

English	Chinese	Pinyin	Part of Speech	Unit
A				
a few; several	几	jǐ	Nu	9.1
a little	一点	yìdiǎn	Adj	2.2
a little (Beijing pronunciation)	一点儿	yìdiǎnr	Adj	2.2
a little while	一会儿	yíhuìr	TD	11.1a
a lot; many; much	多	duō	Adj	2.2a
a short while ago; just now	刚	gāng	Adv	7.1
(a point of) time	时候	shíhou	N	6.2
about; almost	差不多	chàbuduō	Adv	4.2
about; approximately	大约	dàyuē	Adv	11.1
about; around; approximately	左右	zuǒyòu	Adv	7.1
above; on top of	上	shàng	N	2.1
accompany	陪	péi	V	11.1
accountant	会计师	kuàijìshī	N	2.1a
accounting	会计	kuàijì	N	7.1a
acrobatics	杂技	zájì	N	9.2
act; performance; play; to perform	表演	biǎoyǎn	N/V	9.2
address	地址	dìzhǐ	N	2.1a
affair; matter; thing; business	事	shì	N	3.1a
after; afterwards; later; hereafter	以后	yǐhòu	TW	9.2
afternoon	下午	xiàwǔ	TW	1.2a
afterwards; after; later; hereafter	以后	yǐhòu	TW	9.2
again	再	zài	Adv	1.2
age	年纪	niánjì	N	3.2
ago; before; previously	以前	yǐqián	TW	11.1
ahead; front (opposite of 后 hòu)	前	qián	N	10.2
airplane	飞机	fēijī	N	9.1a
airport	机场	jīchǎng	N	7.1a
alcohol; wine	酒	jiǔ	N	6.1a
all along; always; straight through	一直	yìzhí	Adv	9.1
all right; OK	行	xíng	Adj/V	8.2
all together; totally	一共	yígòng	Adv	7.2
all; both	都	dōu	Adv	3.2
allow; may; be able to; can	可以	kěyǐ	AV	5.1
allow; to let; to make	让	ràng	V	12.1
almost; about	差不多	chàbuduō	Adv	4.2
already	已经	yǐjīng	Adv	3.1
also	也	yě	Adv	1.2
also; in addition; as well as	还	hái	Adv	4.1
although	虽然	suīrán	Conj	9.2
always; all along; straight through	一直	yìzhí	Adv	9.1

America	美国	Měiguó	PN	2.1
an aperture of a place; mouth	口	kǒu	N	3.2
and; with	和	hé	Conj	3.1
and; with	跟	gēn	Conj/Prep	4.2
answer (the telephone); to pick up (people)	接	jiē	V	8.1
antique	古董	gǔdǒng	N	11.2
away from (indicates distance between two places)	离	lí	Prep	5.1
apartment	公寓	gōngyù	N	5.1a
approximately; about	大约	dàyuē	Adv	11.1
arrange; arrangement; plans	安排	ānpái	V/N	6.2
arrangement; plans; to arrange	安排	ānpái	N/V	6.2
arrive	到	dào	V	3.1a
arrive late	迟到	chídào	V	10.1a
as early as; right away	就	jiù	Adv	6.2
as late as; not until	才	cái	Adv	6.2
as one pleases	随便	suíbiàn	UE	8.2
as well as; in addition; also	还	hái	Adv	4.1
ask (a question)	问	wèn	V	2.2
ask about; to inquire	询问	xúnwèn	V	5.1
at present; now	现在	xiànzài	TW	5.2
at the back; in the rear; behind (in space or position)	后面	hòumian	N	9.2a
at the time of...; when...; while...	......的时候	...de shíhou	Conj	12.2
at; in; on	在	zài	Prep	5.2
attempt	试	shì	V	6.2
attend (have) a meeting	开会	kāi huì	VO	6.1
attend a school or class; to go to	上	shàng	V	3.1
aunt; nanny; housekeeper; female family friend close to one's parents' age	阿姨	āyí	N	12.1a
automobile	汽车	qìchē	N	2.1a
available; convenient	方便	fāngbiàn	Adj	6.2

B

ball	球	qiú	N	2.2a
ballgame	球赛	qiúsài	N	11.1a
bank	银行	yínháng	N	5.2
bar; pub	酒吧	jiǔbā	N	9.1
baseball	棒球	bàngqiú	N	9.2a
basketball	篮球	lánqiú	N	9.2a
be (is; am; are)	是	shì	V	2.1
be able to do something in time	来得及	lái de jí	V	12.2
be able to; allow; may; can	可以	kěyǐ	AV	5.1
be able to; can	能	néng	AV	5.1
be acquainted with (a person); to know (someone)	认识	rènshi	V	1.1
be afraid; to fear	怕	pà	V	8.2
be at a place	在	zài	V	4.1
be at ease; to set one's mind at rest	放心	fàng xīn	VO	12.2
be called (first name/full name); to call	叫	jiào	V	1.1
be concerned with; to care for or about; concern	关心	guānxīn	V/Adj	12.1a
be done; to be finished	完	wán	V	11.2
be finished; to be done	完	wán	V	11.2

be fond of; to like; to love	喜欢	xǐhuan	V	8.2
be grateful; to thank; thanks	感谢	gǎnxiè	V/N	12.1
be named (surname)	姓	xìng	V	1.1
be on a business trip	出差	chū chāi	VO	6.1a
be out; opposite of 进	出	chū	V	3.2
be present	在	zài	V	5.1
be short by; to lack; inferior	差	chà	V/Adj	5.2a
beautiful	美	měi	Adj	2.1
because	因为	yīnwèi	Conj	11.1
beer	啤酒	píjiǔ	N	6.1a
before; ago; previously	以前	yǐqián	TW	11.1
befriend	交	jiāo	V	9.1a
begin a class; to go to class	上课	shàng kè	VO	5.2a
begin; to start	开始	kāishǐ	V	8.1a
behind (in space or position); at the back; in the rear	后面	hòumian	N	9.2a
Beijing	北京	Běijīng	PN	2.1
Beijing Opera	京剧	Jīngjù	PN	9.2
below; next	下	xià	Adj	6.1
besides; in addition to	除了……以外	chúle...yǐwài	Conj	11.2
beverage (usually non-alcoholic drinks); drinks	饮料	yǐnliào	N	6.1a
big; huge; old in age	大	dà	Adj	2.1a
birthday	生日	shēngrì	N	11.2a
black tea	红茶	hóngchá	N	6.1a
block up; to have a traffic jam	堵	dǔ	V	10.1
blue	蓝	lán	Adj	7.1
body; health	身体	shēntǐ	N	3.2
book	书	shū	N	2.1a
book store	书店	shūdiàn	N	9.1a
boss	老板	lǎobǎn	N	9.1a
both; all	都	dōu	Adv	3.2
bother; to trouble; trouble; troublesome	麻烦	máfan	V/N/Adj	11.1
boy	男孩儿	nánhái'ér	N	3.1
brain; mind	脑	nǎo	N	2.1a
branch factory	分厂	fēnchǎng	N	7.2
branch office	分公司	fēngōngsī	N	4.1
breakfast	早饭	zǎofàn	N	7.1a
bright; the given name of a fictional character in this text	明	míng	PN/Adj	1.1
bring; to take; to carry	带	dài	V	11.2
brothers and sisters; siblings	兄弟姐妹	xiōngdi jiěmèi	N	3.2
build	建	jiàn	V	7.2
Bund (a popular tourist spot along the levy against the Huangpu river in Shanghai)	外滩	Wàitān	PN	9.1a
business	业务	yèwù	N	12.2
business	生意	shēngyì	N	3.2
business card; name card	名片	míngpiàn	N	7.1
business; matter; affair; thing	事	shì	N	3.1a
busy	忙	máng	Adj	1.2
but	不过	búguò	Conj	8.1
but	但是	dànshì	Conj	11.1
but	可是	kěshì	Conj	6.2
buy	买	mǎi	V	5.2a

buy groceries	买菜	*mǎi cài*	VO	7.1a
by chance; by coincidence	刚好	*gānghǎo*	Adv	11.1
by coincidence; by chance	刚好	*gānghǎo*	Adv	11.1

C

cafeteria; restaurant	餐厅	*cāntīng*	N	4.1a
calculator (used in Taiwan); computer (used in mainland China);	计算机	*jìsuànjī*	N	6.2a
call (a taxi); to order	叫	*jiào*	V	11.1
call; to make a phone call	打电话	*dǎ diànhuà*	VO	6.2
calligraphy and painting	字画	*zìhuà*	N	11.2
calligraphy brush	毛笔	*máobǐ*	N	3.1a
campus; school	学校	*xuéxiào*	N	2.1a
can; allow; may; be able to	可以	*kěyǐ*	AV	5.1
can; be able to;	能	*néng*	AV	5.1
can; will; to know how to	会	*huì*	AV/V	2.2
canteen; dining hall	食堂	*shítáng*	N	4.1a
capable	能干	*nénggàn*	Adj	12.1a
car	车子	*chēzi*	N	2.1a
care for or about, to be concerned with; concern	关心	*guānxīn*	V/Adj	12.1a
careful; to do something carefully	小心	*xiǎoxīn*	Adj/Adv	6.1a
carry; to take; to bring	带	*dài*	V	11.2
cellular phone	手机	*shouji*	N	6.2a
chance; opportunity	机会	*jīhuì*	N	7.2
Chang'an Street	长安街	*Cháng'ānjiē*	PN	10.1
character	字	*zì*	N	2.2a
cheerful; happy; joyful	愉快	*yúkuài*	Adj	12.1
Cheers!; to make a toast	干杯	*gān bēi*	UE/VO	8.2a
child	小孩	*xiǎohái*	N	11.2a
child; children; kids	孩子	*háizi*	N	3.1
children; child; kids	孩子	*háizi*	N	3.1
China	中国	*Zhōngguó*	PN	2.1
Chinese characters	汉字	*Hànzì*	PN	2.2a
Chinese language	中文	*Zhōngwén*	PN	2.1
Chinese language	汉语	*Hànyǔ*	PN	2.2a
Chinese New Year; Spring Festival	春节	*Chūnjié*	PN	11.2a
cigarette	香烟	*xiāngyān*	N	3.1a
city	城市	*chéngshì*	N	7.2
city; town	城	*chéng*	N	5.1
classmate	同学	*tóngxué*	N	2.1a
clear; distinct	清楚	*qīngchu*	Adj	5.1
client; customer	客户	*kèhù*	N	9.1a
clock; o'clock; time as measured in minutes or seconds	钟	*zhōng*	N	5.2
close; near	近	*jìn*	Adj	5.1
coffee	咖啡	*kāfēi*	N	3.1a
cola	可乐	*kělè*	N	3.1a
cold	冷	*lěng*	Adj	1.2a
collaboration; cooperation; to cooperate	合作	*hézuò*	N/V	12.1
colleague; co-worker	同事	*tóngshì*	N	2.1a
college; university	大学	*dàxué*	N	7.1a
come	来	*lái*	V	2.1

come back	回来	huílai	VC	5.1a
come in	进来	jìnlai	VC	2.2a
come out	出来	chūlai	VC	9.1a
come to (a place)	到……来	dào…lái	V	3.1
common speech; a reference to Mandarin Chinese	普通话	pǔtōnghuà	N	2.2
common; ordinary	普通	pǔtōng	Adj	2.2
company	公司	gōngsī	N	2.1
comparatively; relatively; rather	比较	bǐjiào	Adv	9.2
comparison marker; than	比	bǐ	Prep	4.2
computer	电脑	diànnǎo	N	2.1a
computer (used in mainland China); calculator (used in Taiwan)	计算机	jìsuànjī	N	6.2a
Computer City	电脑城	Diànnǎochéng	PN	5.1
concern; to be concerned with; to care for or about	关心	guānxīn	Adj/V	12.1a
condition; situation	情况	qíngkuàng	N	12.1
confidence	信心	xìnxīn	N	10.1a
constantly; often; frequently	经常	jīngcháng	Adv	7.1a
consult with someone; to discuss	商量	shāngliang	V	11.2a
contact	联系	liánxì	V	6.1
contract	合同	hétong	N	12.1a
convenient; available	方便	fāngbiàn	Adj	6.2
cook (make dishes)	做菜	zuò cài	VO	2.2a
(cooked) rice; meal	饭	fàn	N	6.1a
cool	凉	liáng	Adj	1.2a
cooperate; cooperation; collaboration	合作	hézuò	V/N	12.1
cooperation; collaboration; to cooperate	合作	hézuò	N/V	12.1
correct; right	对	duì	Adj	8.1
country	国	guó	N	2.1
country; nation	国家	guójiā	N	2.1a
courteous; polite	客气	kèqi	Adj	8.1
co-worker; colleague	同事	tóngshì	N	2.1a
cuisine of a place (e.g., 中国菜 Zhōngguócài=Chinese cuisine/food)	菜	cài	N	6.1a
culture	文化	wénhuà	N	12.1
customer; client	客户	kèhù	N	9.1a

D

dad	爸爸	bàba	N	2.1a
daughter	女儿	nǚ'ér	N	3.1
day after tomorrow	后天	hòutiān	TW	12.1
day before yesterday	前天	qiántiān	TW	7.1
day of the month; number	号	hào	N	6.1
day; sky; used as part of a name in this text	天	tiān	N/PN	1.1
day; the sun	日	rì	N	6.1a
decide; decision; resolution	决定	juédìng	V/N	9.1
decision; resolution; decide	决定	juédìng	V/N	9.1
definitely; for sure	一定	yídìng	Adv	7.2
deliver	送	sòng	V	7.1a
deliver mail	送信	sòng xìn	VO	7.1a
department	部	bù	N	2.2
desire to have (something); to want to; must; have to; need to	要	yào	AV/V	6.1
dictionary	字典	zìdiǎn	N	2.1a

difficult	难	nán	Adj	9.2a
diligent; to work hard	努力	nǔlì	Adj/V	4.2a
dining hall; canteen	食堂	shítáng	N	4.1a
dinner	晚餐	wǎncān	N	8.1
dinner; supper	晚饭	wǎnfàn	N	8.1a
discuss	讨论	tǎolùn	V	9.1a
discuss; to talk	谈	tán	V	9.1a
discuss; to consult with someone;	商量	shāngliang	V	11.2a
disembark from a vehicle	下	xià	V	9.1a
dish (of food); vegetables	菜	cài	N	2.2a
dispatch	发	fā	V	6.2a
distinct; clear	清楚	qīngchu	Adj	5.1
distribute	发	fā	V	6.2a
disturb	打扰	dǎrǎo	V	9.1
do	作	zuò	V	6.2a
do not have; there is/are not; (negative marker)	没有	méiyǒu	V/Adv	3.1
do something carefully; careful	小心	xiǎoxīn	Adv/Adj	6.1a
do; to handle; to tackle	办	bàn	V	11.2a
do; to make	做	zuò	V	2.2a
doctor	医生	yīshēng	N	6.2a
doctor	大夫	dàifu	N	2.1a
document	文件	wénjiàn	N	9.1a
don't	别	bié	Adv	8.2
don't be so polite; You are welcome	不客气	bú kèqi	UE	10.2
door; gate	门	mén	N	10.1
drink	喝	hē	V	6.1a
drink to excess	喝醉	hēzuì	VC	8.2
drinks; beverage (usually non-alcoholic drinks)	饮料	yǐnliào	N	6.1a
drive a car	开车	kāi chē	VO	2.2a
drive; to open; to operate	开	kāi	V	2.2a
driver (of a car)	司机	sījī	N	10.1
driver; master in a given field	师傅	shīfu	N	10.1
drunk; get drunk	醉	zuì	N/Adj	8.2
duration or period of minutes	分钟	fēnzhōng	TD	7.1a

E

each; every	每	měi	Pr	7.1a
early; Good morning!	早	zǎo	Adj/UE	1.2a
(early) morning	早上	zǎoshang	TW	1.2
east	东	dōng	N	10.2
east; the Orient; the East	东方	dōngfāng	N/PN	10.2
the East; the Orient; east	东方	dōngfāng	N/PN	10.2
eat	吃	chī	V	2.2a
eat a meal	吃饭	chī fàn	VO	5.2a
eight	八	bā	Nu	Intro
electric; electrical; electricity	电	diàn	Adj/N	2.1a
electrical; electric; electricity	电	diàn	Adj/N	2.1a
electricity; electric; electrical	电	diàn	N/Adj	2.1a
elementary school	小学	xiǎoxué	N	3.1
e-mail	电子邮件	diànzǐ yóujiàn	N	6.2a

emperor	皇帝	huángdì	N	3.1a
employee; staff; personnel	员工	yuángōng	N	7.2
engage in social activities (when off duty); (work-related) social activities	应酬	yìngchou	V/N	9.1
engineer	工程师	gōngchéngshī	N	11.2a
English	英文	Yīngwén	PN	2.2
enter	进	jìn	V	3.2
entrance; import; to import	进口	jìnkǒu	N/V	3.2
even more	更	gèng	Adv	10.1
evening	晚上	wǎnshang	TW	1.2a
every; each	每	měi	Pr	7.1a
everybody	大家	dàjiā	Pr	8.1a
everyday	每天	měitiān	TW	7.1a
exactly; precisely; just	就	jiù	Adv	9.1
excited	兴奋	xīngfèn	Adj	7.2a
excuse me (an apology); sorry	对不起	duìbuqǐ	UE	5.1
Excuse me…; May I ask…	请问	qǐng wèn	UE	2.2
exercise; to work out	运动	yùndòng	V	7.1a
exercise; to work out	锻炼	duànliàn	V	10.1a
exert one's heart/ mind (polite expression used when asking for help)	费心	fèi xīn	VO	12.2
exit; export; to export	出口	chūkǒu	N/V	3.2
expect; to hope; to wish	希望	xīwàng	V	12.1
expensive; honorific form of "your"	贵	guì	Adj	1.1
explain	解释	jiěshì	V	10.2a
explain	说明	shuōmíng	V	8.1a
export; exit	出口	chūkǒu	V/N	3.2
extremely	……极了	…jí le	Adv	11.1
extremely; very; highly	非常	fēicháng	Adv	7.2

F

factory	工厂	gōngchǎng	N	7.2
family	家庭	jiātíng	N	3.1
family member(s)	家人	jiārén	N	6.1a
family; home	家	jiā	N	4.1
famous roast duck restaurant in Beijing	全聚德	Quánjùdé	PN	8.1
far; remote	远	yuǎn	Adj	5.1
fast	快	kuài	Adj	2.2a
father	父亲	fùqin	N	3.2
fax	传真	chuánzhēn	N	6.2a
fear; to be afraid	怕	pà	V	8.2
feel; to sense	感	gǎn	V	7.2
female	女	nǚ	N	3.1
female family friend close to one's parents' age; nanny; housekeeper; aunt	阿姨	āyí	N	12.1a
few; little	少	shǎo	Adj	2.2a
fifty nine	五十九	wǔshíjiǔ	Nu	3.2
finance	财务	cáiwù	N	11.1a
fine; good	好	hǎo	Adj	1.1
first	先	xiān	Adv	10.1
five	五	wǔ	Nu	Intro

fly	飞	fēi	V	5.1a
for	给	gěi	Prep	6.2
for a long time; long	久	jiǔ	TD/Adj	7.1
for a moment; slightly	稍	shāo	Adv	6.2a
for sure; definitely	一定	yídìng	Adv	7.2
foreign country	外国	wàiguó	N	3.1a
foreigner	外国人	wàiguórén	N	3.1a
forest; a surname	林	lín	N/PN	4.1
four	四	sì	Nu	Intro
free time; spare time	空	kòng	N	3.1a
frequently; often	常常	chángcháng	Adv	7.1a
frequently; often; constantly	经常	jīngcháng	Adv	7.1a
friend	朋友	péngyou	N	2.1a
from	从	cóng	Prep	7.1
front (opposite of 后 hòu); ahead	前	qián	N	10.2
fruit juice	果汁	guǒzhī	N	6.1a
full name of a fictional person in this text	白有天	Bái Yǒutiān	PN	1.1
full name of a fictional person in this text	高明	Gāo Míng	PN	1.1
full name of a fictional person in this text	王英	Wáng Yīng	PN	2.2
full name of a fictional person in this text	张国强	Zhāng Guóqiáng	PN	7.1
full name; given name	名字	míngzi	N	1.1
furniture	家具	jiājù	N	11.1a

G

gate; door	门	mén	N	10.1
general manager	总经理	zǒngjīnglǐ	N	4.1a
get drunk; drunk	醉	zuì	V/Adj	8.2
get sick	生病	shēng bìng	VO	12.2a
get married	结婚	jié hūn	VO	3.1
get off the plane	下飞机	xià fēijī	VO	9.1a
get off work	下班	xià bān	VO	5.2
get out; to go out	出去	chūqu	V	9.2
get up	起来	qǐlái	VC	6.2a
gift; present	礼物	lǐwù	N	11.2
girl	女孩儿	nǚhái'ér	N	3.1
give	给	gěi	V	6.2
give advice (polite expression used when meeting for the first time)	指教	zhǐjiào	V	7.1
give as a gift; to take someone somewhere; to send; to see someone off	送	sòng	V	7.1a, 11.1a
give birth	生	shēng	V	11.2a
given name of a fictional character in this text	明	Míng	PN	1.1
given name of a fictional character in this text	英	Yīng	PN	2.2
given name; full name	名字	míngzi	N	1.1
glad; pleased; happy	高兴	gāoxìng	Adj	1.1
go	去	qù	V	3.1a
go back	回去	huíqu	VC	5.1a
go in	进去	jìnqu	VC	5.1a
go on foot; to walk	走路	zǒu lù	VO	11.1a
go on the street; to stroll on the street (usually for shopping)	上街	shàng jiē	VO	10.1a
go out	出门	chū mén	VO	10.1

go out; to get out	出去	chūqu	V	9.2
go to class; to begin a class	上课	shàng kè	VO	5.2a
go to work	上班	shàng bān	VO	5.2
go to; to attend a school or class	上	shàng	V	3.1
golf	高尔夫球	gāo'ěrfūqiú	N	9.1a
Good afternoon!	午安	wǔ'ān	UE	1.2a
Good morning!	早上好	zǎoshang hǎo	UE	1.2
Good morning!	早安	zǎo'ān	UE	1.2a
Good morning!; early	早	zǎo	UE/Adj	1.2a
Good night!	晚安	wǎn'ān	UE	1.2a
good to watch/read/see; interesting; pretty	好看	hǎokàn	Adj	9.2
good; fine	好	hǎo	Adj	1.1
good-bye; see you again	再见	zàijiàn	UE	1.2
goodbyes; to say goodbye	话别	huà bié	N/VO	12.1
Great Wall	长城	Chángchéng	N	8.1a
green	绿	lǜ	Adj	6.1a
green tea	绿茶	lǜchá	N	6.1a
greet; greetings	问好	wènhǎo	V/N	1.1
greet; welcome; Welcome!	欢迎	huānyíng	V/UE	2.1
greetings; to greet	问好	wènhǎo	N/V	1.1
Guangzhou	广州	Guǎngzhōu	PN	4.1
guest	客人	kèrén	N	11.2a

H

half (an hour)	半	bàn	Nu	5.2
handicraft article	工艺品	gōngyìpǐn	N	11.2
handle; to do; to tackle	办	bàn	V	11.2a
happy	开心	kāixīn	Adj	7.2a
happy; glad; pleased	高兴	gāoxìng	Adj	1.1
happy; joyful; cheerful	愉快	yúkuài	Adj	12.1
have; there is; there are	有	yǒu	V	3.1
have a traffic jam; to block up	堵	dǔ	V	10.1
have a traffic jam; traffic congestion	堵车	dǔ chē	VO/N	10.1
have fun; to play	玩/玩儿	wán/wánr	V	6.1a
have heard it said	听说	tīngshuō	V	4.1
have the knowledge of; to know	知道	zhīdao	V	6.2
have to; need to; must; to want to; to desire to have (something)	要	yào	AV/V	6.1
have to; must	得	děi	AV	11.2
he; him	他	tā	Pr	1.1a
headquarters	总部	zǒngbù	N	4.1
health; body	身体	shēntǐ	N	3.2
hear; to listen	听	tīng	V	4.1
help	帮	bāng	V	6.1
help	帮助	bāngzhù	V/N	12.1a
help	帮忙	bāng máng	VO	6.1a
help; to help	帮助	bāngzhù	N/V	12.1a
her; she	她	tā	Pr	1.1a
here	这儿	zhèr	Pr	5.1
here	这里	zhèli	Pr	5.2a
hereafter; after; afterwards; later	以后	yǐhòu	TW	9.2

high; tall; a surname	高	gāo	Adj/PN	1.1
highly; very; extremely	非常	fēicháng	Adv	7.2
him; he	他	tā	Pr	1.1a
hit	打	dǎ	V	2.2a
hit a ball; to play a ball game	打球	dǎ qiú	VO	2.2a
hold (a meeting/party, etc.)	开	kāi	V	6.1
home; family	家	jiā	N	4.1
homesick; to miss home	想家	xiǎng jiā	Adj/VO	6.1a
Hong Kong	香港	Xiānggǎng	PN	7.1a
Hongqiao Market	红桥市场	Hóngqiáo Shìchǎng	PN	11.1
honorific form of "your"; expensive	贵	guì	Adj	1.1
honorific form of asking a person's surname	贵姓	guì xìng	UE	1.1
hope; to wish; to expect	希望	xīwàng	V	12.1
horse	马	mǎ	N	2.1
hospital	医院	yīyuàn	N	10.1a
hot	热	rè	Adj	1.2a
hot and humid	闷热	mēnrè	Adj	9.2a
hot; spicy; peppery	辣	là	Adj	8.2
hotel	宾馆	bīnguǎn	N	7.1a
hotel; restaurant	饭店	fàndiàn	N	7.1a
hour	小时	xiǎoshí	TD	7.1a
house	房子	fángzi	N	5.2a
housekeeper; nanny; aunt; female family friend close to one's parents' age	阿姨	āyí	N	12.1a
how about; what about	怎么样	zěnmeyàng	IP	9.2
how is…	怎么样	zěnmeyàng	IP	10.1
how many	几	jǐ	IP	3.1
how many; how much	多少	duōshao	IP	4.2
how much; how many	多少	duōshao	IP	4.2
how to…	怎么	zěnme	IP	10.2
human concerns; human resources	人事	rénshì	N	2.2
human resources department	人事部	rénshìbù	N	2.2
human resources; human concerns	人事	rénshì	N	2.2
humid; stifling	闷	mēn	Adj	5.1a
hundred	百	bǎi	Nu	Intro
hundred million	亿	yì	Nu	Intro
hungry	饿	è	Adj	1.2a
husband; Mr.	先生	xiānsheng	N	1.1

I

I; me	我	wǒ	Pr	1.1
ice	冰	bīng	N	6.1a
ice water	冰水	bīngshuǐ	N	6.1a
idea	主意	zhǔyi	N	9.2
if	……的话	…dehuà	Conj	10.1
if	如果	rúguǒ	Conj	9.2
if	要是	yàoshi	Conj	10.1
illustrated magazine or newspaper	画报	huàbào	N	3.1a
immediately; right away	马上	mǎshàng	Adv	6.1
import and export; to import and export	进出口	jìnchūkǒu	N/V	3.2

import; entrance	进口	jìnkǒu	V/N	3.2
important	重要	zhòngyào	Adj	9.1a
in addition to; besides	除了... ...以外	chúle...yǐwài	Conj	11.2
in addition; as well as; also	还	hái	Adv	4.1
in that case; then	那	nà	Conj	1.2
in that case; then	那么	nàme	Conj	6.1
in the direction of; towards	往	wǎng	Prep	10.2
in the middle of; in the midst of	正在	zhèngzài	Adv	9.1
in the midst of; in the middle of	正在	zhèngzài	Adv	9.1
in the rear; at the back; behind (in space or position)	后面	hòumian	N	9.2a
in; at; on	在	zài	Prep	5.2
in; signifies the object of an interest or action	对	duì	Prep	7.2
indicates a capital city	京	jīng	N	2.1
inferior; to be short by; to lack	差	chà	Adj/V	5.2a
inquire; to ask about	询问	xúnwèn	V	5.1
interest	兴趣	xìngqu	N	7.2
interesting	有意思	yǒu yìsi	Adj	4.2a
interesting; good to watch/read/see; pretty	好看	hǎokàn	Adj	9.2
intersection	路口	lùkǒu	N	10.2
introduce; introduction	介绍	jièshào	V/N	2.1
introduction; to introduce	介绍	jièshào	N/V	2.1
investment	投资	tóuzī	N	7.2a
invite; to request; please	请	qǐng	V/Adv	2.2
invite; to make a date or appointment in advance	约	yuē	V	9.1
it doesn't matter; never mind	没关系	méi guānxi	UE	7.1
it's a deal; that's settled then	一言为定	yìyán wéidìng	UE	12.1
it's OK; not bad (a humble expression)	还可以	hái kěyǐ	UE	7.2

J

jewelry; precious gems	珠宝	zhūbǎo	N	11.1
Jiangsu province	江苏	Jiāngsū	PN	7.2
job; work	工作	gōngzuò	N	3.2
jog; jogging	慢跑	mànpǎo	V/N	9.2a
jogging; to jog	慢跑	mànpǎo	N/V	9.2a
joint venture	合资	hézī	N	4.1
joyful; happy; cheerful	愉快	yúkuài	Adj	12.1
just now; a short while ago	刚	gāng	Adv	7.1
just; exactly; precisely	就	jiù	Adv	9.1
just; only	只	zhǐ	Adv	5.1

K

Karaoke	卡拉OK	Kǎlā OK	N	7.1a
keep	保持	bǎochí	V	12.2a
kids; child; children	孩子	háizi	N	3.1
king; a surname	王	wáng	N/PN	2.2
know (someone); to be acquainted with (a person)	认识	rènshi	V	1.1
know how to; will; can	会	huì	V/AV	2.2
know; to have the knowledge of	知道	zhīdao	V	6.2
Kung Pao Chicken	宫保鸡丁	gōngbǎo jīdīng	N	8.2

L

lack; to be short by; inferior	差	chà	V/Adj	5.2a
lady	女士	nǚshì	N	1.2a
language; written language	文	wén	N	2.2
lap top	笔记本电脑	bǐjìběn diànnǎo	N	6.2a
last month	上个月	shàng ge yuè	TW	6.1a
last week	上个星期	shàng ge xīngqī	TW	6.1a
last year	去年	qùnián	TW	7.2
last; previous	上	shàng	Adj	6.1a
lately; recently	最近	zuìjìn	TW	10.2a
later; after; afterwards; hereafter	以后	yǐhòu	TW	9.2
lawyer	律师	lǜshī	N	2.1a
learn; to study	学	xué	V	1.2a
leave	离开	líkāi	VC	5.1a
leave	走	zǒu	V	3.1a
leave early	早退	zǎotuì	V	12.1a
left	左	zuǒ	N/Adj	7.1
Lenovo	联想	Liánxiǎng	PN	11.1a
let; to allow; to make	让	ràng	V	12.1
letter	信	xìn	N	6.1a
library	图书馆	túshūguǎn	N	3.1a
light	灯	dēng	N	10.2
like this; so; such	这么	zhème	Adv	12.1
like; to love	爱	ài	V	10.1a
like; to love; be fond of	喜欢	xǐhuan	V	8.2
likely; possibly; perhaps	可能	kěnéng	Adv	10.1
listen; to hear	听	tīng	V	4.1
"little emperor"	小皇帝	xiǎo huángdì	N	3.1a
Little Wang	小王	Xiǎo Wáng	PN	6.1
little; few	少	shǎo	Adj	2.2a
little; young (for people only); small;	小	xiǎo	Adj	3.1
lobby	大堂	dàtáng	N	8.1
long	长	cháng	Adj	7.1a
long; for a long time	久	jiǔ	Adj/TD	7.1
look for; to search	找	zhǎo	V	5.1
love; to like	爱	ài	V	10.1a
love; to like; to be fond of	喜欢	xǐhuan	V	8.2
low; short	矮	ǎi	Adj	5.1a
luggage	行李	xíngli	N	12.1a
lunch	午饭	wǔfàn	N	5.2a

M

magazine	杂志	zázhì	N	2.1a
make a date or appointment in advance; to invite	约	yuē	V	9.1
make a phone call; to call	打电话	dǎ diànhuà	VO	6.2
make a toast; Cheers!	干杯	gān bēi	VO/UE	8.2a
make a turn	拐	guǎi	V	10.2
make a turn	转	zhuǎn	V	10.2
make an appointment to meet	约见	yuējiàn	V	6.1

make; to do	做	zuò	V	2.2a
make; to let; to allow	让	ràng	V	12.1
male	男	nán	N	3.1
management	管理	guǎnlǐ	N	7.2a
manager	经理	jīnglǐ	N	2.1
Mandarin Chinese (term used in Taiwan); official national language of a country	国语	guóyǔ	N	2.2a
manifest; performance	表现	biǎoxiàn	V/N	12.1a
manufacture; to produce	生产	shēngchǎn	V	7.2
many; much; a lot	多	duō	Adj	2.2a
Maotai (a Chinese liquor)	茅台酒	Máotáijiǔ	N	8.2
map	地图	dìtú	N	2.1a
market	市场	shìchǎng	N	6.1
master in a given field; driver	师傅	shīfu	N	10.1
matter; affair; thing; business	事	shì	N	3.1a
May I ask…; Excuse me…	请问	qǐng wèn	UE	2.2
(May I) disturb/interrupt you a bit	打扰一下	dǎrǎo yíxià	UE	9.1
may; allow; be able to; can	可以	kěyǐ	AV	5.1
me; I	我	wǒ	Pr	1.1
meal; (cooked) rice	饭	fàn	N	6.1a
measure word for actions	遍	biàn	M	10.2
measure word for addressing people politely	位	wèi	M	2.1
measure word for basic units of Chinese currency; spoken form equivalent to 元 yuán	块	kuài	M	11.1a
measure word for bottles	瓶	píng	M	6.2a
measure word for cans or jars	罐	guàn	M	6.2a
measure word for categories	种	zhǒng	M	7.2
measure word for certain machinery, apparatuses, etc.	台	tái	M	6.2a
measure word for business establishments such as companies, stores, or restaurants	家	jiā	M	4.1
measure word for courses of meals	道	dào	M	8.2
measure word for cups or glasses	杯	bēi	M	3.1a
measure word for distance in kilometers	公里	gōnglǐ	M	5.1
measure word for flat objects	张	zhāng	M	3.1a
measure word for frequency	次	cì	M	7.1
measure word for length in meters	米	mǐ	M	7.1a
measure word for minutes when stating a specific time	分	fēn	M	5.2a
measure word for multiple things or people	些	xiē	M	11.1
measure word for nouns that are "bound together"	本	běn	M	3.1a
measure word for objects in general	个	gè	M	2.1
measure word for paintings	幅	fú	M	12.2a
measure word for sentences	句	jù	M	8.1a
measure word for stick-like objects	支	zhī	M	3.1a
measure word for telling time; "o'clock"	点	diǎn	M	3.1a
measure word for the basic unit of Chinese currency	元	yuán	M	11.1a
measure word for things which come in a set or pile, such as reports, newspapers, etc.	份	fèn	M	9.1
measure word for types/kinds/sorts	种	zhǒng	M	7.2
measure word for vehicles	辆	liàng	M	11.1
measure word for years of age	岁	suì	M	3.1
measure word for 事, luggage or clothing	件	jiàn	M	9.2a
measure word meaning a quarter of an hour; 15 minutes	刻	kè	M	5.2

medium; middle	中	zhōng	Adj	2.1
meet; to see	见到	jiàndào	VC	2.1
meet; to see	见面	jiàn miàn	VO	6.2
meeting	会议	huìyì	N	10.1a
meeting room	会议室	huìyìshì	N	9.2a
midday; noon	中午	zhōngwǔ	TW	12.1
middle school	中学	zhōngxué	N	3.1
middle school student	中学生	zhōngxuéshēng	N	3.1
middle; medium	中	zhōng	Adj	2.1
mind; brain	脑	nǎo	N	2.1a
miss home; homesick	想家	xiǎng jiā	VO/Adj	6.1a
miss; to think; think of (doing something); would like to	想	xiǎng	V/AV	6.1
Miss; young lady	小姐	xiǎojie	N	2.2
mom	妈妈	māma	N	2.1a
Monday	星期一	xīngqīyī	T	6.1
money	钱	qián	N	3.1a
month	月	yuè	N	6.1
month	月份	yuèfèn	N	12.1
morning	上午	shàngwǔ	TW	5.2
morning and afternoon	上下午	shàngxiàwǔ	TW	6.1
most likely; probably	大概	dàgài	Adv	7.1
mother	母亲	mǔqin	N	3.2
mouth; an aperture of a place	口	kǒu	N	3.2
movie	电影	diànyǐng	N	4.2a
Mr.; husband	先生	xiānsheng	N	1.1
Mrs.; wife	太太	tàitai	N	1.2a
much; many; a lot	多	duō	Adj	2.2a
must; have to; need to; to want to; to desire to have (something)	要	yào	AV/V	6.1
must; have to	得	děi	AV	11.2

N

name card; business card	名片	míngpiàn	N	7.1
name of a district in Beijing	中关村	Zhōngguāncūn	PN	5.1
name of a fictional company in this text	方正公司	Fāngzhèng Gōngsī	PN	4.2
name of a fictional company in this text	蓝星	Lánxīng	PN	7.1
name of a park-like area in Beijing	后海	Hòuhǎi	PN	9.1
name of a place in Beijing	三里屯	Sānlǐtún	PN	9.1a
name of a place in Guangzhou	东莞	Dōngguǎn	PN	11.2a
name of a place in Shanghai	新天地	Xīntiāndì	PN	9.1a
name of a place known as the Dirt Market	潘家园	Pānjiāyuán	PN	11.2
name of a place known as the Scholars Market	琉璃厂	Liúlichǎng	PN	11.2
name of a road in Shanghai	茂名路	Màomínglù	PN	9.1a
nanny; housekeeper; aunt; female family friend close to one's parents' age	阿姨	āyí	N	12.1a
nation; country	国家	guójiā	N	2.1a
National Theater	国家剧院	Guójiā Jùyuàn	PN	9.2
near; close	近	jìn	Adj	5.1
need to; have to; must; to want to; to desire to have (something)	要	yào	AV/V	6.1
need	需要	xūyào	V	6.1a
need not; not necessary	不必	búbì	AV	6.1a

need not; not necessary	不用	búyòng	AV	6.1a
(negative marker); do not have; there is/are not	没有	méiyǒu	Adv/V	3.1
nervous	紧张	jǐnzhāng	Adj	7.2a
never mind; It doesn't matter	没关系	méi guānxi	UE	7.1
new	新	xīn	Adj	7.2
New Year	新年	xīnnián	N	12.2a
New Year money gift to children	压岁钱	yāsuìqián	N	12.2a
newspaper	报纸	bàozhǐ	N	2.1a
next month	下个月	xià ge yuè	TW	6.1a
next time	下次	xià cì	TW	12.1
next week	下星期	xià xīngqī	TW	6.1
next year	明年	míngnián	TW	3.1
next; below	下	xià	Adj	6.1
nine	九	jiǔ	Nu	Intro
no; not	不	bù	Adv	1.2
noon; midday	中午	zhōngwǔ	TW	12.1
north	北	běi	N	2.1
not bad (a humble expression); it's OK	还可以	hái kěyǐ	UE	7.2
not bad; pretty good	不错	búcuò	Adj	12.1a
not for sure	不一定	bùyídìng	UE	12.1
not necessary; need not	不必	búbì	AV	6.1a
not necessary; need not	不用	búyòng	AV	6.1a
not until; as late as	才	cái	Adv	6.2
not yet	还没(有)	hái méi(yǒu)	Adv	5.2
not; no	不	bù	Adv	1.2
note book	笔记本	bǐjìběn	N	6.2a
novel	小说	xiǎoshuō	N	2.1a
now; at present	现在	xiànzài	TW	5.2
number	号码	hàomǎ	N	6.2a
number; day of the month	号	hào	N	6.1

O

o'clock; time as measured in minutes or seconds; clock	钟	zhōng	N	5.2
observe; to visit; to tour (a company/factory, etc.)	参观	cānguān	V	7.2
of course	当然	dāngrán	Adv	5.1
office	办公室	bàngōngshì	N	3.1a
official national language of a country; Mandarin Chinese (term used in Taiwan)	国语	guóyǔ	N	2.2a
often	常	cháng	Adv	7.1
often; frequently	常常	chángcháng	Adv	7.1a
often; frequently; constantly	经常	jīngcháng	Adv	7.1a
OK; all right	行	xíng	Adj/V	8.2
old (opposite of 新 xīn)	旧	jiù	Adj	7.2a
old in age; big; huge	大	dà	Adj	2.1a
older brother	哥哥	gēge	N	2.1a
older sister	姐姐	jiějie	N	2.1a
on the road	路上	lùshang	N	11.1a
on top of; above	上	shàng	N	2.1
on; at; in	在	zài	Prep	5.2
one	一	yī	Nu	Intro

oneself	自己	zìjǐ	Pr	12.1a
only; just	只	zhǐ	Adv	5.1
open; to drive; to operate	开	kāi	V	2.2a
operate; to drive; to open	开	kāi	V	2.2a
opinion	意见	yìjiàn	N	10.2a
opportunity; chance	机会	jīhuì	N	7.2
opposite of 进; to be out	出	chū	V	3.2
or	还是	háishi	Conj	3.1
or (used in statements)	或者	huòzhě	Conj	11.2
order (food)	点	diǎn	V	8.2a
order; to call (a taxi)	叫	jiào	V	11.1
ordinary; common	普通	pǔtōng	Adj	2.2
original tribe from which 97 percent of ethnic Chinese trace their origins; reference to China	汉	Hàn	N	2.2a
the Orient; the East; east	东方	dōngfāng	N/PN	10.2
other	别的	biéde	Adj	12.1a
ought to; should	应该	yīnggāi	AV	10.1
outside	外	wài	N	3.1a
overly; too	太	tài	Adv	5.1

P

pack	收拾	shōushi	V	12.2
painting	画	huà	N	3.1a
parents	父母	fùmǔ	N	3.2
park	公园	gōngyuán	N	3.1a
particle that implies a supposition	吧	ba	P	2.2
particle that implies suggestion or advice	吧	ba	P	6.1
particle that indicates a past action or state	过	guò	P	8.1
particle that indicates a possessive or descriptive form	的	de	P	2.1
particle that indicates completion of an action	了	le	P	3.1
particle that indicates degree complement	得	de	P	2.2
particle used after 好/是 to indicate agreement	啊	a	P	8.1a
particle used to form a question	吗	ma	P	1.2
particle used to form an elliptical question	呢	ne	P	1.1
pen	笔	bǐ	N	2.1a
people; person	人	rén	N	2.1
peppery; spicy; hot	辣	là	Adj	8.2
perform; performance; act; play	表演	biǎoyǎn	V/N	9.2
performance; act; play; to perform	表演	biǎoyǎn	N/V	9.2
performance; to manifest	表现	biǎoxiàn	N/V	12.1a
perhaps; possibly; likely	可能	kěnéng	Adv	10.1
person; people	人	rén	N	2.1
personnel; employee; staff	员工	yuángōng	N	7.2
pick up (people); to answer (the telephone)	接	jiē	V	8.1
place	地方	dìfang	N	2.1
plan	计划	jìhuà	N	9.1a
plan (to do something)	打算	dǎsuàn	V	9.1
plan; proposal	方案	fāng'àn	N	11.2a
plans; arrangement; to arrange	安排	ānpái	N/V	6.2
play a ball game; hit a ball	打球	dǎ qiú	VO	2.2a

play; to have fun	玩/玩儿	wán/wánr	V	6.1a
play; performance; act; to perform	表演	biǎoyǎn	N/V	9.2
please; to invite; to request	请	qǐng	Adv/V	2.2
pleased; glad; happy	高兴	gāoxìng	Adj	1.1
pluralizes pronouns and human nouns	们	men	Suf	1.2
polite rejection of a compliment	哪里	nǎli	UE	2.1
polite; courteous	客气	kèqi	Adj	8.1
portion (of a larger whole)	份	fèn	N	12.1
possibly; likely; perhaps	可能	kěnéng	Adv	10.1
post office	邮局	yóujú	N	10.1a
precious gems; jewelry	珠宝	zhūbǎo	N	11.1
precisely; exactly; just	就	jiù	Adv	9.1
prefix for ordinal numbers: -th/-nd/-rd	第	dì	Pre	7.1
prepare	准备	zhǔnbèi	V	11.1a
present; gift	礼物	lǐwù	N	11.2
presentation; report	报告	bàogào	N	6.2a
President Li (of a company)	李总	Lǐ Zǒng	PN	4.1a
pressing; tight; urgent; tense	紧	jǐn	Adj	11.1
pretty good; not bad	不错	búcuò	Adj	12.1a
pretty; good to watch/read/see; interesting	好看	hǎokàn	Adj	9.2
previous; last	上	shàng	Adj	6.1a
previously; before; ago;	以前	yǐqián	TW	11.1
probably; most likely	大概	dàgài	Adv	7.1
problem; question	问题	wèntí	N	6.1a
produce; to manufacture	生产	shēngchǎn	V	7.2
product	产品	chǎnpǐn	N	7.2
project	项目	xiàngmù	N	10.1a
proposal; plan	方案	fāng'àn	N	11.2a
pub; bar	酒吧	jiǔbā	N	9.1
put	放	fàng	V	8.1a

Q

| question; problem | 问题 | wèntí | N | 6.1a |
| quite; very; rather | 挺 | tǐng | Adv | 3.2 |

R

rather; comparatively; relatively	比较	bǐjiào	Adv	9.2
rather; very; quite	挺	tǐng	Adv	3.2
read; to watch; to take a look	看	kàn	V	2.2a
read books	看书	kàn shū	VO	2.2a
read books; to study	念书	niàn shū	VO	5.2a
really; truly	真	zhēn	Adv	12.1
recently; lately	最近	zuìjìn	TW	10.2a
red	红	hóng	Adj	6.1a
red envelope	红包	hóngbāo	N	12.2a
red wine	红酒	hóngjiǔ	N	6.1a
reference to Mandarin Chinese; common speech	普通话	pǔtōnghuà	N	2.2
reference to China; the original tribe from which 97 percent of ethnic Chinese trace their origins	汉	Hàn	PN	2.2a
relatively; comparatively; rather	比较	bǐjiào	Adv	9.2

relax; relaxed	轻松	qīngsōng	V/Adj	9.2
relaxed; to relax	轻松	qīngsōng	Adj/V	9.2
remote; far	远	yuǎn	Adj	5.1
report; presentation	报告	bàogào	N	6.2a
request; to invite; please	请	qǐng	V/Adv	2.2
reside; to stay (at a hotel)	住	zhù	V	8.1
resolution; decision; decide	决定	juédìng	V/N	9.1
rest; to take a break	休息	xiūxi	V	5.2
restaurant; cafeteria	餐厅	cāntīng	N	4.1a
restaurant; hotel	饭店	fàndiàn	N	7.1a
restroom	洗手间	xǐshǒujiān	N	10.1a
retire	退休	tuìxiū	V	3.2
return	回	huí	V	5.1
return home	回家	huí jiā	VO	5.1a
return to (a place)	回……来	huí...lái	V	5.1
return to one's own country	回国	huí guó	VO	5.1a
rice	米饭	mǐfàn	N	6.1a
rich; wealthy	有钱	yǒu qián	Adj	4.2a
right	右	yòu	N/Adj	7.1
right away; as early as	就	jiù	Adv	6.2
right away; immediately	马上	mǎshàng	Adv	6.1
right; correct	对	duì	Adj	8.1
road	路	lù	N	10.2
roast duck	烤鸭	kǎoyā	N	8.1

S

same	一样	yíyàng	Adj	4.2
same	同	tóng	Adj	10.2a
San Francisco	旧金山	Jiùjīnshān	PN	11.1a
Saturday	星期六	xīngqīliù	TW	5.2
say good-bye; good-byes	话别	huà bié	VO/N	12.1
say; to speak	说	shuō	V	2.2
say; to speak	讲	jiǎng	V	2.2a
school; campus	学校	xuéxiào	N	2.1a
sea	海	hǎi	N	2.1
search; to look for	找	zhǎo	V	5.1
Second Ring (Road)	二环	Èrhuán	PN	10.1
secretary	秘书	mìshū	N	2.2
see	看见	kànjiàn	VC	9.1a
see	见	jiàn	V	1.2
see someone off; to send; to take someone somewhere; to give as a gift	送	sòng	V	7.1a, 11.1a
see you again; good-bye	再见	zàijiàn	UE	1.2
see; to meet	见到	jiàndào	VC	2.1
see; to meet	见面	jiàn miàn	VO	6.2
sell	卖	mài	V	5.2a
send	发	fā	V	6.2a
send; to see someone off; to take someone somewhere; to give as a gift	送	sòng	V	7.1a, 11.1a
sense; to feel	感	gǎn	V	7.2
set one's mind at rest; to be at ease	放心	fàng xīn	VO	12.2

seven	七	qī	Nu	Intro
several; a few	几	jǐ	Nu	9.1
severe; strong	厉害	lìhai	Adj	8.2
Shanghai	上海	Shànghǎi	PN	2.1
she; her	她	tā	Pr	1.1a
Shenzhen	深圳	Shēnzhèn	PN	4.1
shop	商店	shāngdiàn	N	10.1a
short; low	矮	ǎi	Adj	5.1a
should; ought to	应该	yīnggāi	AV	10.1
siblings; brothers and sisters	兄弟姐妹	xiōngdi jiěmèi	N	3.2
Sichuan province	四川	Sìchuān	PN	7.1
side; used with terms of direction	边/边儿	biān/biānr	Suf	10.2
sign	签	qiān	V	12.1a
signature dish	名菜	míngcài	N	8.1
signifies the object of an interest or action; in	对	duì	Prep	7.2
simple	简单	jiǎndān	Adj	9.2a
sing	唱	chàng	V	8.1a
Sino-American	中美	Zhōng-Měi	Adj	4.1
sit	坐	zuò	V	2.2a
situation; condition	情况	qíngkuàng	N	12.1
six	六	liù	Nu	Intro
sixty three	六十三	liùshísān	Nu	3.2
sky; day; used as part of a name in this text	天	tiān	N/PN	1.1
sleep	睡	shuì	V	6.2a
sleep	睡觉	shuì jiào	VO	8.2a
slightly; for a moment	稍	shāo	Adv	6.2a
slow	慢	màn	Adj	2.2a
small; little; young (for people only)	小	xiǎo	Adj	3.1
smoke	吸烟	xī yān	VO	5.1a
smoke	抽烟	chōu yān	VO	12.1a
smooth	顺利	shùnlì	Adj	12.1a
so; such; like this	这么	zhème	Adv	12.1
soccer	足球	zúqiú	N	9.2a
solution; way to handle things	办法	bànfǎ	N	6.1a
some...some...	有的…… 有的……	yǒude...yǒude...	Adj	4.2
son	儿子	érzi	N	3.1
sorry; excuse me (an apology)	对不起	duìbuqǐ	UE	5.1
spare time; free time	空	kòng	N	3.1a
speak; to say	说	shuō	V	2.2
speak; to talk	说话	shuō huà	VO	2.2a
speak; to say	讲	jiǎng	V	2.2a
speech; spoken language; words	话	huà	N	2.2
spend money	花钱	huā qián	VO	8.2a
spicy; hot; peppery	辣	là	Adj	8.2
spoken language; words; speech	话	huà	N	2.2
Spring Festival; Chinese New Year	春节	Chūnjié	PN	11.2a
Sprite	雪碧	xuěbì	PN	6.2a
square	广场	guǎngchǎng	N	10.1
staff; employee; personnel	员工	yuángōng	N	7.2
stage play	话剧	huàjù	N	11.2a

stand	站	zhàn	V	8.1a
stand up	站起来	zhànqǐlái	VC	8.1a
star	星	xīng	N	7.1
start; to begin	开始	kāishǐ	V	8.1a
station (usually for a bus or train)	车站	chēzhàn	N	5.1a
stay	待	dāi	V	7.1
stay (at a hotel); to reside	住	zhù	V	8.1
stifling; humid	闷	mēn	Adj	5.1a
still; yet	还	hái	Adv	3.2
straight through; always; all along	一直	yìzhí	Adv	9.1
stroll on the street (usually for shopping); to go on the street	上街	shàng jiē	VO	10.1a
strong Chinese liquor; white wine	白酒	báijiǔ	N	6.1a
strong; severe	厉害	lìhai	Adj	8.2
student	学生	xuésheng	N	1.2a
study (mainland China usage)	学习	xuéxí	V	5.2a
study; to learn	学	xué	V	1.2a
study; to read books	念书	niàn shū	VO	5.2a
stuff; things	东西	dōngxi	N	6.1a
submit	交	jiāo	V	9.1a
subsidiary company	子公司	zǐgōngsī	N	8.1a
subway	地铁	dìtiě	N	9.2a
subway station	地铁站	dìtiězhàn	N	10.2a
such; so; like this	这么	zhème	Adv	12.1
suggest; suggestion	建议	jiànyì	V/N	9.2
suggestion; to suggest	建议	jiànyì	N/V	9.2
sun; day	日	rì	N	6.1a
super (Taiwanese usage among youth); very	超	chāo	Adv	3.2a
supermarket	超市	chāoshì	N	12.1a
supper; dinner	晚饭	wǎnfàn	N	8.1a
support	支持	zhīchí	V/N	12.1
support; to support	支持	zhīchí	N/V	12.1
surname	姓	xìng	N	1.1
a surname	张	Zhāng	PN	6.1
a surname; forest	林	Lín	PN/N	4.1
a surname; king	王	Wáng	PN/N	2.2
a surname; white	白	Bái	PN/N	1.1
a surname; horse	马	Mǎ	PN/N	2.1
a surname; tall; high	高	Gāo	PN/Adj	1.1
Suzhou	苏州	Sūzhōu	PN	7.2

T

tackle; to handle; to do	办	bàn	V	11.2a
take a break; to rest	休息	xiūxi	V	5.2
take a cab	打的	dǎ di	VO	12.2a
take a look; to read; to watch	看	kàn	V	2.2a
take someone somewhere; to send; to see someone off; to give as a gift	送	sòng	V	7.1a, 11.1a
take a train	坐火车	zuò huǒchē	VO	7.2a
take; to bring; to carry	带	dài	V	11.2
take (a means of transportation); to travel by	坐	zuò	V	7.2a
talk; to discuss	谈	tán	V	9.1a

talk; to speak	说话	shuō huà	VO	2.2a
tall; high; a surname	高	gāo	Adj/PN	1.1
taste; to try the flavor of	尝	cháng	V	8.2
taxi	出租车	chūzūchē	N	10.1
tea	茶	chá	N	3.1a
teach	教	jiāo	V	2.2a
teach (academic courses)	教书	jiāo shū	VO	2.2a
teacher	老师	lǎoshī	N	1.1a
teahouse	茶馆	cháguǎn	N	9.2
telephone	电话	diànhuà	N	2.1a
television	电视	diànshì	N	7.1a
tell	告诉	gàosu	V	12.1
Temple of Heaven	天坛	Tiāntán	PN	11.1
ten	十	shí	Nu	Intro
ten thousand	万	wàn	Nu	Intro
tennis	网球	wǎngqiú	N	5.2a
tense; tight; urgent; pressing;	紧	jǐn	Adj	11.1
than; a comparison marker	比	bǐ	Prep	4.2
thank you	谢谢	xièxie	UE	2.1a
thank; to be grateful; thanks	感谢	gǎnxiè	V/N	12.1
thanks; to thank; to be grateful	感谢	gǎnxiè	N/V	12.1
that	那	nà/nèi	Spe	2.1a
that's settled then; it's a deal	一言为定	yìyán wéidìng	UE	12.1
theater	剧院	jùyuàn	N	9.2
then	再	zài	Adv	9.1
then; in that case	那	nà	Conj	1.2
then; in that case	那么	nàme	Conj	6.1
there	那儿	nàr	Pr	5.1
there	那里	nàli	Pr	5.2a
there are; to have; there is	有	yǒu	V	3.1
there is/are not; do not have; (negative marker)	没有	méiyǒu	V/Adv	3.1
there is; there are; to have	有	yǒu	V	3.1
thing; matter; affair; business	事	shì	N	3.1a
things; stuff	东西	dōngxi	N	6.1a
think; to miss; think of (doing something); would like to	想	xiǎng	V/AV	6.1
think of (doing something); would like to; to think; to miss	想	xiǎng	V/AV	6.1
Third Ring (Road)	三环	Sānhuán	PN	10.1
this	这	zhè/zhèi	Spe	2.1
this time	这次	zhè cì	TW	7.1
this year	今年	jīnnián	TW	3.1
thousand	千	qiān	Nu	Intro
three	三	sān	Nu	Intro
Tiananmen	天安门	Tiān'ānmén	PN	10.1
Tiantan Road	天坛路	Tiāntánlù	PN	11.1
ticket	票	piào	N	9.2
tight; urgent; pressing; tense	紧	jǐn	Adj	11.1
time	时间	shíjiān	N	3.1a
time as measured in minutes or seconds; o'clock; clock	钟	zhōng	N	5.2
tired	累	lèi	Adj	1.2a
title used to address one who is younger than you	小	xiǎo	Adj	6.1
to	给	gěi	Prep	6.2

today	今天	jīntiān	TW	1.2
together	一块儿	yíkuàir	Adv	9.1
together	一起	yìqǐ	Adv	9.1a
tomorrow	明天	míngtiān	TW	1.2
too; overly	太	tài	Adv	5.1
totally; all together	一共	yígòng	Adv	7.2
tour (a company/factory, etc.); to visit; to observe;	参观	cānguān	V	7.2
towards	向	xiàng	Prep	10.2
towards; in the direction of	往	wǎng	Prep	10.2
town; city	城	chéng	N	5.1
trade	贸易	màoyì	N	3.2
traffic congestion; to have a traffic jam	堵车	dǔ chē	N/VO	10.1
traffic light	红绿灯	hónglǜdēng	N	10.2
train	火车	huǒchē	N	7.2a
travel by; to take (a means of transportation)	坐	zuò	V	7.2a
trillion	兆	zhào	Nu	Intro
trouble; to bother; trouble; troublesome	麻烦	máfan	V/N/Adj	11.1
trouble; troublesome; to bother; to trouble	麻烦	máfan	N/Adj/V	11.1
troublesome; trouble; to bother; to trouble	麻烦	máfan	Adj/N/V	11.1
truly; really	真	zhēn	Adv	12.1
try	试	shì	V	6.2
try the flavor of; to taste	尝	cháng	V	8.2
Tsingtao beer	青岛啤酒	Qīngdǎo Píjiǔ	PN	8.2
Tuesday	星期二	xīngqī'èr	TW	6.1
turn at a corner	拐弯	guǎi wān	VO	10.2
turn right	右转	yòu zhuǎn	V	10.2
twelve	十二	shí'èr	Nu	3.1
two	两	liǎng	Nu	Intro
two	二	èr	Nu	Intro
type (characters)	打字	dǎ zì	VO	2.2a

U

(uncooked) rice	米	mǐ	N	6.1a
understand	懂	dǒng	V	5.1a
university; college	大学	dàxué	N	7.1a
urgent; tight; pressing; tense	紧	jǐn	Adj	11.1
us; we	咱们	zánmen	Pr	1.2a
us; we	我们	wǒmen	Pr	1.2
use	用	yòng	V	10.2a
used after a verb to indicate that an action is only for a moment; a short while	一下	yíxià	TD	9.1
used as part of a name in this text; day; sky	天	tiān	PN/N	1.1
used as part of a name in this text (cf Unit 3.1)	有	yǒu	PN	1.1
used in place of 啊 when the preceding word ends with the sound of *a, o, e, i,* or *ü*	呀	ya	P	7.2
used to inquire about amount	多	duō	IP	3.2
used with terms of direction or localization such as 前面 qiánmian "front," 外面 wàimian "outside," 里面 lǐmian "inside"	面	miàn	Suf	9.2a
used with terms of direction; side	边/边儿	biān/biānr	Suf	10.2
useful	有用	yǒu yòng	Adj	9.2a

V

vase	花瓶	huāpíng	N	11.1a
vegetables; dish (of food)	菜	cài	N	2.2a
vehicle	车	chē	N	2.2a
very	很	hěn	Adv	1.1
very; extremely; highly	非常	fēicháng	Adv	7.2
very; rather; quite	挺	tǐng	Adv	3.2
very; super (Taiwanese usage among youth)	超	chāo	Adv	3.2a
visit	访问	fǎngwèn	V	7.1
visit; to observe; to tour (a company/factory, etc.)	参观	cānguān	V	7.2

W

wait	等	děng	V	6.2a
wait for a moment	稍等	shāoděng	UE	6.2a
walk	走	zǒu	V	2.2a
walk; to go on foot	走路	zǒu lù	VO	11.1a
Wangfu Hotel	王府饭店	Wángfǔ Fàndiàn	PN	8.1
want to; need to; have to; must; to desire to have (something)	要	yào	AV/V	6.1
watch; to take a look; to read	看	kàn	V	2.2a
water	水	shuǐ	N	3.1a
way to handle things; solution	办法	bànfǎ	N	6.1a
we; us	咱们	zánmen	Pr	1.2a
we; us	我们	wǒmen	Pr	1.2
wealthy; rich	有钱	yǒu qián	Adj	4.2a
week	星期	xīngqī	N	5.2
week (= 星期, but more colloquial)	礼拜	lǐbài	N	5.2a
week (= 星期, but more formal)	周	zhōu	N	6.2
weekend	周末	zhōumò	TW	5.2
Welcome!; to welcome; to greet	欢迎	huānyíng	UE/V	2.1
welcome; to greet; Welcome!	欢迎	huānyíng	V/UE	2.1
west	西	xī	N	10.2a
what	什么	shénme	Pr	1.1
what about; how about	怎么样	zěnmeyàng	IP	9.2
when…; while…; at the time of…	……的时候	…de shíhou	Conj	12.2
where	哪儿	nǎr	IP	4.1a
where	哪里	nǎli	IP	5.2
which	哪	nǎ/něi	IP	2.2
while…; at the time of…; when…	……的时候	…de shíhou	Conj	12.2
white; a surname	白	bái	Adj/PN	1.1
white wine; a strong Chinese liquor	白酒	báijiǔ	N	6.1a
who; whom	谁	shéi/shuí	IP	2.2
wholly owned foreign enterprise (WOFE)	独资	dúzī	N	4.1
whom; who	谁	shéi/shuí	IP	2.2
why	为什么	wèishénme	IP	5.2
wife; Mrs.	太太	tàitai	N	1.2a
will; can; know how to	会	huì	AV/V	3.1
wine; alcohol	酒	jiǔ	N	6.1a
wish; to hope; to expect	希望	xīwàng	V	12.1
with; and	和	hé	Prep	3.1

with; and	跟	gēn	Prep/Conj	4.2
words; spoken language; speech	话	huà	N	2.2
work hard; diligent	努力	nǔlì	V/Adj	4.2a
work out; to exercise	运动	yùndòng	V	7.1a
work out; to exercise	锻炼	duànliàn	V	10.1a
work overtime	加班	jiābān	V	9.2a
work; job	工作	gōngzuò	V/N	3.2
(work-related) social activities; engage in social activities (when off duty)	应酬	yìngchou	N/V	9.1
worker	工人	gōngrén	N	4.1a
worry	担心	dān xīn	VO	9.2a
would like to; to think of (doing something); to think; to miss	想	xiǎng	AV/V	6.1
write	写	xiě	V	2.2a
written language; language	文	wén	N	2.2

X

Xiangyang Market (in Shanghai)	襄阳市场	Xiāngyáng Shìchǎng	PN	11.1a
Xiushui Market (in Beijing)	秀水市场	Xiùshuǐ Shìchǎng	PN	11.1a

Y

Yanjing beer	燕京啤酒	Yànjīng Píjiǔ	PN	8.2
year	年	nián	N	3.1
yesterday	昨天	zuótiān	TW	1.2a
yet; still	还	hái	Adv	3.2
you	你	nǐ	Pr	1.1a
you (the honorific form of "you")	您	nín	Pr	1.1
You are welcome; don't be so polite	不客气	bú kèqi	UE	10.2
young (for people only); small; little	小	xiǎo	Adj	3.1
young lady; Miss	小姐	xiǎojie	N	2.2
younger brother	弟弟	dìdi	N	2.1a
younger sister	妹妹	mèimei	N	2.1a

Z

zero	零	líng	Nu	Intro

Index of Sentence Patterns

nǎ guó rén	哪国人	2.1	3
nàme...ba	那么……吧	6.1	6
ne	呢	1.1	4
néng	能	5.1	4
qǐng	请	8.1	1
qǐng wèn	请问	2.1	1
ràng	让	12.1	5
shàng	上	10.1	1
shéi	谁	2.1	2
shénme	什么	1.1	2
tài	太	5.1	3
tīngshuō	听说	4.1	1
xiān...zài...	先……再……	10.1	7
xiǎng	想	6.1	3
xìng	姓	1.1	1
yào	要	6.1	2
yào	要	6.1	4
yàoshi...dehuà, jiù...	要是……的话，就……	10.1	2
yí...jiù...	一……就……	9.1	8
yì nián...liǎng, sān cì (X nián...X cì)	一年……两、三次 (X 年……X 次)	7.1	5
yìdiǎnr	一点儿	2.1	5
yíkuàir	一块儿	9.1	4
yīnggāi	应该	10.1	6
yīnggāi	应该	11.1	2
yīnwèi	因为	11.1	4
yǐqián	以前	11.1	3
yíxià	一下	9.1	1
yìxiē	一些	11.1	1
yìzhí xiǎng	一直想	9.1	5
yǒu	有	3.1	2
yuē	约	9.1	3
zài	在	4.1	2
zài	在	5.1	1
zài	在	8.1	4
zěnmeyàng	怎么样	10.1	5
zhèngzài	正在	9.1	2
zhǐ	只	5.1	7
zuǒyòu	左右	7.1	8

About the Author

Jane C. M. Kuo is the director of the Chinese language program at University of California, San Diego, and Professor Emeritus at Thunderbird, the Garvin School of International Management, where she has taught business Chinese to MBA students for more than 30 years, as well as to professionals in the Executive MBA program since its inception in 1991. Thunderbird is regarded as one of world's top MBA programs for global managers and has been ranked No. 1 in international business by *U.S. News and World Report* for 11 straight years and *The Wall Street Journal* for five straight years.

She has also conducted seminars in business Chinese language and cross-cultural communication skills to executives for various Fortune 500 corporations for more than 20 years. She is a member of the board of directors at Shenzhen Swenco Electronics Co Ltd., in Shenzhen, China.

Kuo has authored two volumes of *Open for Business, Lessons in Chinese Commerce for the New Millennium*, co-authored Business Negotiation: Theory and Practice, written numerous articles in professional journals, and has presented research papers at national and international conferences.